Information Retrieval, British & American, 1876-1976

by

JOHN METCALFE

The Scarecrow Press, Inc.
Metuchen, N.J.   1976

Library of Congress Cataloging in Publication Data

Metcalfe, John Wallace, 1901-
   Information retrieval, British and American, 1876-1976.

   Includes bibliographical references and index.
   1. Cataloging--History. 2. Classification--Books--History. 3. Indexing--History. I. Title.
Z693.A2M47   025.3   75-29154
ISBN 0-8108-0875-7

Copyright © 1976 by John Metcalfe

Printed in the United States of America

CONTENTS

1. INTRODUCTORY, TO 1476   1
   - 1.1 Definitions   2
   - 1.2 Information, Writing and Retrieval   2
   - 1.3 Ancient Times   4
   - 1.4 Alexandria and Rome   5
   - 1.5 Medieval Times   9
   - 1.6 Paper and Printing   11

2. 1476 TO 1876   14
   - 2.1 Transition   14
   - 2.2 Bibliography, Tritheim and Gesner   15
   - 2.3 Philosophical Classification, Bacon and His Adapters   17
   - 2.4 Index Learning   19
   - 2.5 Location Reference   21
   - 2.6 Dryander   22
   - 2.7 Brunet's Manuel   24
   - 2.8 Merlin, Richardson and Sayers   26
   - 2.9 Classification in the British Museum Library   27
   - 2.10 Title Word Indexing; Watt's   29
   - 2.11 Poole and Jewett   30
   - 2.12 Title Word Catalogs: Crestadoro   33
   - 2.13 Indexed Catalogs and Index-Catalogs   34
   - 2.14 Alphabetico-Classed Catalogs   36
   - 2.15 Decimal Systems Before Dewey   39
   - 2.16 IR Notations and Their Uses   41

3. DEWEY AND CUTTER AND CLASSIFICATION   43
   - 3.1 Cutter and Dewey at Home, School and College   43
   - 3.2 Amherst Librarian   45
   - 3.3 The Amherst Plan and DDC   47
   - 3.4 Boston and Business   50
   - 3.5 New York, Albany and Lake Placid   52
   - 3.6 Lake Placid Club Education Foundation   54
   - 3.7 Decimal Classification Beginnings   56
   - 3.8 1873-1876   60

3.9	1873-1876-1885	63
3.10	Subject Insertion; The Procrustean Bed; Divide-Likes; The Index	66
3.11	From Dewey to Cutter	68
3.12	The 35 Base and the Expansive Classification	70

4. CUTTER AND CONGRESS: CATALOG AND CLASSIFICATION ... 73
- 4.1 Cutter's Rules and His Thesis, Antithesis and Synthesis ... 73
- 4.2 What Is a Name, What's In a Name? ... 75
- 4.3 Cutter's Alphabetico-Specific Entry and the Dictionary Catalog ... 77
- 4.4 Cross References and Synoptical Table ... 80
- 4.5 Dictionary Catalog, Specific Entry and Specificity ... 83
- 4.6 Cutter Signs Off ... 89
- 4.7 Library of Congress as National Library ... 89
- 4.8 National, But How or For What? ... 91
- 4.9 Options and Choices ... 93
- 4.10 LoC's New Subject Cataloging ... 95
- 4.11 Logic and Consistency ... 98
- 4.12 Title Entry ... 100
- 4.13 Punctuation and Arrangement of Headings ... 103
- 4.14 Attack and Defense ... 105
- 4.15 LC ... 107
- 4.16 LC's Classification and Notation ... 110
- 4.17 Congress Cards: The Package Deal ... 115

5. BRITISH BATTLES OF THE CATALOGS ... 119
- 5.1 Progress and Calamity: Edwards, Jevons and the Indicator ... 120
- 5.2 James Duff Brown, 1862-1914 ... 121
- 5.3 Glasgow, Sharp and Cranshaw ... 124
- 5.4 An International Battle ... 127
- 5.5 RBU and ICSL ... 132
- 5.6 UDC, Otlet and Special Libraries ... 133
- 5.7 UDC in English and Bradford ... 139
- 5.8 Bradford's Criticisms and Later ... 143
- 5.9 Bradford and Pollard: 1930, 1932 ... 148

6. BLISS AND RANGANATHAN ... 151
- 6.1 Bliss, Chronology and Biography ... 152
- 6.2 Consensus and Classification ... 154
- 6.3 Bliss's Notation, Cataloging, Indexing ... 157
- 6.4 BC's Reception and Adoption ... 160
- 6.5 Ranganathan and Bliss, and Ranganathan's Beginnings ... 161

6.6	The Colon Classification and Chain Procedure	165
6.7	Ranganathan's Influence in Britain	168
6.8	BNB, Its Classification, Notation and Indexing	170

7. **PRE-COORDINATE INDEXING WITH PERMUTATIONS AND COMBINATIONS** — 174

7.1	Definitions	174
7.2	Kaiser's Systematic Indexing	175
7.3	Farradane's Isolates and Their Relations	184
7.4	Coates' Chain Procedure Cross Reference	189
7.5	Sharp's Selective Listing in Combination	191
7.6	Austin's PRECIS	195

8. **POST-COORDINATE INDEXING AND MECHANIZATION** — 198

8.1	Definitions and Limitations	198
8.2	Batten's Optical Coincidence and Taube's Uniterm Number Coincidence	203
8.3	Edge-punched cards, Notching, Needle-sorting and Mooers' Zatocoding	205
8.4	Photography, Shingling, and Roles and Links	208
8.5	The New Thesauri	211
8.6	Computers and IR	213

ABBREVIATIONS AND ACRONYMS	218
REFERENCES AND NOTES	220
INDEX	239

Chapter 1

INTRODUCTORY, TO 1476

Of eight chapters this first one deals with principles and definitions and then with the slow development of information retrieval through about 5,000 years until the introduction of printing in Europe less than 500 years prior to our period of principal coverage, 1876-1976. This latter period coincides with the second century of the United States of America, during which were intensified earlier efforts to carry out one of Washington's urgings in his Farewell Address: "Promote then, as an object of primary importance, institutions for the general diffusion of knowledge."

The second chapter is on the approach from about 1476 to 1876, including such illustrious names as Francis Bacon and the development of other systems before those of Dewey and Cutter published in 1876, some of which, like them, still persist through survival and revival--especially the title-word or concordance indexing systems, now aided by mechanization and bearing such acronymic names as KWIC and KWOC. The third chapter begins with the classifications of Dewey and Cutter, and the fourth with the alphabetical indexing of Cutter, his specific entry, and the Library of Congress (LoC) and its classification. What follows then is shown in the page of contents.

As a whole the outline is necessarily historical or chronological, though not always rigidly so--an arrangement which could be of use to students and to those writers on the present who cannot resist questionable flashbacks, for example from computers to Crestadoro in 1856. Development out of the past explains the present, and even 1876 had a past, whereas 1976 is hardly here. Even in 1876 Cutter's specific entry and what became known as Dewey's classification were already known. No revolution seems immediately in sight today; what is needed is refinement, development, consolidation of major advances in the past twenty-five years; like 1876, 1976 cannot be seen clearly without hindsight.

1.1 Definitions

Information retrieval (IR) as a term was not introduced until 1949-50;[1] it means recovery of recorded documents or items of information such as books, chapters in them, articles in periodicals, reports, pamphlets and so on; their recording is their indexing or cataloging in library catalogs or indexes, or in bibliographies and literature indexing at large, all of which may be termed compilation, as distinguished from consultation. Item is preferred here because it can refer to documents or entries of them in catalogs or other records and has had some use in IR terminology or jargon. Items, then, are the material of libraries and librarianship. The word library is misleading as a general synonym for collections; libri- means such material and -ary a place of collection or a collection. In many neologisms biblio- is used, more than libri-, as in bibliography, and the bible was originally the bibliotheca sacra or biblia sacra, the sacred library or sacred books. Volume in origin was volumen, meaning a roll or scroll of writing material such as papyrus, later parchment or vellum and later still, paper; whereas volume in later usage, first called codex, is something consisting of hinged leaves. Library or librarianship should not be identified with any particular material, or form of written record of writing, or period; Roman gentlemen shunned the codex used by Christians, and Renaissance princes have been said to have excluded printed books from their libraries. The form can change again; in fact, has changed already.
In part it may be some form of screening from a computer or from microfilm, may be a videotape, may be a book for use in some form of transistorized television. But the essentials of what is recorded and communicated are not changed. (IR here does not include recording and retrieval of such data as may be kept of financial transactions.) And informative literature item searching may have to follow on retrieval, using any internal indexing an item may possess and often involving a close reading of the item. IR at best is not close indexing of items, though it may give leads on what to look for.

1.2 Information, Writing and Retrieval

Information, writing and retrieval have a reciprocal relationship: one of mutual promotion. Information needs to be recorded and communicated, and has been without writing; by speech, through tradition, explanation and demonstration. But it developed needs for independent records, especially administrative; not, as often supposed, to preserve and communicate literature, which remained "unwritten" for a long time. These records developed first in pictographic and ideographic forms, and, as far as is known, first in the Middle East, in Mesopotamia and Egypt from about 3,500 B.C. on, and then, apparently quite independently in the Far East, in China, about 100 B.C. By then, in the Middle East they were being superseded by alphabetic writing, which was established as the first writing of European countries, especially Greece, and in turn of their colonies. However, the places of record, looked after by clerks or scribes who were in holy orders, were in temples or monasteries, and later in convents and cathedrals, the particular repositories being in modern terms libraries and/or archives, that is, administrative record repositories; this continued to be the case until early modern times. The most famous of the early temple libraries was that in the Museum in Alexandria, Egypt, then a Greek or Macedonian colony. The first part of its name meant the Muses as minor deities, the last part a temple. But this library was not formed until the third century B.C. and long before it there was the Ramesseum of Rameses II, divine native ruler of Egypt, also known as Ozymandias; on the evidence of tradition there was a library in the Ramesseum.

Writing, including printing, is the factor which tends to produce those accelerations in the production of information which have sometimes been called explosions. To what extent the first writing produced an explosion, there is not now sufficient evidence to tell, but certainly when final decipherment of Egyptian hieroglyphic, hieratic and demotic writing--all versions of the same writing--showed what knowledge the Egyptians had, there was disappointment; Egypt had not been another Greece. There was undoubtedly an acceleration of learning, knowledge, information in Greece in the fifth, fourth and third centuries B.C., promoted by men using the much easier alphabetic writing. Though not so spectacularly, this continued with Rome, and in Christianity and the Middle Ages, with steady development towards the Renaissance and modern times. Printing, itself, in the 15th century was an explosion or acceleration of the alphabetic writing of which it was a deliberate mechanization; this helped greatly to generate literacy, and in turn the technology which produced the developments to which the name explosion was first given in the second half of the 20th century. And from about 1876 to 1976 there has been an explosion of IR.

Yet there have been suggestions, even assertions that we have been merely going around in circles. For example, as late as 1974, it was claimed that "the history of cataloging is exceptional in that it is endlessly repetitive. Each generation rethinks and reformulates the same basic problems, reframing them in new contexts and restating them in new terminology."[2] Either this needs at least qualification or the statement made just before it and this outline of development before and after 1876 are quite wrong. The reader must judge for himself. In fact, there seems to have been a reciprocal development in several fields including technology generally, science and various other areas. IR, then, appears as a function, defined in Webster's Collegiate Dictionary, 1973, as "one of a group of related actions contributing to a larger action."

1.3 Ancient Times

Ancient times see the beginning of writing--not, of course, in English and not beginning with the alphabetic-- and, it may be presumed, a beginning of IR at the same time, round about 3,000 B.C. But there is much that is only tradition, assumption and guesswork, even into medieval times. The Ramesseum library already mentioned is said to have had an entrance inscription describing it as a Dispensary of the Mind, but this is a tradition in alphabetic writing about 1,200 years later, when such writing was well established in Greece and Italy, although not yet in native Egypt. What these early hieroglyphics were or may have meant, if anything, would be a guess; the source is Diodorus Siculus, a Greek historian, writing more or less about the time of Caesar and Augustus in well established alphabetic writing while the pictograph was still part of the way of life in once powerful Egypt. The legend includes chests or cupboards with wall inscriptions amounting to a catalog, classified of course. But all this can mean in retrospect is intuitive and rudimentary subject and/or form arrangement of writings not distinguished as information, literature or archives, and probably written according to the order of the monarch; classified did not precede alphabetical arrangement according to some conscious choice, as sometimes seems to be implied. Such was the charm clinging to classical antiquity, said Edwards in 1859, that a treatise on libraries must begin with Greeks and Romans or even Egyptians, "slender as may be the trustworthy information concerning either, and remote as must needs be the relation between such collections,

Introductory, to 1476 5

and those of modern times."³ And Edwards was writing a century before computers.

The clay tablets and cuneiform or wedgeshaped impressions on them, especially those found at Nineveh, the capital of Ashurbanipal (669-633 B.C.), and taken into the British Museum, seem much more promising. Evidence of classification has been asserted by many. Richardson, for example, said, "that Assyrian and Babylonian libraries were classified is certain."⁴ Hessel, in his History of Libraries, said that the books were well arranged by subject, and bore stamps indicating their position in the collection.⁵ The latter seems more certain from a note in Hessel which quotes conflicting opinions: the tablets, being short separate pieces, had to be related in some way in series; more so than papyrus sheets in rolls or, later, bound together leaves with page numbers; and as late as 1929 there wasn't certain evidence of arrangement which amounted to classification or notation.⁶ It has to be remembered that monarchs could have had written down what they wanted, and the collections at Nineveh may have been information recorded to order, something like the much later Chinese encyclopedias. Time was marching on and the next major stop is the temple library in Alexandria, undoubtedly the greatest in antiquity, and probably until the Renaissance. There is little reliability in statistics, however, because of confusion between voluminae or roll counts and estimates, and estimates of the number of works. Homer's Iliad in a bucket could be twenty-four rolls or "books," but is only the length of a modern medium-sized novel and certainly not much larger than Milton's Paradise Lost in its twelve "books."

1.4 Alexandria and Rome

Alexander the Great of Macedonia (356-323 B.C.), in his conquests, established Alexandria in Egypt in 332-331 B.C., intending it to be his world capital. After his death in 323 he was entombed there and one of his generals established a colonial kingdom and dynasty, the Ptolemies, with queens known as Cleopatra, the last of the line, who died with Marc Antony in 30 B.C., being the one who is usually remembered today. The first of the Ptolemies, Ptolemy Soter (323-283), and his son Ptolemy Philadelphus (285-246) established and built up the first Alexandrian library, mainly of Greek literature, Greek having become the official language. Callimachus was long supposed by scholars to have been the second librarian; Edwards claimed so in England in 1859, [7] and Richardson in America as late as 1930. [8] He is still often quoted as the librarian, mainly on Richardson's authority, though scholars reckon him as a bibliographer of Greek literature and a teacher of rhetoric who became something of a consultant in the library, probably suggesting desiderata as well as using its collection in his bibliography. This bibliography, said to have been in 120 books, has only survived in fragments, references and extracts. The individual bibliographies were called Pinakes, a name which might suggest literary portraits, or it could mean painted tablets. In modern modern Italian a pinacoteca is an art gallery, and Pinacotheca means the same in German.

Callimachus appears to have placed writers in "genres," by form rather than subject--Richardson gives these as Poets, Lawmakers, Philosophers, Historians, Rhetoricians or Orators, and Miscellaneous--and then under writers, used title catchwords in alphabetical order. Turner, Professor of Papyrology at University College, London, said in 1968, "this is how works were entered in Callimachus' Pinakes, which could have been used as a short-title guide to the authors contained in the Alexandrian library."[9] Richardson called the catchwords a true "Abbreviations notation,"[10] a term I have not come across elsewhere. Some of the subjects listed by Richardson, such as Fishes, Cheesecakes and Feasts, seem to be trivial subjects of poems rather than informative literature. But though he had to guess at the classification in substance and outline, Richardson decided that the historical tradition of modern classification began with Callimachus, on the discredited assumption that he drew up a classification for the Alexandrian library and classified it. On the authority of Richardson, Sayers called the system designed by Callimachus, the greatest Egyptian librarian, "the earliest recorded system of any dimensions," and this is repeated in the further posthumous edition of his <u>Manual of Classification</u> in 1967.[11]

Of some IR interest also is Turner's discussion of the arrangement of Euripides' plays in buckets according to initial letters of titles, each play being on a roll, and the buckets being a common form of storing them. He also mentions made up rolls of letters received in administration in Ptolemaic Egypt; pasted together end-to-end, each letter could then be given a file reference representing, for example,[12] book box or tub 3, roll 9, sheet 72. He refers to actual rolls which have survived.

Ideas of the Alexandrian library as the collection of a cultured royal gentleman in competition with a rival in Pergamum in Asia Minor, whose supplies of papyrus, practically an Egyptian monopoly, he cut off, forcing him to turn to parchment (in its best form, vellum), and of Antony seizing this library as a gift for Cleopatra, are not to be uncritically accepted. The library, and others in Alexandria, had economic justification in a flourishing booktrade, especially with Roman gentlemen who wanted scholarly editions of Homer and other Greek writers, and this was where such men as Callimachus came in. Reichmann says that despite a great trade in book making and selling, not only in Rome itself but in some provincial cities, Alexandria maintained its position in the Greek book trade.[13] It had the raw material, papyrus, and the library had the texts from which copies could be made; and this seems to have been the calculated imperial purpose of the libraries, not information retrieval; though it must have included scientific writings such as those of Eratosthenes (c. 276-194), who not only measured the diameter of the earth but also became the second librarian of the chief Alexandrian library.

With the Roman Empire based on Rome by Octavius rather than on Alexandria by Marc Antony, Alexandria, along with Egypt, became a Roman colony, but it supplied grain as well as books and papyrus to Rome, and remained the second city of the Empire. The libraries had their ups and downs and complete reconstructions; they suffered Christian destruction of pagan literature, and Mohammedan too, until the final end seems to have come with Mohammedan Arabic conquest in 642 A. D. Omar (c. 581-644) is supposed to have ordered complete destruction, but there was informed pillaging and some books survived, though scattered as far afield as Baghdad.

If the Glory that was Greece produced so much in its Hellenestic, post-Alexander period in a Macedonian colony, it may seem reasonable and has been assumed by many that the Grandeur that was Rome did better, but it was second-rate in culture and literature and a borrower from Greece. It had libraries, some of them in some sense public, but identification with the later public and popular libraries of the 20th century, and their techniques at their simplest, has to be rejected. Its mixture of temple libraries as show places and its archives is hardly relevant here; and they suffered in the decline and fall. The important libraries by which culture was transmitted into the medieval period seem to

have been private ones, something like the later ones of
Renaissance princes and dictators. Irwin, reporting on technique, quotes authority that in the Ulpian library, something
of an official archives, there were in a sixth book press
'librum elephantinum,' meaning engravings on ivory plates of
archival significance. The presses were evidently numbered
serially and though Irwin does not express any opinion of Roman libraries as some retrospective patriots have done, nevertheless, with typical British interest in classification, he says
this numbering may "indicate some kind of classified arrangement."14 In the context, however, all that seems to be indicated
is numbered location of miscellaneous things, and simple location numbering is not even evidence of the later and now
generally superseded fixed location numbering, in which the
numbered location had subject identification.

Cassiodorus (c. 490-c. 585) is regarded as a transition
figure from ancient to medieval. He was of a Syrian family
settled in southern Italy, which became wealthy and influential in the 5th century A. D. , holding important public positions. They were Christians, or Cassiodorus was a convert.
Amongst several written works that are relevant here is his
Institutiones Divinarum et Humanorum Literarum, a sort of
anthology or encyclopedia about literature, sacred and profane, and libraries, compiled for monks in two monasteries
which he established on family estates. He may thus to
some extent have anticipated and influenced his contemporary,
St. Benedictine (c. 480-547), founder of the Benedictine order.
He saw as one of his tasks assisting the studies, especially
of commentaries on the Bible, by student monks, who were
not always very literate in Latin.

The standard book early adopted by Christians had become the codex, the present day hinged-leaf book which differed significantly from the roll or volumen but was still
called a volume. Through medieval times it usually lacked
the later apparatus of title page, table of contents, clearly
divided chapters and headings, and a concluding alphabetical
index. In Latin it began, of course, in manuscript, with the
Latin word incipit, meaning "here begins," followed by a
description of what might be a complete if short, pamphlet-
sized work, or a book or a chapter in a collection of works
such as the Bible, which began as the Biblia Sacra (sacred
books) and only by binding got its reputation as a unified
work in its two principal parts, the Old and New Testaments.

Irwin says Cassiodorus was led into introducing "a

Introductory, to 1476 9

system of classification symbols ... the earliest, I think, of
which we have any detailed knowledge." To enable the student to identify the many patristic commentaries these are
marked in red ink at the beginning of each codex with appropriate symbols. For example, commentaries on the Octateuch
are marked OCT. He says there is no direct reference to a
catalog of the library, but in this passage, "(1.26), the use
of the word indices ('I have set down relevant symbols as indices for the codices...') may suggest a shelf list thus
marked."[15] But in Latin, index meant indicator. It could
extend to a list, and Irwin himself spoke of it as not implying necessarily an organized catalog. It seems to have meant
the tag or Sittyba hanging out of a roll in a pigeonhole for
identification; this word became corrupted into syllabus. In
late Latin a manuscript's page of contents was called a tabula generalis, and an index a tabula alphabeticum, and for
some time the term alphabetical table was used for an alphabetical index in English, even in printed books. However,
the identifying marks of commentary on particular books in
closely written bible commentaries, the red abbreviations
described by Cassiodorus, while listed at the beginning of a
codex, must have had marginal repetition to catch the eye of
the reader, and these would probably be like the rubrication
of illuminated manuscripts which persisted in printed prayer
books. The writing of Cassiodorus himself in Latin and as
translated into English suggests this. Irwin compared the
Cassiodorus symbols with an indexing system used by Grosseteste (c. 1175-1253), but Richardson refers to a true abbreviations notation in Callimachus. If what was already arranged in a book followed the order of the Bible, however,
they could hardly be a classification. This shows again a
tendency to jump at numbers as notations, necessarily implying classification, and a tendency to assume that such
words as index in Latin or Greek must have meant what they
meant later.

1.5 Medieval Times

In medieval times in Europe the monastic library replaces the temple library, and the codex or hinged-leaf book
the roll or volumen, though the word volume is still used
and the volume in its apparatus was not that which developed
with printing. Savage described cooperative bibliography in
the Middle Ages but he did not present this as general. He
described registers maintained by Franciscans of copies of
works they found in monastic libraries they visited and used

especially in biblical studies, and pointed out that these were
not catalogs.[16] In monastic libraries there were some divisions of books into such classes as sacred and profane, and
according to languages, Latin, Greek, Hebrew. But monastic
orders placed great emphasis on their books and libraries as
property which was not cheap or easily replaced; what have
been loosely described as catalogs were rather inventories
used in annual checks or audits of what were not identical
copies of works according to standard bibliographical descriptions as in later printed editions of works, but individual
copies with differences which could make them good or bad.
It was not very easy for a not very literate monk to identify
even a work, much less a particular copy. A practice grew
up of putting identifying marks in volumes and in the inventories, and there have been the same old assumptions that
these were or could be classification notation. Authorities
have warned against this.[17,18] The libraries were not large
by later standards in volume count, and the volumes were
largely composite volumes of works of pamphlet size. The
catalog or shelf list often consisted of statements that the
volume numbered XLVI contained ten or more works which
might be listed, but there is little evidence of indexing.
Where such a listing did not exist, during the decline of the
monasteries books of importance were often lost for centuries.

What was more productive in many ways was the verbal indexing of the Bible to aid the study of concordance or
harmony in the use of words in it. The name of the purpose
of the indexing (concordance) was unfortunately later con-
ferred upon the method, used for general subject indexing of
books by title word. With some forerunning the first concordance was organized by Cardinal Hugh of St. Cler, who
died in 1263. A Dominican monk, he is said to have used
five hundred monks on the task, not having at hand the services of the computer, still about six hundred years in the
future. Stephen Langton (d. 1228) is said to have divided
the Bible books into chapters, so reference was to book and
chapter, the familiar "chapter and verse" reference coming
later.[19] No context of the words indexed was given, as became the practice later, and reference appears to have been
to St. Jerome's version. The alphabetization was probably
not exact, but to index such a great work at all was a great
advance and could be said to have advertised the possibilities
of indexing. Concordances before and after Cruden's in English must have shown many, including librarians, the possibilities of alphabetical indexing alongside classification. The
original concordance bible indexing was verbal, of words as

Introductory, to 1476

words; it could of course also be subject indexing but could miss real concordance indexing. (The German language uses the word concordance more precisely than English.) An English example, C. R. Joy's Concordance of Subjects, indexes passages on charity as a subject even though the word doesn't appear in such passages; this, of course, helps preachers. As Bibles have continued to rely on this chapter and verse indexing, many of them are still without pagination, even in print. And if a text is fixed, such as that of the Authorised Version in English, then the same reference serves all printings.

1.6 Paper and Printing

Paper gets its name from Egyptian papyrus, once sometimes referred to as paper. Papyrus, parchment and vellum, and clay tablets were treated materials, but they were not broken down and reconstructed, as materials are for paper. Papyrus was strips of the pith of the plant, placed crosswise to each other, stuck together by their own sap or some adhesive, then smoothed down for writing on one side or sometimes both. If papyrus were broken down into its fibers, or if any other vegetable material were treated in the same way, and the fibers then floated together into a felt with drying and pressing, the result would be the later paper, invented in China and used for various purposes as papyrus was in Egypt. Its Chinese use for writing dates from about 100 A.D.; printing on paper in China dates back to about 1000 A.D. Paper is not a textile, not woven, but is technically a felt, originally made from textile fibers from discarded rags. With no thought of printing, Europe needed something that could be manufactured like paper, without waiting on vegetable and animal growth as with papyrus or parchment and vellum, and it began as a cheap, despised substitute, coming through China but made in Spain and Italy probably through Arab transmission in the 11th century.

The relationship of printing development and paper as seen in retrospect was hardly apparent at the time. Gutenberg printed forms of indulgence for the church on paper, as did Caxton in England. Both wanted to print fine books, and did, but Gutenberg began with a Bible on vellum, in the style of the best illuminated manuscript books, with the color work added by hand. By Caxton's time it was becoming apparent that the printed book had to develop a style of its own, and would need to use paper, though it came to depend on slow growing trees and became short in supply as papyrus had. However, what seems clear is that, unlike paper, printing did not come from China. Chinese printing was a simple mechanization of Chinese writing. Ideas or concepts such as stars, rats and arts were represented by ideograms carved on small wooden blocks. Water colors could be smeared on a group of these blocks, and paper lightly pressed on them and peeled off with an impression on it. The European printers saw their problem as one of mechanizing alphabetic writing, and had the advantage of an alphabet of only about twenty-six letters compared with the hundreds and even thousands of Chinese word or idea representations by what were basically pictograms.

The letters A, R, S, T are all in the alphabet, and are all in the words stars, rats, arts, and in others such as tsar and tars. Hence the possibility of interchangeable type or letter stamps, called movable type; there had to be many more than one of each letter, and more of some than others, but if molds could be made of the letters in their different styles and used successfully, any number of the same letter could be made from each mold. The technical problems were not easily solved, especially as what was envisaged was printing from the letters in type or stamp form, without enlargement or reduction of what was printed. Metal workers succeeded where wood carvers or engravers had failed, except for some illustrating; metal workers accepted the weight of metal type and so the Chinese way of impressing paper or parchment or papyrus on the type--a whole page of it--and distinguished their printing as letterpress. They held the composed type together in a form or frame, used oil paint as ink on it, and with a heavy screw press, thought to have been modeled on winepresses, impressed their sheets of paper on the type with a careful turn of the screw. In the light of later developments this entirely hand and screw press method was very slow, but producing a written page, even only one at a time on a leaf of paper, at a single impression or stamping, was quicker than the slow drawing of the letters one by one which was called writing. Even typewriting one letter at a time, which was not practicable enough for commercialization until 1874, is of course quicker than handwriting of letters.

Printing meant that existing works could be readily duplicated in exact facsimile, and this created a demand for new works which could be printed. The relation of libraries and the production of informative literature and its availability

Introductory, to 1476

was changed, but on the whole for the good. And, as happened in Greece when it got alphabetic writing, there was an information explosion or acceleration, one which continued much longer and still continues. Gutenberg quickly had imitators, including Caxton, a late one who was printing in Bruges about 1475. The four centuries from 1476 to 1876 bring us well into modern times, but in this period printing was at least a factor in developments in IR which continued in influence and use after 1876, despite the great developments of that year; whereas with the printed book there is undoubtedly a cut-off from the medieval period and its books and their writing, Bible concordance indexing being probably of more influence during that period than anything else.

Chapter 2

1476 TO 1876

2.1 Transition

By 1476 printing was not only established but had reached the stage where attempts to imitate manuscripts had been virtually abandoned. Gutenberg had begun with a deluxe bible which was not intended to deceive but to let churches, monasteries, and convents buy relatively cheaply a bible similar to the best they were familiar with. Gutenberg first used hand illumination in spaces left in the printed pages, which were left unbound until illustrated; then perhaps in his Psalter of 1457 used some color printing. The Roman styles of type which later became standard, even in Germany, were developed in particular by Jenson in Venice.

For IR, other developments were more important and came more slowly; in printing and publishing--both themselves new developments both in technique and as trades-- were developed what became known as preliminaries, though they were printed last. These consisted of introductory matter placed before the actual text, which hitherto had begun with its "incipit" or "here beginneth," and had ended with its "here endeth" or "explicit" and/or its colophon, usually contributed by the scribe. These latter items became the information set out on title pages, particularly on the verso of the full title page, which was now often more the publisher's than the author's. The preliminaries could be printed as a separate section and were probably mostly used as separates for advertising what was perhaps the first more or less mass-produced, machine article to be sold off the shelf. There had been some manuscript production of this kind, especially for student use, though it was usually not very good. Good or bad, the printed book had the advantage that it was the same in all copies, the process only being stopped for some minor corrections.

The preliminaries of IR importance included the con-

1476 to 1876

tents page and the index, if any, though it became the English custom to print the latter at the book's end. Changes in titling, of books as a whole and of what were still called chapters--a word derived from the Latin capitulae, for headings --may be called bibliographical. As a result of these, books were eventually to be described bibliographically, but the changes were not made with the development of standard bibliographical description in mind. There are, then, two meanings of bibliography: first, the description of books and parts of them which appears within the books themselves; and then, cataloging description based on these descriptions. A third meaning is the listing of books apart from libraries; within libraries, much the same description happens to be called cataloging. In library catalogs and in bibliographies at large it is also sometimes called indexing, especially if it includes analytical indexing of parts.

At the turning point which came with printing, and with the religion turmoil and its effect upon monastic libraries, there was now reason for some bibliographical survey of available literature such as Callimachus had attempted about 1700 years before. If this seems an incredible gap in light of the great speed-up in modern times, it was to take yet another four centuries, from 1476 to 1876, before the next two great and still-persisting leaps forward, though there was acceleration of most of the prior development in the fourth of these centuries, from 1800 on. However, whatever the reason, in the first century of printing, even in its first half-century, modern bibliography in the sense of simply the listing of books began with Tritheim (1462-1516) and Gesner (1516-1565).[20]

2.2 Bibliography, Tritheim and Gesner

Conrad von Gesner, a Swiss scientist (1516-1565), was displaced by Johann Tritheim as the father of modern systematic bibliography on the authority of Besterman in his Beginnings of Systematic Bibliography (1936).[21] Tritheim took over a run-down monastery at Sponheim in Germany, 1483-1505, when the library had only ten volumes; he was in some ways like Cassiodorus and Callimachus; he regenerated the library, and it was probably looking for desiderata that led him into systematic bibliography; there was, however, a decline again and the library seems to have disappeared in the Reformation troubles. His printed bibliography was lost sight of. Edwards had an account of him but not a clear one of the bibliography, which he may have confused with a catalog of the library.[22] The bibliography was arranged alphabetically, with an alphabetical index of authors. Edwards suggested that he salvaged many manuscript books by exchanging newly printed books for them, and this might well have been his motivation as it had been that of Callimachus and the Alexandrian library with Greek books.

Edwards thought publishers' classified lists were the earliest catalogs of printed books, but classification has always had merit for trade bibliography as an aid to book selection. Edwards cited a couple of lists with a mixture of languages, form and broad subjects, and then said that in 1548, "we arrive at what some writers have termed the first bibliographical system published with a view to the use rather than the sale of books; it is that of Conrad Gesner, and appeared in the shape of an index of matters to his Bibliothèque Universelle, under the title of Pandectarum sive partitionum universalium librari xxi." This looks like typical cart before the horse; the Bibliothèque Universelle arranged alphabetically seems at least as much bibliography as the complementary classification. But Edwards and other British writers present Gesner as first and foremost a classification maker and classifier, and both Richardson and Bliss in America seem to see him only as a classification maker;[23, 24, 25] and they too made their influence in England rather than America. Edwards usefully distinguished classificatory systems as being either of a philosophical basis or mainly practical;[26] and was followed in this by Sayers.[27] It is however of some importance to distinguish systems which may have had no bibliographical application, at least as referred to.

Richardson referred to Cassiodorus' use of the seven liberal arts curriculum of the Middle Ages as a classification, but gives no evidence that Cassiodorus used it as a bibliographical classification;[28] and Bacon's and other philosophical classifications, though adapted for bibliographical use, were not primarily bibliographic classifications. In his first enunciation, in 1907, of what he called "canons of classification," Sayers attempted an identification of evolutionary and historical order and the extension and intension (or denotation and connotation) of logic, which was absurd, as Jast pointed out.[29] In 1924, in the first edition of his Manual of Classification, Sayers seems to have had no knowledge of the seven liberal arts as a university curriculum and was in difficulty in explaining Gesner's classification as philosophical,[30] but he caught up and found out that "the Trivium and the

Quadrivium appears ... in almost every scholastic and philosophical classification and most strikingly in ... Gesner."31 The originally Greek encyclopedic curriculum is obvious in Gesner, though he does not follow it rigidly. But between 1907 and 1924 Sayers had completely altered his canons. Brunet's later manual is another bibliography which, like Gesner's, was subsequently treated as though it were no more than a classification. Gesner did not fit his system with a notation for practical use, but his system was used, notably in the Wolfenbüttel library under Leibnitz, though Leibnitz also had his own ideas on classification.32

2.3 Philosophical Classification, Bacon and His Adapters

Gesner, with wide attainments in languages, history and science, made a reputation in the beginnings of biological science, especially in botany and zoology, in a classificatory way. Branching into general bibliography, he made a classification as others have done for bibliographies and for library catalogs. Sayers, beginning in ignorance of the ancient Greek circle of liberal studies, or cyclopaedia, exaggerated its philosophy. However, philosophical or not, it was a classification for books, and had some influence, notably on Savigny in France in 1587.33 And Savigny has been said in France to have influenced Bacon, which on comparison and other evidence seems most unlikely.

Bacon, like Gesner, would have become famous without his classification, if only as an English lawyer and politician. Born in 1561 when Gesner was 45, he died at 65 in 1626. Christophe de Savigny published his classification in 1587. Bacon, first publishing in 1605, could have been aware of both Savigny's and Gesner's classifications, but was he influenced by them? First, his classification was one for philosophy, learning and knowledge; it was partly epistemological but more metaphysical. It was a classification for the objects of knowledge and learning, and of writing about them of which Bacon was aware; but he did not present it as a bibliography or library classification. It did not resemble Gesner's, nor Savigny's either, which was similar to Gesner's. Though the fact never seems to have become what could be called common knowledge, Bacon had a source for his classification which he does not seem ever to have acknowledged. Bibliographical acknowledgments were not so common in the scholarship of his day as they became in later pretensions to scholarship, and his source--somewhat like

Freud's psychological theories from about 1920 to 1950--
was so well known as to be possibly taken for granted.

Pierre Charron (1514-1603), one of 25 children of a
bookseller, might have become a bookseller himself. Had
he been a successful advocate, he might have remained a
lawyer, but he was not successful. He entered the Church and
found success at last as a preacher. Becoming a friend of
Montaigne's he also became a defender of the Roman Catholic
faith, then unexpectedly in 1601 published what he called de
la Sagesse, "a complete system of moral philosophy." It
was subject to attacks, censorship and suppression until his
death in 1603. It did include a psychology, which was sen-
sational in two senses; dividing the intelligent soul into three
faculties, he shows, in the manner which Francis Bacon subsequently adopted, the branches of science corresponding with
each of the faculties. This division Bacon stated in his Ad-
vancement of Learning in 1605 when he said that "the three
parts of human learning have reference to the three parts of
man's understanding, which is the seat of learning: history
to his memory, poesy to his imagination, and philosophy to
his reason." What emphasis Bacon placed on order is not
clear, but an accompanying chart gave the same order in
1605: I. History, including natural history; II. Poesy; III.
Philosophy. The order remained the same in his expansion,
De Augmentis Scientarium, in 1623. It may be said to have
a scientific rather than a philosophic basis, hence some of
the variations of it.

At least in some ways Bacon seems to have made
more appeal in France, where social and philosophical revolution were building up, than in England, and he in his turn
was subject to adapters. The French scientist d'Alembert
(1717-1783), who became associated with the French encyclo-
pedist Diderot, in the Discourse Preliminaire on social arguments, in Diderot's encyclopaedia on science, turned Bacon's
order into: I. History; II. Philosophy; III. Poetry. His version became accepted as Bacon's, even in America, which
was also moving into revolution, and even Edwards in England seems to have fallen into confusion and given d'Alembert's version as Bacon's. In America d'Alembert's version
was accepted as Bacon's and E. W. Johnston (1799-1867)
used it finally in the St. Louis Mercantile Library. Then
even the American authority Leo LaMontagne seems to have
become confused, [34] stating that W. T. Harris (1835-1909)
inverted Johnston, which would produce: first, History, including Natural History; then Philosophy, including Natural

Philosophy or Science; and finally, Literature. What becomes apparent, however, from Harris's own account is that in 1870 he went right back to the original Bacon, inverting his order, leaving what he called Art still in the middle, but placing what he called Science first and History, no longer including natural history, third. The importance of this is that it is what Dewey adopted as the "inverted Baconian" arrangement in 1873-76, as discussed in the next chapter. LaMontagne in 1961 suggested an American belief that there was a leap from Bacon in the early 17th century, through Harris's inversion, to Dewey in the third quarter of the 19th, Harris thus becoming the father and Dewey the son in American classification. This also seems to have been the British belief. But in fact American history from 1776 to 1876 seems to have been richer than this theory suggests. 35, 36

2.4 Index Learning

Alexander Pope (1688-1744) originated the phrase "index learning" in his Dunciad, published in 1728, in which he satirized contemporary literary critics and men of letters. Among other things he referred satirically to index learning "that turns no student pale, yet holds the eel of science by the tail." But Joseph Glanvil (1636-1680) in his Vanity of Dogmatizing had said, "methinks 'tis a pitiful piece of knowledge that can be learnt from an index, and a poor ambition to be rich in the inventory of another's treasure"; and Swift (1667-1748), in his Battle of the Books written in 1697, attacked alphabetical indexing of books with metaphors of entering a gentleman's house by the back door, putting salt on sparrows tails to catch them, and tickling fish. 37 Pope seems to have read Swift. But when the Chambers's Encyclopaedia was published in alphabetical form when there was still prejudice against this arrangement and in favor of classified, it quoted Pope in support of alphabetical arrangement despite his earlier satire. Books such as Foxe's Book of Martyrs, that could be said to supplement the Bible for protestant preachers, and the Histriomastix by Prynne (1600-1669) had their indexes. Prynne, indeed, was said to have betrayed himself by saying in his index that Christ was a Puritan, and lost his ears for it. Here, at least, was negative acknowledgment of the value of indexing.

The literary reaction of Swift and Pope to indexes also had its opposite, as Wheatley showed in his How to Make an Index, 1902. This, like his How to Make a Catalog of a

Library, 1889, was a good if not adequate state of the art book, and quoted supporters of indexing. It is interesting that many of these books explained indexing as something new. Marbeck's First English Concordance of the Whole Bible in English (London, 1550) was described as "A concordance, that is to say, a worke wherein by the order of the letters of the A. B. C. ye may readily find any words contained in the whole Bible, as often as it is there expressed or mentioned." It might therefore be said, despite all the talk, that in modern times alphabetical IR preceded classified. Analytical indexing of books is different from cataloging or indexing books as wholes, and not so simple. Whereas whole books usually have fairly easily discernible subjects, many related or incidental may lie within a book, and they are not easily reduced to a principle or method. In general, book indexes are not good, and this is often because of an author's limitations or particular interest in the use of words.

The index learning controversy shows that cataloging was seen as cataloging of books as wholes, and inquirers heard of or found reference to these as the works of specific authors and expected them to be cataloged in this way if a library had them. As late as 1876 W. Stanley Jevons, in his Principles of Science, a Treatise on Logic and Scientific Method,[38] was basically interested in subjects and yet saw authorship as a better characteristic for the cataloging of books than anything else, though he did not object to subordinate cataloging, provided this was not classified. In this he followed another distinguished logician, De Morgan, and said, unfortunately without sufficient qualification, that the classification of books by subject is a logical absurdity--which may well be strictly true. A later logician, in 1957, referred to librarians' idea of classification following on the mere splitting up of topics as being a superstition which has prevailed "with disastrous consequences."[39]

Author cataloging, of course, cannot be a substitute for subject cataloging, which itself can be alphabetical. Nevertheless, subject cataloging was not seen as a necessity by the literary men of the generations of Swift and Pope, nor even by some much later. The conflict which was coming up, however, was not between author and subject cataloging. The index learning controversy, as indicative of attitudes, was not irrelevant to IR. Book indexing as an aid in searching literature for specific information existed and was going to continue, but it involved technical problems. Some of these are relevant here and pertain to what may be called location reference, a question not solved by alphabetical arrangement of subject names or words in themselves.

2.5 Location Reference

Clearly putting CHARITY in alphabetical order does not say where in the Bible the word and probably something on the subject appears. Context helps, as in CHARITY--"But c. edifieth"; but "I Cor viii, 1" gives the location in the Authorized version of the Bible in English of the verse which says, "Now as touching things offered unto idols, we know that we all have knowledge. Knowledge puffeth up, but charity edifieth." How did this chapter and verse indexing come about, and why isn't it more used?

To begin with individual manuscripts, though of the same text they often differed in their spacing out, and this difference remained with printing--not between single copies but between editions. The Bible, however, had come to have fixed content and arrangement according to the "canon," and though there were differences in layout in different editions of an Anglican or Episcopalian version, any book chapter and verse would be in the same relative place. There was thus no need for page numbers and in some Bible editions they are still not given; only in front is there a list of the originally separate books of the Biblia Sacra, in their proper order and showing the number of chapters in each; for example, I Corinthians 16.

Later, this relative location numbering became accepted in classification numbering or notation. But books generally, as they appeared in print, came to have numbered pages, to which index references could be made. The index, however, would often be applicable only to one edition, and a whole page might have to be searched for a word used often. In addition, there might be references from the same word on many pages, and no contextual help in the index.

Printed library catalogs, however, did allow this kind of reference from subjects, or authors, or titles, to entries which might be identified by headings, or by words in the titles given in the entries. An entry in such a printed volume--the predecessors of card catalogs--might have the shelf number of a book, called a press mark, but these might only be written in some copies of the catalog or in a "finding list" which supplemented the catalog. Later notations, which among other things have given a number used as a shelf number, have also been used with classifications and taken for granted, especially with relative location as shown in the next chapter with particular reference to DDC. In classification schemes classes were usually numbered for reference in catalog use, but earlier thinking is indicated in Edwards' Memoirs of Libraries, 1859. His chapter on classificatory systems gives their classes and numbering for catalogs which he assumed to be in printed volume form, but he has a quite separate and unrelated chapter on what he calls "local arrangement" and its applications.

    In ordinary books, paragraph numbering used in indexing seemed an improvement but the paragraph numbers on a page are not as easily found as the page numbers, which are regularly placed. Also, since a new edition of a book is usually altered and expanded, there is no longer the advantage that Bibles have had. In Sayers' Manual of Classification (3rd ed. revised, 1959), a paragraph (202) on Cutter's Expansive Classification was about sixty lines over two pages; in the posthumous edition edited by Maltby in 1967, it has been more than halved, though it retains much the same substance, including the questionable statement which LaMontagne's book in 1961 amply disproved: that the 1876 Bureau of Education Report on Public Libraries showed that until that time classification was not a common study in America. The new paragraph number is 119, but having read LaMontagne, Sayers' editor in a new paragraph 113 says, "the real beginnings of library classification, as we know it today, took place in the nineteenth century and most of the important steps forward were made by libraries in the United States"; there must, in light of this, have been some interest before 1876. Although there might have been the same difficulties with page number references, these examples from Sayers show that paragraph numbering, from one edition to the next, is no more helpful. Two French classification systems, influential in different ways--Brunet's and Merlin's--and before them an English one, Dryander's of Banks' library, may now be considered.

2.6 Dryander

    Jonas Dryander (1748-1810) was a Swedish botanist of note who became librarian to the wealthy English naturalist, Sir Joseph Banks, who accompanied Cook in his discovery of the East coast of Australia and became the last amateur Pres-

1476 to 1876

ident of the Royal Society from 1778 to his death at the age of 77 in 1820. Banks' natural history collection eventually passed to the British Museum, but before that Dryander had made a catalog published in five volumes, 1796-1800. For some at least these were opulent days, and the catalog was typical in being one of a private collection. It even had its own classification, three quarters of a century before the first one separately published for general use, DDC in 1876, and it anticipated library use of card catalogs at a time when printed volumes were taken for granted.

The classification was simple, following the natural history of the day, with four main subject class volumes, and one general author index volume, and the notation was simple class numbering. What was unusual was the subject alphabetical indexing of each class volume; but this was not classification indexing such as in DDC. To exemplify, there were, beginning on page 107 of the Zoology volume, items headed "208--de Cetis Scriptores," meaning items on whales. One of these is entitled "An essay upon the natural history of whales, with a particular account of the Ambergris found in the Sperma Ceti Whale." Another entry of this item might be expected in a subclass Medica, with a subsubclass Ambra, containing items on Ambra grisea. But the index refers from Whales to page 107 for the 208 general class on whales, and to the same page for Ambergris, the intention being that the latter word can be found by scanning the entries on the page.

Several points here are relevant to historical development. By having a subject index at all Dryander's catalog anticipated developments and practice in Great Britain by nearly a century, but the index mixes books cataloged and subjects, and with references to page numbers, not class numbers. The catalog has only a single entry for each item, so that here we have a mixture of alphabetical subject indexing by the title word method and class indexing. Those who advocated classed catalogs welcomed Dryander's as a good example. H. B. Wheatley, who was still expressing hostility to classified catalogs in his How to Catalogue a Library (1889), did not mention Dryander's; nor did Edwards in his Memoirs of Libraries (1859), though he was in favor of classificatory systems in general, but perhaps more in the systems per se than in their use. Some copies of the catalog may have had location reference numbers written in, but they were not printed with the entries. A catalog was a catalog, and a common method of actually locating books was to have an extra finding list, arranged alphabetically by authors.

Edwards said of the <u>Catalogue of the Library of the London Institution</u>, which was systematically classed, that it was "one of the best productions extant in its kind." Referring to it as first printed in 1835 and completed in 1852, Wheatley said in 1889 that it was very useful as a bibliography but that "what shows the general uselessness of a classified catalogue for the work of a library is that in actual practice an alphabetical finding list has been in more constant use than the fuller catalogue." In his index Wheatley had the following entry: "Catalogue - Classed, nearly useless." Such prejudice was soon to change in Great Britain. 40

The ultimate in the finding list idea may be that of a collection of bibliographies which are checked for subject references which are then checked in a library's catalog. This idea has been tried and not forgotten. One trouble in the past has been that bibliographies have differed widely in arrangement, each of which has had to be mastered before consultation could be relied on. The finding list in this instance becomes the library's author catalog. This is the idea which came to pass with periodical indexing with some uniformity of indexing, especially in indexes such as those of the H. W. Wilson Company. Librarians take it for granted that they note references and then check their holdings. And something like this has been done with the BML subject index and, later, the <u>British National Bibliography</u>. The advantage of the self-contained catalog with location references has been for the man in a hurry; he finds or has found for him what a library has on a subject, and at least gets that.

2.7 Brunet's Manuel

Brunet's <u>Manuel</u> was used as a bibliography complementary to libraries' catalogs. Jacques Charles Brunet (1780-1847), son of a bookseller, compiled a bibliography he called <u>Manuel du libraire et de l'amateur de livres rares</u>; published in 1820 in three volumes, it was finally in six volumes in a 5th edition, 1860-1865, with a supplement, 1878-1880. Like Gesner's work it was an author or title catalog, which he called "Dictionnaire Bibliographique," in 5 volumes, plus a short title classified catalog which he called "Table Methodique." As with Gesner, Brunet has been most notably considered as the author of a classification, and its relation to an alphabetical author and title catalog has been forgotten. In both an early and a later period, what LaMontagne called "the Brunet" was a rival of "the Bacon" in America.

The classified titles or groups of items are numbered, so that it may be calculated that it included from 45 to 50,000 items, an equivalent of the later library of about a million. There is cross-reference from the detailed bibliography entries to the classified short-title entries by their numbers, but without the purpose being clearly stated. The subject classification of a known item could be ascertained, however, and it might be found grouped with others which a bookseller might be able to supply. Harris said that the Manuel was clearly made for the antiquarian booksellers in Paris rather than its libraries and whether Brunet remained connected with the trade or not, his thinking seems to have been informed by it. His classification has been considered practical rather than philosophical, but it was philosophized to the extent that all general classifications tend to be in their order, as they must be to accommodate literature which reflects prevailing social philosophies. At one period accustomed to close association of church and state, ecclesiastical or church history seems obviously a part of general political history; at another, it is accepted as clearly belonging with religion. Science in the present is first distinguished from merely descriptive natural history and seen as natural philosophy, but with its development and application is seen as closely related to the useful arts, which are renamed technology or applied science.

A detailed classification, Brunet's is hierarchical, and while it has no subject index it has a closely printed "Order des Divisions" in 36 columns, and there is hierarchical notation. For example: III - Science; 4 - Zoology; E - Invertebrate animals; a - Crustacean to f - Intestinal worms. There are also entry numbers here, 6668-6174, but this item numbering with cross reference from the alphabetical section is not part of the notation. The subject notation would have been "mixed, cumbrous and obsolete" if, as Sayers seemed to think, Brunet intended such combinations as III4Ef as a class number for intestinal worms; but he apparently had no such idea.[40] The correspondence here is with similar notation in the contents listing of some books, and with their subnotation of sections and subsections in chapters. Later Brunet versions, especially in a period of what LaMontagne called Brunet remodeled, in America, 1880-1882, had notations influenced by DDC. Mixed notation such as Brunet's provided few problems of variations, because he could use both roman and arabic figures and letters in upper and lower case, and his subsections rarely ran over ten.

2.8 Merlin, Richardson and Sayers

R. Merlin, the cataloger of the library of Silvestre de Sacy, is identified with philosophical classification in the sense of classification derived from one principle--a principle which was becoming known as evolution. This was not meant necessarily in the strict, biological sense, where the term is identified with the emergence of biological species and with Darwin, whose theories on the idea were finally accepted after the publication of his Origin of Species in 1859, the same year as Edwards' Memoirs of Libraries. The idea was not new and clearly Edwards was one of those who did not accept it; he even described it as a philosophical blunder,[41] going beyond his proper limits as a writer on libraries and bibliography. A conference of librarians was held in New York in 1853, and might have been but was not the beginning of the ALA, which had to await the stimulus of the centenary of 1876. Merlin did not attend but he wrote to that 1853 convention.

Many years later, in 1900-01, Dr. Ernest Cushing Richardson lectured to the New York State Library Association Alumni on "Classification Theoretical and Practical According to Merlin's Philosophy." The lectures, 44 pages and going into three editions, were filled out with a bibliography of classifications. On Merlin he said, "it is amusing at this day to note" Edwards' criticism, and concluded that it "seems clear that if M. Merlin had been more successful as a promoter ... we should have been much further advanced in the matter at the present day."[42] Richardson preached the Merlin doctrine for about half a century, with more influence on theory than practice, and more in Great Britain than America, where it was accepted that Cutter's alphabetical subject cataloging was not scientific.

His lectures included a sketchy page of "Criteria of a practical book classification." An important point was that such a classification must follow the order of things, and "must therefore, follow the order or the complexity of history, or, if you please, of evolution"--which isn't very definitive.[43] In 1907 Sayers first stated what he called some "Canons of classification" applied to the Subject Classification, meaning Brown's. These canons were much more elaborate and better organized than Richardson's Criteria, but were also unsound. Sayers was then 26, and Richardson was his major authority. British librarians, particularly in public libraries, resisted the recruitment or employment of graduates, but they were impressed by doctorates. Americans like Richardson and Bliss came equipped with doctorates in philosophy; in England itself, there was Bradford with a doctorate apparently in science; and then there was Ranganathan from India with a doctorate apparently in mathematics.

Wyndham Hulme, with a bachelor's degree from Oxford or Cambridge, hardly rated in such company, but he seemed fairly sound on logic. In discussion he said, "Book classification was not a science. It was an art like that of fitting a child's puzzle together," a thesis he developed in his LAR articles of 1911-12. Jast, at the same meeting with Hulme and thirty members in London, and much better in his self education than Sayers, said "he was inclined to think that neither Doctor Richardson, nor the late Mr. Franklin Barrett, if he were alive, nor himself would be able really to find themselves in this rehash of what they had individually stated." He found especially hopeless Sayers' attempt to equate not only history and evolution but also the logical concepts of extension or denotation and intension or connotation of terms in logic. Briefly, Jast was declaring that Sayers didn't know what he was talking about. But instead of dropping his canons as he might have done, Sayers went on using them, especially in his Manual of Classification, but with increasing modification and muddle from edition to edition. He stuck to Richardson, who had not introduced the logical term ideas of extension and intension; but that was hardly any matter. Evolution as a popular idea and Sayers' textbooks in a centralized examination and certification system were to last for about forty years. 44

2.9 Classification in the British Museum Library

The first account of classification in the BML seems to have been in a "Synopsis of Numbered Rooms and Contents," with which went, in 1808, an "Analytical Syllabus," containing five classes--Theology, Jurisprudence, Science and Arts, History, Belles-Lettres. There seem to have been common origins with Brunet, but there are a variety of different explanations of this origin. 45

An attempt at an actual classified catalog was the work of Thomas Hartwell Horne (1780-1862), a theologian and bibliographer of contemporary note. Edwards praised his outline and it was apparently deserving of such praise. It was more up-to-date than Brunet's though Edwards did not approve

Horne's moving of ecclesiastical history out of general History and into Theology and Religion. Horne's attempt was dropped and Esdaile, never lacking in extravagant praise of Panizzi, said that his hand "may surely be seen in the massacre of Horne's classed catalog." Panizzi was not a classification man. But the catalog--eventually to be an author catalog complemented with a later alphabetical subject index and shelf arrangement and notation--and classification were still separate considerations.

Of Thomas Watts (1811-1869), not to be confused with Dr. Robert Watt (1774-1869), Esdaile says he was overshadowed by Panizzi, as others were who perhaps lacked Panizzi's unexpected "charisma." Those who worked with Panizzi, however, differed in their opinions, some describing him as a tyrant and a steamroller. Watts, of lowly social origins and largely self educated, nevertheless became involved in movements of stock as the library grew until its famous round reading room and iron library, for which Panizzi got much credit, were finally inadequate in their quadrangular prison. Watts is said to have suggested this building in a quadrangle, which was later copied in Melbourne. He made a new adaptation of the classification, but with an actual physical and numerical warrant for its classes, which were identified with large two-level book presses. These presses were given a gap system of numbering, allowing interpolation, and eventually the BM was in luck when a system of suspended presses was found which was adaptable to its iron library. It had, of course, to be possible actually to insert a press when dividing the contents of one into two; some volumes could be left in one press with numbers unaltered, others would be renumbered in a new press, and following presses and their contents would be left unaltered in their numbers. The main consideration was the catalog location references, and these, according to Garnett, were not interfered with. This was called Watts' elastic system, and even after the later introduction of relative location and numbering in America, it was considered superior by some librarians there. In 1953 Hill, of the BML, said that "had it been realised that the numeration could have been applied directly to the books, leaving presses unnumbered, greater flexibility would have resulted ... the practice of numbering the presses has been discontinued." But in the time of Watts and Panizzi, this was the state of the art, and they had shown innovation. The BML also had a closed access system. In other libraries, notably the small public libraries, change from closed to open access was an important factor in the development of closer classification; with its closed access, the BML did not see the advantage of the closer classification which was being advocated by many.

In 1891 Geo. W. Harris--not to be confused with T. M. Harris (1768-) of Harvard, or W. T. Harris (1835-1909) of the St. Louis Public School Library--was librarian at Cornell University in 1891. He persuaded himself that the BM classification, being more or less Brunet and with its elastic shelving system, was a good compromise with the existing fixed location and was better than DDC. His adaptation, known locally as the Harris scheme, became increasingly unsatisfactory, however, and finally, in 1947, replacement with LoC was begun at great cost. [46]

Esdaile, as Secretary of the BM, got himself involved in comparisons in his estimation of Panizzi. Panizzi's only competitor, he thought, was Putnam, but Panizzi, according to Esdaile, was "felix in opportunate vitae." Panizzi was fortunate in that he did not come to England as an ordinary migrant like Crestadoro; fortunate, too, in his contact with Brougham, a trustee of the BM who helped him in. He had administrative ability, difficult as he was, and an interest in techniques as well as scholarship, and a career in a national library, and a British one, helps to enhance British reputation. But Putnam also was "felix in opportunate vitae." Young, appointed in 1897 as the first librarian of the new LoC library, had administrative ability, but he died an accidental death in January 1899 before he was sixty; while Dewey had retired to the Lake Placid Club. Was Billings, for example, of the US Surgeon's General Library and Index Catalog, and then of the New York Public Library, a lesser librarian than Panizzi or Putnam? Esdaile's comparisons need some tempering.

2.10 Title Word Indexing; Watt's

On title word indexing Edwards and Panizzi were within ten years of being on opposite sides. In 1849 Panizzi advocated what he called an index of matters based on information "as far as it can be collected from a title page, which is all that can be expected in a catalog." Referring to Dr. Robert Watt's Bibliotheca Britannica of 1824, he said, "the usefulness of [it] must be acknowledged by everyone conversant with bibliography. That it would not be so useful had any systematical arrangement been followed seemed undeniable."

Watt's extraordinary life of labor is detailed by Mason in his article entitled Bibliographical Martyr. 47 Watt seems to have become obsessed with an expansion of a teaching aid for medical students, which was eventually published in 1824, and is usually in two volumes, one for Authors and one for Subjects. He called it Bibliotheca Britannica; or, A General Index of British and Foreign Literature.

Edwards, after being at odds with Panizzi in the BML from 1839 to 1850, began the section of his Memoirs on catalogs by comparing the Bibliotheca Britannica and classified catalogs. Within five pages Edwards was dismissing catalogs on the Watts plan with copious examples of the evils of synonymous and homonymous entry words. As one example, he pointed out, a kind of sword fighting and fencing are synonymous, while fencing as enclosure and fencing as the receiving of stolen goods are homonymous. Watts entered a book called The Complete Fencing Master under FENCING, and also one called The Use of Furze in Fencing the Banks of Rivers. In detail, Watt's method, which may have been based on the catchword entry of anonymous books, was to use the essential title word as a heading, and only its initial in the printed page entries, in which space had to be considered. Of course, in 1859 Edwards had no anticipation of alphabetico-classed or alphabetico-specific entry, not necessarily by title words; and his next chapter of over 70 pages dealt with classificatory systems with little consideration of essential IR problems, such as the indexing of classifications.

Users of Watt's Bibliotheca Britannica for at least half a century after its publication in 1824 were accustomed to sorting out homonymous and synonymous meanings and apparently felt little difficulty. The catalog still has historical value. Its method, which can be related to Bible concordance indexing, may be called by the later acronym KWOC, because it is Keyword out of content in its headings, and because, while there could be multiple entry--for example of Furze and Fencing and Rivers--there seems to have been no idea of title transposition and permutation.

2.11   Poole and Jewett

William Frederick Poole (1821-1894) was an American counterpart of Dr. Watt in Scotland, in more ways than one. From his upbringing--he worked to matriculate and pay his way through a university--he became habituated, like

Watts, to work. He also became identified with periodical indexing. But his general reputation, in librarianship and bibliography as well as in other things, amply justified his funeral text: "Know ye not that there is a prince and a great man fallen this day in Israel."

In his day student reading, especially of the extra-curricular variety, was not encouraged and thus fraternity libraries were important. After a variety of arduous manual jobs, Watt became an assistant to Edmands (1820-1915)[48] in the library of a fraternity known as the Brothers in Unity. Edmands had produced a pamphlet on Subjects for Debate, with References to Authorities. Poole went a step further and got George Palmer Putnam to publish in 1848 an index of pamphlets and periodical articles. It was called An Index, Alphabetical, to Subjects Treated in the Reviews, and it bore the motto, "Qui ubi sit scientia, habenti est proximus" (he who knows where knowledge dwells has it within his reach).

When at last he graduated from Yale and was thinking of law he organized with personal financial risk the publication of what was to become a household word for librarians as Poole's Index. It used a title word method, combining title word indexing with title description, and using title word transposition or permutation. Examples are "Caterpillars, Preservation of. (S. H. Scudder), Am. Natural. 8:321"; and "Caterpillars, Venomous (A. Murray), Nature 8:7." In "Caterpillars; My Summer Pets. (M. Treat). Lippinc. 4:25," the subject indexing entry word is supplied. An example of a cross reference in Poole is "Cathari see Albigenses."[49]

In 1853 Poole was associated with Charles Coffin Jewett in running the 1853 Librarians' Conference which might have anticipated the founding of the ALA in 1876. Jewett (1816-1868), a professor of modern languages at Brown University, had gone on to establish a reputation as its librarian. While Poole had got the first edition of his Index published in 1853, Jewett had become Assistant Secretary in charge of the library at the Smithsonian Institution, which was finally founded in 1846, with Joseph Henry (1797-1878), distinguished as a scientist, as its Secretary. Jewett had ambitions and plans to make the Smithsonian Library a national library, and to offer a central cataloging service using stereotypes to print entries on pages, not cards, the stereotypes being made of something like clay. He had support, but Henry succeeded in maintaining the view of its founding benefactor that the Smithsonian's purpose was the diffusion of knowledge by research and publication, though he was not opposed to a national library. In 1853 Jewett seemed on his way in both respects, toward the national library and the stereotyped catalogs, but he lost out in conflict with Henry in 1854, losing his assistant secretaryship and becoming the Boston Public Librarian. The final blow was that what Poole called his "mud catalogs" did not work; the stereotypes broke up.50

While at Boston, Jewett used a mixture of independent headings and title words in the Boston catalogs, and Cutter credited him with an improvement in setting out his entry words with author alphabetical subarrangement, though Watt had done this in 1824. Cutter's comment51 is important, however, when he says that "the effect of this trifling difference is obviously to give greater prominence to the subject idea; it impresses the reader as a list of authors who have written about a topic rather than of books which have a certain word in the title. It was a slight change, but it meant that Jewett was thinking more about those who are seeking information than who are searching for a book." This was hardly established but in 1876 it was an interesting comment.

The newly founded ALA set up a committee on a new edition of Poole's Index but took no responsibility for it, and Poole went his own way. One proposal was apparently very elaborate and outside his methods, but Poole did comment that if it were matured "and issued as a separate publication like Roget's Thesaurus it would be an admirable undertaking." This did bear some fruit, slowly and on later thesaurus lines, but though it seems the first use of the word in this way, its use by Poole seems to have been forgotten when it was later revived.52 Poole's Index was finally superseded by the indexes of the H. W. Wilson Company, not so much because the title word method was dropped but because Wilson solved the cumulation problem by the use of metal linotype slugs for entries.

Poole settled down to be an able librarian and used his title word method successfully in some public library catalogs, but he was too contemptuous of what he thought to be unnecessary bibliographical refinement, and he never quite realized that inexperienced young men could not be trusted to work as he himself had, with insufficient experience and inadequate instruction. This merges into the Cutter-Boston Athenaeum catalog story and the emergence of Cutter's alphabetico-specific entry. In the meantime, the center of title word indexing interest had shifted to London.

1476 to 1876

2.12 Title Word Catalogs: Crestadoro

Andrea Crestadoro (1808-1879) was an Italian contemporary of Panizzi's, though not as well connected socially and certainly not a political refugee when he came to England in 1849. From a public school in Genoa he went on to the University of Turin where he graduated with a Ph.D. In British librarianship in the 1870s he was known as Dr. Crestadoro. In the University of Turin he was a professor of natural philosophy and in the usage of the day was probably as much entitled to be called professor in the University of Turin as Panizzi was in the University of London. Throughout his life he published on economic and social questions, and ultimately received the order of the Crown of Italy from Italy's king.

His purpose in migrating to England was to push his mechanical inventions, some in aeronautics, but he made no money out of them and apparently in the mid-fifties became an employee of Low, who had been involved in trade bibliography, indexing with author entry and subject title listing in broad classes. Developing to entirely alphabetical indexing by title words, Low said in 1854 that "under the old system of classification the difficulty has been to find a given title, although enabled to find a group of books published within a scientific definition. The present plan, it is hoped, will, by following out the author's own definition of his books and presenting a CONCORDANCE OF TITLES, combine both of these advantages."53 Here, then, is a tangled skein; what ideas came from Poole's indexing and what were Low's own, and what if any Crestadoro's? Low would have well known that book titles were not always their authors', but might have let Crestadoro, himself an author, think so. Cutter thought the dates of Low's and Poole's indexes suggested independent development. But Poole's first index was published and had become known in London, and Low would also have been likely to have been familiar in 1853 with Norton in America, a bookseller and publisher-promoter of the 1853 Library Conference, and publisher of Poole's 1853 index and of a trade journal. Further, in a review, "concordance" had been used with reference to Poole's indexing. More research and documentation in this area seems needed.

Nevertheless, Crestadoro certainly could and did develop ideas in what might be called an academic way; in 1856 he wrote a substantial pamphlet called The Art of Making Catalogues of Libraries, or a Method to Obtain in a Short Time a Most Perfect, Complete and Satisfactory Printed Catalogue of the British Museum Library, by a Reader Therein. This was published by or from the Literary, Scientific, and Artistic Reference Office, no. 10 Brownlow Street, Holborn. Panizzi was probably made aware of it but there is no record of his acknowledging Crestadoro, who could well have been the publishing agency and have been attempting to establish himself as a consultant. A contemporary authority has said that while Crestadoro suggested a concordance use of titles in his 1856 book, Luhn in 1959 showed how the computer made it a really feasible exercise; this is what used to be called arrant nonsense. Crestadoro was employed by the Manchester Corporation to make a catalog of its reference library, Edwards as its librarian being apparently absorbed in classification; and interested users such as Jevons considered both the title word subject indexing in the index to the British Catalogue of Books and the Manchester Free Library's reference library cataloging under Crestadoro's direction the best they knew. Friction brought an end to Edwards' employment in Manchester, as it had to his earlier association with Panizzi in the BML, the common judgment in both cases being faults on both sides. Manchester thereupon made Crestadoro its librarian and he held this position, apparently without friction, until his death in 1879. 54

Referring to Low's concordance of titles proposal, Cutter said, "not a word about subject information, which indeed was not to be expected, the British catalog being merely intended as a ready guide for booksellers and others to the publisher's name and the price of each."55 But clearly Crestadoro developed other ideas, setting himself up as a consultant and contractor for library cataloging. His brief biography by Axon in DNB notes that, perhaps unconsciously, he used a method applied to the cataloging of manuscripts, but there seems no need to go beyond the Bible concordance idea for his inspiration. Axon also speaks of the marked and beneficial influence Crestadoro had upon the progress of the free library movement. 56

2.13 Indexed Catalogs and Index-Catalogs

Crestadoro's Art of Making Catalogs has had little exposition or criticism, but it does go more thoroughly into cataloging problems than might be assumed, as Cutter showed in his page or two on it in his 1876 PLUSA chapter. At one point Cutter called the plan admirable, but said it had, however, "one defect--its close adherence to title." Crestadoro could not get around inconsistencies of title, and in practice did not apply all the remedies he proposed, but in his thinking he was well beyond Poole and the equal, or more than the equal, of Cutter himself. 57 Axon was fuller and fairer in his Handbook of the Public Libraries of Manchester and Salford, 1877, which was partly reprinted in the Library World in 1921-2. 56

Crestadoro's theory began with what he called an inventorial catalog, an accession or acquisitions register which could be added to at the end and have numbered entries, an important consideration in the days before card catalogs. This was to be indexed from the titles, briefly but completely as to authors, titles and subjects, the latter either as expressed in title words or, if necessary, in words supplied; such an index could be comparatively cheaply printed and reprinted. The Manchester committee, however, had insisted on an author catalog, but the entries had to be numbered for easy cross reference from the indexing. Axon said the catalog could be even classified, but Crestadoro was clearly not a classification man, for one reason, because he didn't agree with it. Also he appears to have assumed closed access, and probably the arrangement was by the numbers so that staff could get books directly by reference to the index.

The numbering is reminiscent of Brunet, but worked the other way. Examples show fullness in author entries, to which Poole did not pretend, but one book is called the Elements of Conchology, another the Natural History of British Shells, and another is the description of a percussion shell to be fired horizontally from a common gun, and the books' numbers were 3053, 7130 and 15909. The index had "Conchology. Elements. Brown. Lond. 1816 8vo ... 3035"; "Shells, British. Donovan. 5 vols. Lond. 1803-4 8vo. 7130"; "Percussion. Miller. Lond. 1827. 4to." Books on the same subject are not indexed together. There is, however, nothing wrong with the sequence SHELLS and SHELLS, PERCUSSION arising out of homonymity, whereas conchology and shells in the other two present the problem of synonymity. Bradford, in his Documentation, referred to the "classical error" of a librarian putting "Lead pipes" just after "Lead kindly light," and there is the old joke about "Mill on liberty" and "Mill on the Floss." This sort of thing happens in any alphabetical catalog or encyclopedia, but Bradford was just too eager to praise classified catalogs, especially UDC, by damning alphabetical.

As Cutter pointed out in his Rules, there is little or no economy in references. Extra entries take up no more room than references if there is the basic economy of title-a-line with ruthless title cutting. Presumably on the same line of argument, Crestadoro developed his Index-Catalogue, especially for small circulating libraries, "on the principle of a dictionary," with such entries as "Conchology Elements 6150" and "Brown, Capt. T. Elements of conchology 6313"; but, as "Mayo (C) Lessons on shells 6450" and "Shells. Lesson on, By Mayo 64550" shows, the problems of synonymity in title names do not disappear. Billings finally adopted the title Index Catalog for his U.S. Surgeon-General's Library in printed form since users of the card form called it an index catalog because in addition to cataloging books it indexed periodical articles. There was no question of economy in entries. This was a dictionary catalog on what might be called the grand scale.

British public libraries used Crestadoro's index-catalog method as a matter of course, with catalog references to the accession numbers by which the books were arranged behind a circulation desk. This was usually aided by the use of an invention called an indicator, which showed the numbers one way round and in one color if the book was "in," and the other way round in another color if it was "out," and which could be changed at the flick of a circulation assistant's finger. With the increasing change to open access about 1900, there had to be classified shelf arrangement, although economy still had to rule. The cheapest form of classified catalog was really a shelflist with, of course, single entry. Crestadoro's indexing was still used, but with reference to class numbers; the reference might be to a class but it might, in effect, be to an item which should have had added entry. Titles in the class, then, had to be read through to find one which had within it the title word referred from. This was scarcely an improvement on Crestadoro's reference to entry numbers, but it persisted until about 1950 when Ranganathan's chain indexing, with all its complications and questions, provided some amelioration.

2.14 Alphabetico-Classed Catalogs

The alphabetico-classed catalog was in 1868 distinguished by Cutter[58] as a fourth kind following on three which he distinguished as "classification with minute subdivisions," "classification without subdivisions," and the dictionary system which he developed as his alphabetico-specific. In the latter the subject under which an item is entered is its specific subject as nearly as possible, not necessarily the subject as named in an author's or publisher's title. There might be three items specifically on domestic animals variously called Pigs, Hogs, Swine; but all three would be entered under the name best expressing their subject, at least for users of the catalog.

The fourth system, called the half-way or mixed, Cutter thought best called alphabetico-classed. In this, Domestic animals might be a heading, with Cats, Dogs, Horses, Sheep, Pigs or Hogs or Swine as subheadings; or the heading might be Animals, with Domestic animals as a subheading and the special names of Domestic animals as sub-sub-headings.

Coates in England, in his Subject Catalogs, Headings and Structures (1960), stated reasonably that "the cataloger can best serve the enquirer by uniformity of method and decision based on a few all-embracing rules." And on that point, being a classifying man, he thought "the whole justification for the alphabetico-specific catalog" rests, "for it is known that many enquirers use a class term approach in the first place." They do indeed, for example asking for items or patents on engineering when their interest turns out to be mousetraps. Coates' whole or only qualifying justification for alphabetico-specific entry may still be questioned, but the class term approach is nevertheless common. Despite this, said Coates, "the alphabetico-specific catalog uses specific terms because of the sheer difficulty of deciding under which of its possible hierarchical class terms a specific subject is to be entered."59

After Cutter had gone to succeed Poole as librarian of the Boston Athenaeum Library he might have preferred an alphabetico-classed catalog, but felt he had to salvage what he could of the title word cataloging of his predecessor. He cited a Report of the Harvard Library Committee and his own 1868-1869 article as supporting the arguments of his own PLUSA chapter of 1876, but did say in the latter that he was convinced "that there is very little difference for a person who understands both. The Abbot system is best for the thorough investigation of subjects; the dictionary system for finding quickly what relates to a person or other special topic."60

This raises the question as to whether library catalogs are used for the systematic investigation of comprehensive topics, or whether the student goes from textbooks to catalogs for particular topics. One trouble with the alphabetico-classed catalog was that it was mixed in more senses than one, using specific entry because of uncertainty about including classes. It could be said that once Cutter developed his alphabetico-specific catalog, and it was mainly only on cards, the alphabetico-classed catalog fell between two stools; although Abbot at Harvard, with Cutter's assistance, for about eight years developed it as a card catalog. One catalog, presumably based on the Harvard one, was done at LoC in two printed volumes in 1869, and another was the BML Subject Index which was begun in 1881 and was published until about 1970 in five-yearly cumulations. This might be said to have been mixed in most possible ways.

Fortescue, somewhat like Watts, not far advanced in formal education, became by merit Superintendent of the BML Reading Room and wanted a subject index. In 1881 he got started on the one already referred to, which continued in five-yearly cumulations until about 1970. He was probably aware of Cutter and was certainly aware of Anderson in the Public Library of New South Wales, who produced a subject headings list and subject index supplementing an author catalogue about 1896, using specific entry principles. This was the idea Fortescue favored but Bond, who had begun a classified catalog of manuscripts, was Principal Librarian of the BM in 1878-88 and is said to have insisted on the classified approach. 61 The Index does not seem to have been considered as part of the Catalog--which was an author catalog--but as a reference tool with entries often made from accession list titles. At least, it was begun by the overtime labors of Fortescue, and in its results it is very mixed in class and specific entry, with, for example, such headings as "Sport" and "Aeronautics" but also "Lawn Tennis" and "Gliding." It also developed a policy of what it called decentralising: "Manslaughter" began under "Crime" but could later become a separate heading. The index's method of publication made this possible.

References, of course, up and down, but mainly up, make the alphabetico-classed catalog work. But why should the enquirer have to work up to "Cereal Crops" for "Wheat," or "Domestic Animals" for "Sheep," when he can make a simpler reference from one index in a classified catalog, or find information on wheat or on sheep directly under those headings in an alphabetico-specific catalog, or in an encyclopedia without cross-reference or indexing at all? What does he gain in finding pigs, in which he is not interested, with sheep; maize, in which he is not interested, with wheat?

2.15 Decimal Systems before Dewey

Legends have persisted that decimal classification was invented by a young man who was a genius, something like Newton or Leibnitz, in 1876 or even 1873, he being also something of a saint. To begin with what decimal systems are, in simple terms they are applications of numbering things in tens, with particular reference here to books. But, as LaMontagne somewhat facetiously said, following a custom of long standing when discussing decimal classifications, "it is necessary ... to advert briefly to the systems of La Croix du Maine and Nathaniel B. Shurtleff."[62] These happen to be about 273 years apart, but the custom seems to date only from Sayers (1881-1960).[63] Drawing on a French writer on books, Albert Cim, he referred to Francois Grudé, Sieur de la Croix du Maine (1552-1592), who is regarded as a founder of French bibliography and is said to have suggested to Henry III of France a perfect library of 10,000 volumes in a hundred presses or bookcases and ten alcoves divided into classes, but not decimally. Sayers then moved forward to Nathaniel B. Shurtleff, apparently of Welsh descent, a graduate of Harvard, a distinguished physician, Mayor of Boston and chairman of its library committee, who actually had put into its library his system, with a notation which Sayers said "bears no relation to that of Dewey." But doesn't it?

Edwards mentioned Shurtleff's pamphlet called a Decimal System for the Arrangement of Libraries (Boston, 1856); he said he was "unable to discern the propriety of applying the term 'decimal system' to an account of manipulations and arrangements which have been well known in European libraries for scores of years," but gave no details nor mentioned any examples.[64] Sayers did not mention Poole who, in 1876 in his PLUSA chapter, discussed shelf marks or shelf numbers for books in systems dating back before 1876, some of which were variations of a plan he called the decimal system. Decimal is from the Latin adjective decimas, for tenth; Man has ten fingers, or in Latin, digits; and it is reasonably assumed that decimal systems are related and are digital because man, having ten fingers, counted with them in tens.

A typical Latin number however is MDCCCLXXXV, which is M, one thousand; D, five hundred; CCC, three hundred; L, fifty; XXX, thirty; and V, five; this corresponds to the later arabic numeral figure 1885. While the Latin figures were used for record, for example in inscriptions, they could hardly be used in calculation. The Romans had what they called an abacus (apparently of Indian origin), meaning a low table or tray used, among other things, for calculating; it was dust or sand covered so that marks could easily be made on it and altered, or small stones or pebbles could be used called <u>calculi</u>; hence calculation and the term still used in medicine for stony accretions in the body. The abacus was a digital computer, though not electronic. Beads on bamboo rods or wire could be moved faster, and skilled manipulators have been said to equal the speed of mechanical calculators on the same principle. With the abacus counting was done with strokes or pebbles or beads, up to about twelve; then one stroke or pebble or bead was moved to represent one ten, leaving only two representing two units. In the adding machine a wheel with ten cogs is revolved right around and then it moves one cog on another wheel representing ten and its own revolution is started again, and so on; the more the abacus changes the more it is essentially the same thing.

Its method was reduced to writing with the place method learnt in junior school, only easy when you know how; the place of origin was apparently still India, but the digits, or figures or numerals which began coming into Europe about the tenth century were the arabic 1 to 9. Strictly, only 1 to 9 are digits with quantitative values; the none sign or zero, 0, and the decimal point are not, and one thing of importance which emerges is that the notation called decimal does not have ten digits. Dewey went on saying that he solved the general notation problem by using only "the simplest symbols known to the human mind, arabic numerals with their usual arithmetic values"; of course as symbols of simplicity 1, 2, 3, despite his continued assertion, are of the "simple when you know how" kind, and even more so (not less, as Dewey asserted) than A, B, C, despite their primary use being complicated by inconsistent spelling. And when in his second edition, 1885, he converted the zero into digit use to really make ten, Dewey had obviously abandoned the established arithmetic values of 1 to 9, and also in his "form" use of 0 got his system into unforeseen difficulties which are still plaguing it, together with the complications of his mnemonic ideas and especially his use of 9 as a terminal form number for locality and history.

1476 to 1876   41

2.16 IR Notations and Their Uses

IR notations must be familiar for general and even for most special uses. Users do not know classifications in any detail. They relied originally on preliminary listing and then on indexing, first by page numbers as already shown (2.6 Dryander), and then, when classifications were criticized for lack of indexing, by already known notations. This was necessary to meet the competition of alphabetical catalogs which are self-indexing. The only two generally familiar notations are the more or less decimal numerical and the alphabetical, used "purely" or in mixtures, which are either actual number mixtures of the A1 kind essentially, or basically one notation which might be called block complementation by another.

A basic use of notation, not confined to IR, is ordinal, meaning to indicate the order of things, such as books according to subject arrangement or classification or classes in catalogs. There has always been this use with numbers, but not so much with letters. This may seem unexpected, but, as already shown, close alphabetical arrangement of words did not begin with alphabetical writing and established order of the letters; it only became fixed with the advent of printing and index learning.[65] Finding words including vowels in alphabetical order is helped by syllabification, as in "Con-sti-tu-tion," and even then there is a lot of casting around, even by educated people, in dictionaries, encyclopedias, telephone directories or electoral rolls. The principle of exact order with reference to the alphabet is not well understood; for example, that Cyanide, Cybernetics, Cyclones will be in that order exactly and why. There have been attempts at vocalized classification notations largely because they are pronounceable, for example in D. J. Foskett's <u>London Education Classification.</u> But obviously this greatly limits possibilities.

The alphabet of 26 letters is a straight notation not used in any way like the numerical in its primary arithmetical use. It therefore conforms to the formula that the number of "numbers" possible with scale or base or radix is, with single digits, the number in the base, 26 in the case of letters; but this is squared with two digits, so AA-ZZ is 26 squared, which produces 676, and with three digits, such as AAA-ZZZ, it is the number cubed, producing 17,576. If DDC is accepted as having a base of ten digits including its use of the zero, its three-digit numbers are ten cubed or a thousand, 000-999. But a, e, i, o, u and y are the only six vocalizing

letters and purely consonantal combinations in which these
are not used greatly reduce the possible total. They have
to be used, however, in an extensive classification, but combinations such as FXY are not found as readily as FOX or
FEX. The reverse problem of literal combinations with of-
fensive meanings is a minor one.

   The peculiar use of both notations in IR classifications
has been their hierarchical or expressive use in relation to
the classes numbered. This has already been considered
with Brunet's classification, in which his class numbering
through classes, subclasses and so on is comparable to the
same sort of thing in some books. He did not intend the
numbers "III, Science," "4, Zoology," "E, Invertebrate animals," "a, Crustacea" to "f, Intestinal worms" to be combined. But in DDC, 595.121 is an ordinal number and also
expressive of hierarchy or class; 5 is Science; 9, Zoology;
5, Other invertebrates; 1, Worms and related animals; 2,
Platyhelminthes and Nemertea; 1, Cestoidea including tapeworms. Thus 595.121 denotes the specific order and finding
number for these in zoology. In medicine the number is
616.964, a hierarchy made up of: 6, originally Useful arts
[in the 18th edition, Technology (Applied sciences)]; 61, Medical sciences; 616, Pathology; 616.9, Other diseases; 616.96,
Parasitic diseases; 616.964, Diseases due to tapeworms
(Cestoda). This sort of thing, including the analogical use
of letters, may be considered development and refinement of
the Decimal systems, related to subject developments which
certainly could not be anticipated. It was and even still is
assumed--with only the LoC classification as a supposedly
primitive exception, relying on gaps in straight ordinal numbering because it had adopted alphabetical cataloging--that a
notational hierarchy must be related to what it begins with.
The examples show that extension was necessary and was
supposed to provide for what has been called hospitality.
But difficulties and doubts began to arise, and are considered
in following chapters. The conflict of what he called Hospitality and Expressiveness is well discussed by A. C. Foskett
in his Subject Approach to Information.

Chapter 3

DEWEY AND CUTTER AND CLASSIFICATION

Dewey, though the younger (1851-1931), was before Cutter (1837-1903), and much more successful, with classification, accepting the proposition that nothing succeeds like success. Dewey did not attempt direct alphabetical subject cataloging, which was what made Cutter's reputation. So Dewey is first here, but for the sake of contrast, with an opening paragraph on Cutter.

3.1 Cutter and Dewey at Home, School and College

Charles Ammi Cutter (1837-1903), the second son of a second generation dealer in fish oils in Boston, was, according to his nephew biographer, William Parker Cutter, frail in body, nearsighted, and so, intended for the church. From early childhood he lived with cultured and devout spinster aunts; he went to a school endowed for boys who would, if they could, enter Harvard College and then its Divinity School. There was no doubt that he could, and through serious out of school reading he became informed in more than its classical and biblical curriculum. He was able to matriculate at 14, in 1851, and graduated A.B. in 1855, then worked as an entrance examination tutor for a year before entering the Divinity School in autumn 1856. He graduated in 1859, winning "the famous Bowdoin prize for an essay entitled 'Persecutions for Religion's Sake during the Colonial Period in New England'." He preached a few sermons, but did not become ordained, which, as his nephew said, was fortunate for the Forbes Library, of which he became the first librarian in 1893; the founder, Judge Forbes, had willed that no ordained minister be employed in any capacity in the library.

In the meantime he had done some bibliographical work for the Divinity School Library, apparently being advised by and attracting the attention of Abbot, described by W. P. Cutter as head cataloger of the Harvard College Library. In

1860 Cutter became Abbot's assistant in the College Library and, as already noted, his assistant in the compilation of an alphabetico-classed catalog until 1868. During this period he wrote an article on the catalog for the North American Review, and at the end of 1868 he became Librarian of the Boston Athenaeum Library, succeeding Poole, whose title word indexing and cataloging has been discussed earlier.

Dewey, born December 10, 1851 and dying December 26, 1931, was in his tenth year when the Civil War broke out. Joel Dewey, his father, was colonel in a New York Regiment, a man of property, owning several small farms, conducting a general store in Adams Center, in northern New York State where Melvil was born, and a manufacturer of footwear, making boots and leggings for northern troops, and employing several men. Melville Louis Kossuth Dewey, christened and devout in the Baptist Adventist Church, was not, as might appear in the light of different standards and conditions more than a century later, a Huckleberry Finn but more a Tom Sawyer in social and economic standing. He went as a young child to a select or private school run by an Aunt and showed great speed in mental arithmetic, an instinct for system and a growing dislike for weights and measures of the inches, feet, yards kind. He is said to have studied bookkeeping and satisfied himself that his father's store didn't pay. Perhaps it didn't in the Civil War years; perhaps the soldiers' boots and leggings did. He got two certificates for elementary teaching when he was about 17 and taught for two or three terms at Toad Hollow and Bernhard Bay. About this time his father seems to have been easily persuaded to sell out the store, and was able to retire to Oneida in the south of New York State where Melvil Dewey, as he became through simplified spelling, had better opportunities for secondary education and college matriculation.

He thought of Harvard, even writing to its young President, C. W. Eliot (1834-1926), and considered Rochester as well as Amherst in Massachusetts. There is a suggestion that he chose the latter because of its compulsory physical education, certainly an interest of his. He seems finally to have gone to Amherst on a conditional basis, apparently on condition that he matriculated, but talks he made at school lyceums in Adams Centre and Oneida show how well he followed his own lines of interest--which might be summed up in the words efficiency and economy. He spoke, and very well, against tobacco and alcohol and for the decimalization

of weights and measures, or the metric system. In 1870 he
attacked the roman notation in favor of the arabic, a method
of writing numbers, he said, which was accurate, simple,
and probably as nearly perfect as man can invent, while the
other was almost incapable of being used in rapid calculations, in which he shone. Taught the arabic system as it is
and roman figures as they were used mainly for record, he
does not appear then or later to have become aware that the
Romans used an abacus method for calculation. [66]

At Amherst he lived in the town with a widow called
Pratt and seems to have concentrated on his degree from
1870 to 1874 for reasons of thrift inculcated in him in childhood and because he was determined to pay back what his
father had advanced for fees. He kept out of things and decided on a career--not as a foreign missionary, for which
Amherst was noted, but in public education including libraries.
In 1872 he recorded his reading of Memoirs of Libraries
(presumably Edwards') as strengthening his devotion to free
or public libraries. This was when he was 21. He was becoming sure in reliance on his own judgment about ends and
means, and did not want to hear people as renowned as Emerson, or go to town meetings. This probably prevented him
from becoming interested in public politics and the compromise they required; he was to become, instead, astute in
what may be distinguished as private politics.

The college librarian was nominally the professor of
Romanic languages, Montague. He was not noted for drive
or efficiency, and young Dewey, when in 1872 he was made
a paid assistant, getting about $12.50, proved something of
a tiger by the tail. Montague, not lacking generosity, paid
him more substantial sums, probably out of an allowance he
got as librarian. With a degree certainly not "cum laude,"
Dewey was made assistant librarian, and later librarian. [67]

3.2 Amherst Librarian

While still not graduated or yet librarian, Dewey in
1873 was interested in two hardly congruous things, shorthand and library cataloging and classification. Falling behind
in his studies of Latin and mathematics, Dewey became fascinated by shorthand, in particular a system known as Lindsley's takigraphy. It takes application to learn any system
of shorthand and still more to practice it so as to be able to
use it; but by December 1873 Dewey was using takig, as he

called it, for all his notes, his diary, and for dropping what he called "breves," the abbreviations he had invented himself. But the major interest remained firm: efficiency and economy of time, and with his missionary spirit he began interesting other students. After graduation he organized classes, on his own initiative; but the faculty had its own ideas about who decided which subjects could be taught and by whom. Commenting on this opposition, Dewey wrote in his diary that he had got his things mostly arranged so that he could leave town very easily if they served him any more mean tricks. This is typically Dewey; he is doing a good thing and anyone trying to stop him is playing mean tricks; never he but always the regiment is out of step. His biographer attributes it in this case to youthful sensitivity, but Dewey changed little with age, especially as shown by his school of librarianship tactics at the age of 36.

However, in January 1875 he saw a graduate of Amherst, Burgess, who had become a professor and supported Dewey because he supported library reform in relation to teaching. Burgess arranged a compromise with the faculty but Dewey accepted it as though he were making a sacrifice and losing money; besides library work, for which he claimed to be unpaid, he taught shorthand four hours a day. In March 1873, while he was still working to finish his degree, he wrote in his diary, "my heart is open to anything that is either decimal or about libraries ... for my interest and faith in 'decimals' is unlimited. " As his biographer said, this leads into a subject which is technical. [68]

On May 8th 1873, he made a submission on a new catalog and classification for the library. This wasn't new in American or even British librarianship, but his particular proposals were. They led to him inspecting other libraries in New England and New York State, practically the whole area of effective librarianship in America at that time. He became known, and what became known as the Amherst plan in the making created increasing and widening interest down to the centenary library conference and the establishment of the ALA in 1876. And as Dewey went his way with an amazing diversification of simultaneous interests--if not always simultaneous activity in them--librarians developed feelings about him which ranged from adulation to suspicion and detraction. It must be emphasized that Dewey never became widely known outside librarianship, perhaps not because of any lack of ability on his part but because of the limitations of librarianship in the public eye.

Dewey and Cutter

Adulation of Dewey increased over the years, however, partly because of his achievements, and partly because of two posthumous biographies which are very much in his favor. Both call him a genius and one, the first, added saint. This latter is <u>Melvil Dewey: Seer, Inspirer, Doer, 1851-1931</u>, by Grosvenor Dawe (Lake Placid Club, 1932). It is nearly 400 pages of chaotic, inadequately indexed, pollyanna-ish panegyric commissioned by his second wife and others associated with the Club in which he finally lived and died, and in which there is a stained-glass chapel window of him as the Seer. Dawe had controlled access to documents but completed the rambling work in a few months of 1932; it is mainly useful if it is read critically for what may be said to be between the lines.

The other work is <u>Melvil Dewey</u> by Fremont Rider (Chicago: American Library Association, 1944).[68] Rider was a librarian and a friend, genial and a generalizer. "Geniuses cannot in fairness by judged by the standards we apply to ordinary folk," he said, and apparently meant in anything. He likened Dewey, often called a "dynamo of energy," to a fifty-ton tank. Dewey's son Godfrey (1887-   ), without metaphor, said in 1951 that "one did not say 'no' to father, unless one was prepared to make a life work of it," and seemed generally to accept Rider's evaluation.[69] If one cites accepted examples of genius: Roger Bacon, Francis Bacon, Leibnitz, Newton, Goethe, Jefferson, Franklin--mostly mathematicians, as Dewey never was, and most of them with some achievement in librarianship or IR, on which however their reputations do not rest--could Melvil Dewey be seriously counted in such company? This is a question to be considered, perhaps by his next biographer. But a first question about Dewey as a librarian, especially in Amherst, is that of how the Amherst classification got into the world, not only under Dewey's name, as DDC, but also as his property by virtue of a copyright granted to him.[69]

3.3 <u>The Amherst Plan and DDC</u>

Instead of getting into a tangled web with questions about the classification itself, only the question of the Amherst Plan's emergence into the world is considered here, and tangled as it is may best be presented in short enumerated statements:

1. On May 8, 1873 Dewey submitted to a College

Committee ideas for a new catalog and classification for what was becoming his library; this was not an unusual thing to do.

    2. His proposal was for a card catalog, which was still unusual, and had the defect of not existing in more than one copy, as compared with the multiple copies of printed catalogs--in which the classification could be studied. Some one, apparently not Dewey, proposed eventual printing of Dewey's classification scheme for student use; the scheme, of course, was not then the formidable length of later editions.

    3. By 1876 Dewey, with the full-time aid of Biscoe and library and faculty aid, had a more or less complete scheme being applied in the library; but despite his assertions, this was not the decimal fraction scheme he had proposed in 1873.

    4. Even in 1932 it was a question of some concern to the committee instructing Dawe, Dewey's biographer, as to how the Amherst Plan's conversion into DDC was to be presented.

    5. Dawe consulted Biscoe, Dewey's assistant and successor,[70] who said that neither he nor Mr. Dewey, as far as he could recall, had any thought of laying down a system that would be worldwide in its application. They were simply trying to solve the problem of Amherst. But when that was solved Mr. Dewey leapt beyond the Amherst situation into the wider world; but why then did he only give this world the Amherst Plan?

    6. Dawe also quoted correspondence in 1876 between Dewey and Professor Montague in which Dewey repudiated the idea that the copyright in the classification should have been the College's. He took the line that from start to finish it was his.

    7. Rider gave no opinion on the copyright question, but though the basic idea was Dewey's, he said, "its development was a long process in which, from the first, many minds cooperated."[71] And Comaromi said that who contributed substantially to the final form of the first edition ... and to what extent ... will likely never be known.[72]

    8. Comaromi's thesis was based in part on papers in the Melvil Dewey Collection at Columbia but it was in the Dewey office in LoC that he found an application by Dewey

dated March 22, 1876 to enter for copyright a little work just passing through the press with the title "A Classification & Subject Index with Directions for their Use," but asking the LoC Copyright Office for advice. What may have been in his mind is not clear, but he could only have been referring to the Amherst classification, and its printing for student use, and the advice he got was that he had to supply two copies of the best edition already printed for publication. This seems to have been entirely unilateral action. Professor Montague, however, became aware of it, and presumably informed the College trustees, who cut back Dewey to his regular salary with the loss of a promised final bonus of about $1,000.

9. This put Dewey so much in the red in his business ventures in Boston, where he had gone early in April 1876, that he said he would accept anything from Montague which was "not an absolute charity," mentioning $300 which Montague had offered him out of his own pocket. 73

10. Dewey attempted to justify his action with the argument that the classification was "no more the property of the college than any of the books published by members of the faculty and prepared during their salaried time as college officers." There have been many variations of this right down to the present; but the classification wasn't all his work. He particularly had the assistance of Biscoe and faculty members, and he was being generously paid over and above his salary as librarian.

11. His finances being in the state they were, how did he get his edition printed? Although such might have been the intention, Ginn and Heath did not become his publishers. On Comaromi's evidence he appears to have had one and even two editions of the tables and the index run from the typesetting paid for by the college primarily for students. One edition may have been for Ginn and Heath who advertised in American Library Journal in November 1876 their edition of what they called The Amherst College Classification and Subject Index and apparently had this available before Dewey's.

12. Dewey had to or wanted to add a Preface. It ran to ten pages, and gave himself all credit. Like others, he may have confused copyright in a text with patent rights with questions of prior publication and invention. This preface was used for or was taken from his PLUSA account, in

an early paragraph of which he said, "A description of the plan as in actual use in the Amherst College Library would be its best explanation. " He did not say it was the Amherst Plan, and went on to say that it could be adapted, if desired, in connection with very different catalogs and methods. 74

13. In what Comaromi called the ambiguous final paragraph of the introduction he said it was reasonable to assume that Dewey was protecting himself from accusations that he was not original in producing his classification; it may also be assumed that Dewey was especially concerned about his copyright claim. 75

14. Comaromi also said that whether the College Trustees, while aggrieved about the copyright question, "learnt of the extra printing, is not known. " He suggests further bibliographical complications in different versions of the first edition, but for him and his thesis "the DDC was now in the world, " where it has remained, with a history of editions of ever-increasing size over a century and with unsolved complications and weakness stemming from the first. But that, like the development of the classification itself up to 1876, is another question.

15. Dewey's copyright might have been contested by the College but wasn't, and finally Dewey received his master's degree for the classification. By fair means or foul he had nevertheless brought lustre to the College name, and for the College this might have seemed a better bargain than attempting to carry on the classification itself; and what was involved as time went on may support that conclusion.

3. 4 Boston and Business

On April 10th, 1876 Dewey went out of librarianship in Amherst and into business in Boston, which he had already visited in 1873, discovering that Cutter strangely put books on the horse under HORSE and not under ZOOLOGY. 76 On April 19th, whatever talks he may have had before, he talked with Fred Ginn and with Cutter about starting a library bureau and publishing a library monthly; and more concretely, on April 20th, about a business in which Edward Ginn would have half interest and Fred and he one fourth, but with Dewey as manager and drawing $2, 000 a year from the firm. Much later the second Mrs. Dewey said that because of other interests "he never worked for nor drew a salary from the

Dewey and Cutter 51

company." But this might have been a mutual decision. He had started his own business in his own premises, the Library Journal was to be Leypoldt's and Bowker's in New York, not Ginn's in Boston, and perhaps he wanted to keep the classification to himself; or perhaps the Ginns and their partner Heath had realized that, in Dewey, they would have a tiger by the tail. He was paid a substantial honorarium for editing the journal, but there was trouble about his copy getting in. He did bring investments to the Ginns, however, and the loan of money from Mrs. Pratt back in Amherst; since he was the go-between it was questionable that he should have placed her money with Ginns and not with some agency in which he himself was involved, but "something for both of us" was an abiding principle with Dewey.

In the new association, the ALA, Foster called him one of the five men of 1876; at 24 he was the youngest, along with Winsor, 45; Poole, 55; Cutter, 39; and Bowker, 55. 77 Besides being the first secretary of the ALA and other things, Dewey ran what was called the Library Supplies Committee, and he was as usual meticulous about its accounts, until it was closed down as a supply agency and Dewey's own business in Boston took its place. The impression is sometimes given that the Library Bureau stemmed directly from this, but the record seems different.

He certainly helped to organize and carry on the ALA in association with the centenary in 1876, despite the distrust of some older men, notably Poole. He also had a hand in organizing a Simplified Spelling Association, with March as President, and the Metric Bureau, with Barnard of Columbia College as President. What he organized in Boston at 32 Hawley Street was common offices in which these two organizations were located, along with what he called the Economy Co., a commercial corporation manufacturing labor-saving devices for readers and writers. Each society had a supply department, and Dewey was secretary of all three. He wasn't making much, however. What he needed apparently was capital, and in December 1879 he organized the Readers and Writers Economy Company, with Cutter and six others, "as an outright commercial firm to manufacture and deal in library supplies and equipment."

For a time the Company was very successful. Dewey said that under his sole management, growth was very rapid in selling and manufacturing, with stores established in Boston, New York, and Chicago, and 120 employees, but "the rich promise of the business had drawn into an element caring nothing for my educational work, which to me was the main thing ... in January 1882 it was closed down entirely."[78] What was emerging was that although Dewey could manage, he would not stick to business management, and would either attempt too many things at once or would become immersed in one thing to the neglect of others. Also, he was apparently little disturbed about the livelihood of 120 employees, though that perhaps went with the times. Rider says that Dewey was not disheartened. He proceeded to start up the same business all over again, this time under the name of the Library Bureau, and again at the same Boston address. This seems to dispose of suggestions of continuity with the ALA Supplies Committee which he had managed from the same address, but which was closed off in his accounting in 1879. Rider said that then something happened: Dewey had to get a job and two young men, H. E. Davidson and Parker, had realized the potential of the closed-down business and offered to revive it, granting Dewey a substantial stock interest in it if he left actual day-to-day management to them. Dewey then left Boston for New York.

3.5 New York, Albany and Lake Placid

Dewey and Cutter were more associated in IR, in classification notation, and in business than seems to have been generally realized. As already noted, he had been in Boston in 1873 and had learned about Cutter's specific entry. After his return to Boston in 1876, he visited the suburb of Cambridge to talk to the Harvard Library staff and others about his system; this was on April 18, and one of those listening to him was Ann Godfrey, the first librarian of Wellesley, a non-graduate with no library experience, but an able woman. Cutter was assisting her and she could have been called his protégée; Dewey helped her too, and on October 19, 1878 Ann Godfrey became Mrs. Dewey. She died in August 1922 and Mrs. Emily McKay Beal became Dewey's second wife in May 1924. Ann Godfrey helped him in Boston in his accounts, and worked at indexing in Harvard and elsewhere to help keep the home fires burning. But when the Economy Company had failed and the Library Bureau was still only another unproven venture, Dewey had to get employment.

Barnard, who had become his Metric Bureau President, was President at Columbia College in New York, and Burgess, who had supported Dewey's library reorganization at Amherst, had become a professor at Columbia and was urging complete updating of its library services, as was happening elsewhere. Dewey was asked to advise on a librarian appointment or invitation. In British countries, apart from some internal senior appointments, positions at all levels were more and more advertised and applicants considered by committees. In America appointment by invitation persisted, and in Columbia Burgess, Barnard and others promoted an invitation to Dewey, apparently not without some prompting by him. However, the records seem to show that wherever Dewey went into a library job he did it well, improving the librarianship and the services, especially those to university undergraduates or the general public. It was in other things that he got into difficulties.

He introduced women into the Columbia library, six women graduates from Wellesley, and became devoted to women as assistants, probably because librarianship still didn't seem to offer a career to men; but this use of women became mixed up with ideas of teaching librarianship. Just as Wellesley was exclusively female, so most of the other colleges were exclusively male. Dewey fought to introduce a co-educational school of librarianship into Columbia, but his methods, as so often with Dewey, were in some degree underhanded. When he was denied the use of designated classrooms he triumphantly occupied a disused loft above a chapel, even bringing in furniture from his home for it, and started his own school, which had to pay for itself. 79 Suggestions were made that Dewey's enthusiasm for women in library work may have had a sexual basis, though the economic value of their low pay may have loomed larger in his mind. At any rate, some men humorously advised young girls to beware of Mr. Dewey when going to library conferences. At the same time, Dewey's early teaching seems to suggest some sexual ambivalence in him; he was a complex character in more ways than one.

It is an Australian metaphor in politics that one should bore from within like the white ant, and one politician is said to have replied he bored from within and bored himself right out. Dewey was close to boring himself right out at Columbia. There are stories that he was under criticism for demanding vital statistics of applicants for the school of librarianship. What he was actually criticized for was running an employment agency for the Library Bureau, without it being known that he was also running the school of librarianship which provided the Bureau's applicants. This and other things bored him right out.

He then got himself in 1887 a job as secretary to the Regents or Councillors of the University of New York State, who had responsibilities for secondary education. With this development went the transfer of his school to the library of the state legislature, of which Dewey became librarian. In the meantime he had become involved in the development and management of a country club called Lake Placid and, through it, in investment in land round about. Then, instead of being just a secretary to the regents, he entered into the arguments about public education, and during the course of these was accused of anti-semitism in the club which he controlled through a family holding company. Of course, many shared his racialism and sectarianism but did not lay themselves open to attack. Dawe only writes vaguely of "racial rules governing the club." To Dewey's credit, had he been opposed to anti-semitism he would have opposed it, but Rider was convinced he supported it.[80] The result of the public controversy was that Dewey was left only as librarian and director of the school, and was then given the choice of giving up management of what the Regents significantly called his business or resigning. Rider said that Dewey loved the club too much to give it up, but his own account seems to show that its finances were so involved that Dewey could not neglect them, and from 1905 he lived in and for the club.[81]

3.6 Lake Placid Club Education Foundation

Dewey finally decided or was forced or persuaded to give up the holding company for the Lake Placid Club which was worth millions of dollars, and according to Dawe, it was provided that "only dividends on $60,000 of stock a year should be available for Mr. Dewey himself."[82] This was about 1922, Dewey having retired into the club in 1905-6; but five per cent would have yielded $3,000 a year, at least equal to $10,000 in purchasing power fifty years later. Dawe added that "during the last year of his life he did not receive a cent of personal income." What Dewey and his wife gave to the Club went to the Lake Placid Club Education Foundation, which from 1922 also had the copyright of the classification--in effect, owned it. This all sounds like some kind of settlement rather than an untrammelled gift, and in 1931, the year of Dewey's death, the depression had really bitten.

Dawe said that "his activities in Boston with the Readers and Writers Economy Company and the Library Bureau loaded him down with $22,000 of debt that was still round his

Dewey and Cutter 55

shoulders as late as 1892." Rider said that "the Depression caught the club in a greatly over-extended position, its habitual position. With Dewey at the financial helm it had weathered dozens of storms; had he been still alive, his daring and adroitness might have pulled it through even the trials of 1929-39." But men at least as able and well connected as Dewey had become financially could not pull great companies through. Rider continued: "the club passed into a sort of not unfriendly receivership, and was eventually reorganized, a process not completed until 1943. The reorganization left the Club, physically at least, substantially intact." But what about its educational foundation, which seemed to have begun to rely very much on the classification? It had become clear that Dewey had become a financial juggler, who might well have proved in 1892, when he appeared to owe $22,000, that he only owed in cash about $10. The Library Bureau went through financial difficulties, but helped by Dewey, it apparently came out well, though remaining entirely in Dewey's private estate as far as he had extensive holdings in it.

Three editions of DDC were published or prepared for publication while Dewey was in the Lake Placid Club: the 11th in 1922, the 12th in 1927, and the 13th in 1932, which was made a memorial edition. Dewey was undoubtedly involved but much of the editing was done first by May Seymour, whom he called for 34 years his co-worker, and then by Miss Fellows. Both contributed to the Foundation, May Seymour dying in 1922 and leaving $40,000. Dewey, meanwhile, managed the Lake Placid Club, in New York State and in Florida; Rider said that its great growth began in 1905, when for the first time Dewey made it his main interest and all-year place of residence; before that it had been, for himself and his wife, a summer refuge from hay fever. Dawe somewhere gave the Club a value of nearly four million dollars; besides the Club proper it consisted of farms, cottages, recreation areas and so on, and, Rider said, hundreds of employees.

At about 55 years of age in 1905-06 Dewey might in those days have gone on being a distinguished librarian for another twenty years; certainly, he was a distinguished consultant, with a reputation made and increasing with that of DDC, but he did not want to be or wasn't invited to take charge of another library of importance. He was also regarded as an efficiency expert and as a founding member of the Efficiency Society advised on efficiency methods in government offices. He took on too much, though, and Rider couldn't resist showing him as a figure of fun, with five

fountain pens in a waistcoat pocket and more on his desk,
using different colored inks, "each one adapted--or so he
persuaded himself--to meet some special purpose." One of
Rider's stories is that when Dewey was on war work a member of his committee arrived at the Club unexpectedly to confer with him and witnessed the disorder of his office. He
had papers swept into a huge clothes hamper and hidden in
a nearby closet; "the office presented a fine impression of
clean-cut efficiency--but it took the Dewey secretarial staff
a week to straighten out the contents of that hamper." At
least he was resourceful and Dewey's son supported Rider's
assessment of his "incredible skill in rationalizing."

As might be expected, the Club itself was no ordinary
one. In addition to Jews, hard liquor and smoking were not
accepted; music was cultivated; called a university of the
woods, it was something of an adult education institution for
its members, a pleasant one, complete with lecture hall or
theater as well as a chapel with stained glass windows, one
of the Seer and one of the Sower, both of them, of course,
Dewey. [83]

3.7 Decimal Classification Beginnings

"Decimal Classification Beginnings" was the title given
to recollections by Dewey published in Library Journal, Feb.
15, 1920 when he had turned 69. He referred back 47 years
to 1873, to his Archimedian Eureka experience, the place,
however, not being in his bath or a library but in church
during a Sunday sermon. Up to a point, though with some
discrepancies, this agrees with what he said about 1873 in a
paper for PLUSA on the Amherst Plan--the same paper which
served as a Preface for A Classification and Subject Index,
bibliographically anonymous but bearing on the verso of the
title page the notice, "Copyrighted 1876 Melvil Dewey."

In 1920 he compared the use of arabic numerals for
notation with that of the alphabet for indexing, but his arguments were specious and lacked plausibility; of course a
verbal index must consist of letters and be alphabetical in
order, but whereas letters can be used for notation, mixed
or unmixed with numerals, numerals cannot be used for spelling. Dewey could have used letters wholly or in part, both
for his notation and in an index. His opposition was false
but it remained in what became, after his death, the standard
version of his introduction to DDC, reprinted in all editions

up to the 18th in 1971, although not likely to be included in later editions, except possibly a centenary 1976 edition. He could not know, of course, what his Lake Placid Club promoters of the genius-saint legend would publish after his death in 1931.

In 1876 he claimed with some exaggeration that besides making over fifty personal visits to libraries--which should have included the Boston Public Library where Shurtleff's Decimal system was in operation--he had studied library economy in some hundreds of books and pamphlets. The Eastern states had hardly produced that many, however, and the Western states few indeed at the time. His reading was to inform his mind, but a bibliography of what he actually read, with an indication of what had impressed him, would have helped; but unlike Cutter, he wasn't that kind of librarian.

It was the revelations of others with different interests that questioned his reputation and suggested that he might have taken his classification, usually meaning his notation, from some writer not mentioned by him. In 1945 there was an article by Leidecker on the debt Melvil Dewey owed to William Torrey Harris, already considered in association with Bacon. And as late as 1972 Maass asked, rhetorically, in the Wilson Library Bulletin, "Who Invented Dewey's Classification?" His almost unqualified answer was that it was Blake (1826-1910), a geologist who organized the 1876 centenary exhibition in Philadelphia and in February 1873 sent out widely an advance publicity pamphlet for the exhibition. Dewey, while claiming he developed the Amherst or Dewey Classification of 1876, did not mention either Harris or Blake, or submissions which he made to the Amherst library committee on May 8, 1873, or a letter to Harris on May 9th of the same year. But Dawe made much of the submissions and reproduced them as documents of historic value--which they are. These are contemporary documents, against which the claims which Dewey made for developments in 1873, and the claims made for Harris and Blake and possibly others whom he may have read at that time, may be compared; and against which what he published as his classification in 1876, and its development at least as far as the second edition of 1885, can be measured.

According to Dawe, Dewey wrote other papers which were apparently considered by the committee but those Dawe reproduced were apparently the basic three submitted on May 8th. The most relevant here is the first, called "Library

Classification System," little more than one page of print.
Rider called this a memorandum, quoting with omissions and
including a few lines from the second paper, called "The
Merits of the System." Rider doesn't make clear its limitations or explain certain typographical difficulties in it, but
these are explained up to a point by a facsimile reproduction of
a page of the manuscript original, which Dawe enthusiastically
included, apparently without realizing its implications.

"Classification," as Dewey talks about it here, is ambiguous. In the first section of Dewey's own standard introduction, on "Origin and Growth," there is confusion between
classification and indication of classification (notation), but in
that he does go on to say that what he called the outline of
his system--apparently meaning the numbers only--could have
headings different from those of DDC or the same headings
in different order, and also makes the point that DDC could
be a relative index system "if the classification were marked
wholly by letters or other symbols." Decimal, he says,
"means simply that heads are grouped and numbered with common arithmetic figures used decimally." These common arithmetical figures are related to a decimal scale, though the use
of place is confusing, but decimal, as used by him and others
before him, seemed to mean merely a way of expressing subject relation or hierarchy. He did not attempt, as Ranganathan and some others did for a time, to use decimal to de-
note any scale or radix fraction. Rider was tempted into
this in 1944. But the simplicity of arabic numerals was much
too much a part of Dewey's advocacy.

Dewey's submission to the committee was in manuscript, possibly with some copying ink duplication. James
Watt had patented the screw press for this ink copying in
1780; typewriting with stencil duplicating came only about a
century later. Dawe's reproduction is obviously of what was
basically handwriting. The first sentence of the submission,
in Dewey's economical style, is "Select the main classes,
not to exceed nine and represent each class by one of the
(ten digits) nine significant figures." The manual typesetter
of Dawe's book was doing his best. What the manuscript
facsimile shows is that Dewey had written, "Select the main
classes not to exceed ten and represent each class by one of
the ten digits...." But the first "ten" had "nine" overwrit-
ten, and "ten digits" in the third line is bracketed out and
interlineated above it is "nine significant figures." The conclusion seems inescapable that Dewey had not realized or had
forgotten or overlooked that his simple 1, 2, 3 system did

not have ten digits. Nine cannot be exceeded at any point in a number; if it is, then there is a transfer to the "place" on the left, and ten is represented by the first digit and the circle sign, which was introduced to avoid confusion in spacing and became known as the zero or cipher sign, but not as a digit. The reproduced manuscript suggests hurried alteration just before, or perhaps during, the meeting.

The substitution of 9 made the system hierarchically nonary, not decimal. Dewey had then gone on to propose extension of his basic digits by decimal fraction subclasses, omitting the decimal point but arranging as if it were written after the first figure. John Napier (1550-1617), however, had established the decimal point to show transitions of numbers from integers or whole numbers to decimal fractions; without it a number extended from integers to fractions on the same decimal base could be misunderstood as entirely an integral number. Apparently Dewey had realized this, or had it pointed out to him, and had then bracketed out the words about omitting the point.

The facsimile page ends at this point, but the printed version of the submission goes on to suggest that the zero may be used with its "regular zero power, i.e., indicates no classification," if it indicates form, not subject; for example, encyclopedias in general. But this is mathematically, arithmetically, a quibble; if the zero represents any literature, whether "form" or "subject," it no longer has the purpose of the zero of arithmetic.[84]

Dewey may have seen the exhibition pamphlet which was widely circulated in February 1873; this shows Blake using the roman numbers I-X for what he called Departments, corresponding to Dewey's basic classes. But this would not mean that Dewey, as Maass suggests, got his whole decimal idea from Blake. It has been pointed out that Blake in 1867, at the age of about 40, translated from the French an article advocating of metric weights and measures, but to be fair, Dewey in 1867 advocated the metric system when he was only 16. The exhibition pamphlet may, however, have been the source of the idea--apparently not Dewey's--that eventually, if and when he produced a classification, copies should be printed for the convenience of catalog users. Maass does not seem to have proved his case, that "beyond the shadow of a doubt that Melvil Dewey studied this pamphlet ... and derived from it the draft of his Decimal classification" and "cunningly covered his tracks."[85]

3.8 1873-1876

As has been shown, Dewey put forward a scheme on May 8th, 1873, and said in his 1876 explanation that the plan was developed early in 1873. The simple answer seems to be that this is not true. He began in 1873 talking about ten classes but, with alterations of his submission, finished with nine, plus decimal fraction extensions; in 1876 he had nine classes without decimal fraction extension. "Practically, it is desirable that the classification be as minute as possible without the use of additional figures, and the decimal principle on which our scheme hinges allows nine divisions as readily as a less number." This seems a contradiction of the decimal idea. However, "It has seemed best in our library to use uniformily three figures in the class numbers." This appears in the PLUSA account, which is fuller than the DDC introduction because it is more general. But the system as published in 1876 has three figures in the class number, and these are only class numbers for nine classes, and without decimal fraction extensions. With three-figure class numbers there were to be book number extensions, such as 513.1 for the first book on Geometry, 513.2 for the second and so on.

In 1873, however, the proposal was to use authors' names, which seems to follow Harris's proposal, and even his text. This is all right since there are several ways of distinguishing authors, but numbers such as 513.1 seem deliberately to exclude decimal extensions of subject. The point he made was that numbers like 513.1, etc. were for books in classes, with relative location, not shelf marks. He allowed some bracketed subdivision in a catalog--for example, of counties of England--but this was to disappear in actual arrangement, in which 942 would embrace them all. Unfortunately, this explanation appeared on cover pages of the scheme, and was lost in binding in many copies.

In 1873 Dewey was influenced by Harris, whose proposals appeared in 1870. He accepted Harris's arrangement of items within classes by authors' names, and he presumably preferred his "Hygiene - 57 c," with very limited hierarchical division, to his "Sci. X.5. c." Neither, however, was his own 613, with 6 for Useful arts, 1 for Medicine and 3 for Hygiene. With only nine classes this gave him only 729 three figure numbers, to which he added 99 preliminary numbers vaguely for form: 1 to 99 with about forty blanks. While admitting some congestion in history and geography he still felt that he could use 794 for his personally favored chess, and four numbers for outdoor sports excluding football and baseball, already established in America, and even for a time cricket. But a total of 829, he felt, gave him numbers to play with. Meanwhile, he had dropped Harris's author names for numbers like 513.1 to indicate the first book in geometry, and had thus blocked decimal extensions.

These developments came after 1873, with uncertain history. But he had read Harris and wrote to him on May 9th, 1873, effusively offering exchanges for information on what Harris was doing in St. Louis schools. This letter, turning up later, led Leidecker to assume that Dewey's scheme was derived from Harris,[86] but there was the weakness that Harris, while using the numbers 1-100, did not use them hierarchically or as a decimal system, and Dewey took the inverted Baconian classification with little acknowledgment to either Bacon or Harris. Whereas others, before and after, fitted a notation to a classification, Dewey did the reverse. That he might have been misled about ten digits by Blake has been considered above. For Dewey, the first and last thing was his decimal or hierarchical notation, which was nonary rather than decimal in his first edition. It also had an index referring to class numbers, not shelf marks, and in this sense was relative. A head note ended with the advice that "where a class number ends in a cipher the subject will be found, on reference to prefixed classification, to be subdivided." This meant, for example, that 630 would be divided or extended by 1-9 in place of the zero, but it would not be extended beyond that; hence, 636 for all domestic animals. It seemed more than enough at the time, but without the further extensions of the second edition the scheme would probably not have survived. Nevertheless, these were not developed in 1873, and if the index is considered an essential part of the Classification, as Dewey began to think, it was not part of the plan developed in 1873.

This index in 1876 was probably relative as he first intended it, though he did not use the term. The index references were to class numbers relative to each other, not to fixed shelf marks. In 1873 he had used the term subject index, but not with reference to an alphabetical index. He said, "the shelf catalog (with cross references--all on cards) affords at the same time the best devised subject index," and, though not explicitly, he seemed to reject the alphabetical index idea. In 1876 he had a classification table index with reference to class numbers such as 636, but since extension did not go beyond three figures, CATTLE, HORSES, PIGS, SHEEP all refer to 636 without any distinction.

Dewey's Preface to his first edition was written against a deadline and increasingly so with reference to the submission of his work for copyright beforehand. The so-called acknowledgments are in the last paragraph, as follows:

> In his varied reading, correspondence and conversation ... the author doubtless received suggestions and gained ideas it is now impossible for him to acknowledge. Perhaps the most fruitful source of ideas was the Nuovo Sistema di Catalogo Generale of Natalie Battezzati, of Milan ... though he copied nothing from it. The plan of the St. Louis Public School Library, and that of the Apprentices Library of New York ... were not seen till all the essential features were decided on [that is, of his own]. In filling in the nine classes of the scheme the inverted Baconian arrangement of the St. Louis Library has been followed. ...

Little has been said on this because few commentators have known enough to comment, and there was the first stumbling block or red herring of Battezzati. Even Comaromi in 1969 said that neither he, "nor as far as he can determine, anyone else has seen Battezzati's scheme," though on the strength of Dewey's reference it has been listed as a library classification. In his own despair this writer got in touch with an Italian correspondent, Enzo Bottasso, and learnt from him of his substantial paper on "Le Origini della Classificazione Decimale," 1965, unfortunately not translated into English. The full title of Battezzati's work, dating back to 1871, is Modello di un nuovo sistema di catalogo bibliografico generale disposito per autore, per materia e per aditore ad uso praticodel librario per conoscere tutte le publicazione giornalmente. The word librario means booksellers and giornalmente means daily. Battezzati's scheme was used for service supplied by publishers, using colored slips and some Brunet classification. Dewey had become aware of it and knew there was some exhibition of it in 1876 in the Philadelphia exhibition; he made reference to it in Library Journal,[87] but only in this context and without relation to library classification or to library catalog card service.

As Comaromi said, it is certain that the skeleton of Harris's classification provided the bones of Dewey's; his

source was the book classification paper in which Harris said
explicitly that his scheme was being completed for the St.
Louis School Library. As Comaromi says, there is insufficient resemblance to suggest that Dewey got anything from
Schwartz's New York Scheme. Comaromi said that it is reasonable to assume that Dewey was protecting himself from
accusations that he had not been original in what he called
"the ambiguous final paragraph" and that "who contributed
substantially to the final form of the first edition ... and to
what extent ... will likely never be known." Biscoe, however, was certainly a substantial collaborator.

Dewey also did not as he wrote know where he stood
or was likely to stand on his copyright claim, and it may
be assumed that the first and last paragraphs of his Preface
were meant to impress in that direction and that, like others,
he was not clear on differences between copyright and patents
of inventions, requiring some evidence of priority. Comaromi's adjective, "ambiguous," is kind; other applicable terms
might be evasive, equivocal, spurious. Dewey had to have
his little work in print for a copyright claim, but he had
learned that he could have printed on his title page verso,
"Copyrighted 1876 Melvil Dewey." The speed at which he
was working and the ways in which he must have been improvising through that year may even excite admiration for
what has been called his genius, though the brand was not
that of other men so-called.

An English version of Battezzati's scheme had been
done for exhibitions, apparently first for the Vienna Exposition of 1873, and this was presumably the version Dewey saw,
and did not misunderstand.

3.9 <u>1873-1876-1885</u>

Dewey was right in distinguishing his class and book
numbers, such as 513.1 for the first book on geometry and
so on, from the shelf mark which it superseded, in which
513.11 was a shelf mark signifying not the 11th book on
geometry in the library, but the 11th book on shelf 513; or
alcove 5, range 1, shelf 3, as in most libraries. This was
admirable progress but, again, it was not proposed in 1873,
nor was what he changed to in his second edition, 1885, where
decimal fraction extensions of three figure numbers were no
longer the simple item numbering introduced by a point which
could be confused with decimal fractions. His 513.11 in the

1876 edition was obviously not the author's name distinction
adopted from Harris in 1873, nor was it a decimal fraction
number, 513.11, which in the 1885 edition became a subject
number for "Right Lines in Plane Geometry." He had had to
drop the book numbers to allow for decimal fraction extensions and, typical of the way he went from one extreme to
another, he described "the table of classification mapt out in
logical order and skilfully arranged to show in no less than
four ways, viz: by sizes of type, face of type, indentation
and number of figures prefixt, the exact rank in the classification of the thousands of headings." This, he said, was "an
essential part of the subject index," and in his pretence that
there had been few changes in the development of the system, said that "the prefatory matter of the first edition is
reprinted as the introduction in the second, with modifications
and additions inserted in brackets." But unfortunately this
was careless and inconsistent. There had obviously been
major changes from 1873 to 1876, and again from 1876 to
1885. In the second edition, Horses were 636.1; Cattle
636.2; Sheep, Goats 636.3; Swine 636.4; but the index gave
class inclusions--for example, Horse, domestic animal
636.1; Zoology 593.7--and this has been taken to be what he
meant by relative indexing, and general indexing of subject
relations, although clearly he only indexed class inclusions.
It is all development without which his original decimal base
would not have worked, but to say that there were few
changes from 1873 is rubbish.

  Dewey did carry over from 1873 some of his ideas
about the use of the zero. In 1876 he wrote of a class 0,
for a cyclopedia or periodical not limited to any one subject
class. He said that they were assigned to a class 0, but
that there would be no difficulty in following the arithmetical
law and omitting the initial zero, so these numbers were
printed 31, 32, etc., instead of 031, 032, etc. So, in obe-
dience to the law, he had ninety-nine single to two-figure
numbers, 1 to 99, including 51 for American periodicals.
But 51 could be read for Mathematics instead of American
general periodicals, and users had found it better not to omit
the initial zero; therefore, despite the arithmetical law, he
found it better to use the initial zero. The effect, which he
might not at first have realized, was that he had a tenth
digit, though not one sanctioned by his arithmetic, and in the
second edition, instead of only listing nine classes as in the
first, including his preliminary numbers he listed 0-9 instead
of 1-9, ignoring the fact that he had altered the value of the
arithmetical figures, 0 coming to mean first and 9 meaning

tenth. It didn't matter much in practice in some ways, but in fact he had converted the signs. His 0 became General works. The practical value was that 051 for a general periodical could not be confused with 510 for Mathematics. At the same time he found it convenient to use 0 in the second place for a subclass or division number for general works further divided by the terminal 1 to 9; but "they apply only to the general treatises, which, without them, would have a class number ending with two zeros."

In the second edition he began extending 0 numbers for form across the decimal point. This was Dewey, in whom thrift had been inculcated, not realizing the trouble he was causing. What he never seemed to realize was that he was not engaged in an arithmetical exercise. He was using ten symbols of known shape and ordinal value; their basic arithmetical quantity values were of no value, and his hierarchical or "decimal" orders of class values and subordinations added nothing to arithmetic. Any other ten symbols which were more or less generally familiar would have served as well, but of course the letters of the alphabet were the obvious alternative because of their great extension in number. The scale or base of ten had more disadvantages than advantages, and decimal was not really a magic word. To the end, however, he tried or pretended to see advantages in the arithmetical uses of his symbols.

Clearly his use of the zero was no great invention of his; it was something like the means he found of printing his first edition--a chance offered itself: in this case, the use of the initial zero by others to escape such ambiguities as that of 51 for an American periodical and 510 for Arithmetic. He conveniently forgot his arithmetical law, and came out with his ten class 0-9, and mixed up the Introductions of the first two editions to show how few changes there had been. His original Preface, with all its second edition expansion, and an appendix called "Variations Practicable" are in his last version, the 12th edition in 1927, and are reprinted in all editions up to the 18th. But the Introduction is expanded from the 16th on, and in the 18th this ominous Prefatory note about Dewey's Introduction appears: "... Many of its statements and examples are obsolete, or even in direct contradiction to the Editor's Introduction, and it should be read in the context of its time." It should also be read in the context of the man Dewey, but of course it remains an important historical source.

3.10 Subject Insertion; The Procrustean Bed; Divide-Likes; The Index

Dewey, on his "waste not, want not" principle, decided to use his two noughts in his nine basic class numbers for what he called form divisions and sections, but this meant that if the noughts were dedicated to form then they could not be used for subjects between, for example, 621 and 629, these being dedicated to branches of engineering. This sort of thing left no spaces for common subject aspects, and he realized too late, if ever, that space for subject insertions was most needed at the beginning and end. He made some use of 9 for "other branches," most notably in 629, but did not do so systematically with what Ranganathan later called his "Octave Device," and to make matters worse, proudly using the mnemonic parallels, 09 became his local and history form extension for subjects. Still struggling in the 17th and 18th editions, his editors cleared the little-used 04 number (previously for essays) for what were called general special concepts applicable to a subject sequence of things such as the oceans. This sort of problem, of course, could happen without ill-informed, inexperienced use of any notation, but the shortness of the decimal or nonary base with which Dewey began didn't help.

What appears to have been the first application of the "Procrustean Bed" metaphor seems to have been in LJ Feb, 1885, by Schwartz, and Dewey was able to attempt an answer under the heading "Decimalism" in his second edition and later edition introductions. Clearly he was stung but he would have done better to have ignored the criticism instead of advertising it, with his argument that decimals were servants not masters and his metaphorical nonsense about railroads.

After the second edition DDC grew in size under editors Miss Seymour and Miss Fellows, his immediate pupils, and the complications and makeshifts to meet growing needs increased. One of these was "divide-likes," which really began when he crossed the Rubicon of his decimal point for form numbers. They were a space-saving device, an easy way of classification extension, and mnemonic, and they could be doubled and even trebled. An example of a double divide-like, producing 636.5920896942 for "Erysipelas in turkeys," is seriously given in the 18th edition (v.1:29). Ranganathan in India could think of catalogers laboriously number-building and incidentally saving precious paper, but American librarians couldn't or wouldn't. An obvious solution seemed to be indexing, and in the index of DDC there appeared: "Dogs, drawing techniques 743.6974442," a combination of a simple animal drawing number, 743.6, and a divide-like for dogs from Zoology, 599.74442. The procrustean bed is not escaped, however, and the index cannot be inflated for thousands of animals in this way; there has to be great reduction of this and some use of the literary warrant principle. Already before the 1970s many libraries, at least among those using DDC outside America, could not afford a one-volume abridged edition, let alone what became a two-volume full edition with the 16th and a three-volume 18th edition following a crisis over the indexing of divide-likes in the 17th. Another divide-like weakness is that the classification used for dividing may hardly be suitable. For example, are perennials in gardening really usefully divided by their botany numbers, making as a mild example, 635.93347 the number for cactus?

The saving answer, if not the best and final one, was copy cataloging; that is, with the book in hand, getting a number given to it by LoC as a clerical operation, and some administrators used techniques to bypass their cataloging departments when this copy cataloging proved possible.

DDC rolled on with little interruption up to the time of Dewey's death, although before this Hulme in England, its most able and most neglected authority on IR (2.8), criticized the seventh edition, 1911, for having too many numbers for "snippet" literature without what he called "literary warrant."[88] What may be called crisis editions for the Lake Placid Club Education Foundation, which has had the copyright from 1922, began with the 15th edition, 1961.

Comaromi said the Standard (15th) edition was to be one of three versions but most librarians seem only to have seen or heard of the one which appeared. It was edited by a not very impressive committee, except possibly for Rider, and seems to have been influenced by his generalization about too much classification being too much of a good thing. Divide-like and other "advice" was almost eliminated, "in the belief that the user does not need to be told how to arrange his collection" (Intro., xxi). But then does he need any classification? The idea was to simplify, especially by reducing number length, an idea which Rider realized in his 1961 International Classification, partly by using the much longer alphabetical base. The Foundation was shaken by the reaction, many librarians staying with the 14th edition or

going over to LC, and one result was that editing DDC was
taken over by LoC where Custer promoted its recovery with
the two-volume 16th edition, 1958. Custer then produced
controversy by a somewhat slashing attack on the divide-likes
indexing question, leading the Foundation to replace the Index
for the 17th edition, 1965. That Custer was basically right
was becoming apparent and there was little opposition to his
reduced indexing in the 18th edition, 1971; but by this time
there were more DDC numbers on LoC cards and copy cataloging from LoC cards was catching on with administrators.

3.11 From Dewey to Cutter

From Dewey to Cutter in classification is not merely
a chronological step, of immediately leaving Dewey's DDC
for Cutter's EC, the Expansive Classification with which he
has been commonly identified. Besides having business talks
with Ginn and Cutter in 1876, Dewey said that on April 18
that year he talked about his classification at Harvard and
"they made me give a lecture ... to their first assistants
and to the librarian of Wellesley College," Ann Godfrey, who
later became his wife and then was under Cutter's tutelage.
Dewey was able to write to her on July 7, 1876, sending a
proof of the library scheme (the first edition of the Decimal
Classification), the preface of which he had dated "June 10th,
Amherst College."[89] This seems to imply that he had got
his copyright certificate and been able to go on and complete
the title page, its verso and his Preface.

Cutter wrote to Ann Godfrey on June 28th saying that
Dewey had explained his system, answering all his objections,
and that he intended to try it out in a projected Athenaeum
extension, designed to hold 125,000 volumes.[90] What impressed him most was the index, and the mnemonic corres-
pondences. The relative location idea he did not think new,
but Mr. Dewey's movable decimal system, first used at Amherst, was the most widely known. To have it adopted by
Cutter was a major triumph, but as Cutter tried it in his own
library he became dissatisfied, finding it, as others did,
cramping. He was even occasionally cramped using a literal
notation of 26 letters, but had the idea, which he retained,
of using single figures for form divisions.[91] At this point a
different man might have gone along developing a quite acceptable classification with a literal subject notation, and
there is evidence that one reason why the first edition of DDC
did not sell rapidly was that many were waiting to see what
Cutter might produce.

Dewey had some reason to be alarmed. His 2nd edition was still about six years in the future and something that might anticipate it and appear better than his first edition in notation and capacity would not have helped his business interest in DDC. Cutter's interest was the usual one of a classification simply for his own library or a part of it, but he had received suggestions and presumably requests that he publish what would have been the Athenaeum Classification, or AC. It was in character when he said in 1881 that "the idea of publishing the classification in form similar to Mr. Dui's Amherst system has been given up for the present, as I prefer to subject my ideas to the test of actual use before fixing them by type." He obviously did not think this had been sufficiently done with DDC.[92] But in much that was going on and that transpired right to the end of Cutter's Expansive Classification, one man at least seems to have thought Dewey a genius: this was W. P. Cutter, Charles Ammi Cutter's nephew, assistant, and author of a too short and too reticent biography of his uncle. It seems clear, however, despite his circumspection and reticence, that he thought Dewey his uncle's evil genius.[93]

Back in 1879 Cutter was becoming a partner in the Reader's and Writer's Company which, after a burst of glory, failed to be succeeded by the Library Bureau when Dewey was obliged to take a job, the Columbia College Librarianship. But Dewey and Cutter must have seen a lot of each other, and in their discussions about classification Dewey probably got more from Cutter than Cutter did from him, except for the 35-base notation. Having later in 1879 shown that he was making good progress towards a classification with a literal notation and some use of figures, Cutter said that while "he was working this out, Mr. Dewey was devizing something better still," and referred to Dewey's articles earlier in the year on "Principles Underlying Numbering Systems."[94] These articles show at least some appearance of scholarly impartiality and of learning.

Dewey considered notations briefly, saying that at Amherst, after careful consideration, "the balance of advantages rested with ... the simplest numerical scheme," but he would like to see letters thoroughly tested by someone else. In the second article he began considering what have been called mixed notations, in which letters and numbers are complementary, simple examples being B7 and 7b. But then in the same paragraph he went straight on to say that "to get the fullest advantage of compactness," by which he meant shortness of numbers, the two systems must be merged in one of 35 characters; counting 0 as one in 0-9 this provides ten, and the alphabet, after omitting O, makes the total 35.

Dewey never used this notation, sticking for his own reasons to his numerals only. He did not say he invented it and Schwartz seems to have been using it as a notation for the titles of voluminous authors, simply to provide numbers. And, as related above, when Schwartz used the term "procrustean bed" in criticizing Dewey's decimal base, Dewey reacted furiously in the Introduction to his 2nd edition and went on doing so in later versions. In 1879, of course, Dewey had no library in which to present an improved classification; but Columbia in 1883 gave him opportunity, as did Wellesley College, perhaps. These both became scalps for the system he owned and wanted to develop as a business asset, and any theoretical second thoughts about classification and notation he might have had remained mute.

3.12   The 35 Base and the Expansive Classification

The 35 base has to be understood not as one base complementing another, but as two bases made into one, like tying two pieces of string together. Ten numerical digits are simply ten numbers; in pairs they are ten squared or a hundred, in threes ten cubed or a thousand, the maximum of Dewey's three-figure numbers. The same formula applied to 26 letters gives 676 and 17,576, respectively. Now assume 35 digits, forgetting how they are made up; then 35 squared is not a hundred plus 676, it is 1,225. The characters look unusual, but Cutter found that attendants and library assistants could easily learn to find them. If they came into open access, though, the public found them confusing. In 1882 Cutter wrote a short article on "Thirty-five versus Ten" and in conclusion said, "let it be remembered that the 35 base was of Mr. Dewey's own suggestion; and if he is beaten it is with a weapon furnished by himself."[95]

But if he were not beaten? Larned said in 1884 that when the 35 base is mixed, as it has to be for a large collection, with subject, form and time distinctions, the necessary combinations "exhibit a most forbidding cryptographic appearance and show nothing in themselves that promises a key to their meaning."[96] In 1887 Cutter traversed the story and admitted that no other library after his own was ever likely to adopt a classification on the 35 base.[97] By then--

and he was now talking of a notation for small libraries--he had lost half a dozen years towards the development of his Expansive Classification and effective competition with Dewey, whose decimal base at least satisfied small libraries. And Larned had become an influence, much more to the good.

Going, like many, into a library with a good mind but no experience and training, Larned is said to have been the first to have DDC adopted completely for shelf and catalog in what became the Buffalo Public Library.[98] He remained satisfied for some years but his mind was too good, and in 1884 he published the results of experiments with the use of different letter combinations or permutations in what he called "A Nomenclature of Classification." For example, two consonants with a vowel between is one set of permutations and a vowel between two consonants is another, and he proposed using one of these for geographical numbers. In 1887, with acknowledgment to Larned, Cutter proposed alternatively to add to what Larned proposed, single-figure numbers for the usual form divisions and a much more extensive series of two-figure numbers with expansions at will. However, before clearing up the Expansive Classification, as regretfully must be done since it has not survived, reference may be made to a title page which has survived in draft from 1879. It reads, mainly in Cutter's handwriting, "Melvil Dewey's/35 character notation/applied to/Book Classification/by/C. A. Cutter/with enlarged edition of Dewey's Index/Boston/Economy Company/1879."[99] This seems never to have been published but there was some interest by Dewey in an idea of publishing an index for common use, though always with his numbers.

As Cutter had spent time over the 35 base so he spent time over the idea of the expansive or expanded editions given the name Expansive Classification. His first publication was apparently <u>Expansive Classification, Part I: The First Six Classifications</u>, Boston 1891-3. This volume is printed but is not otherwise well produced, with rambling attempts at simple explanations at different levels, though there is some cohesion and an embracing index by Miss Harriet E. Green. Of what use there was of EC, a lot had to be based on the sixth expansion because the final 7th Expansion only came out piecemeal after Cutter's death. At the 2nd International Conference in London, 1896, Cutter talked on "Reasons for Using the Expansive Classification in International Bibliography," with exaggerated claims of evolutionary order, not quite on Richardson's lines, and again at the Brussels Bibliographical Conference of 1897.

But thinking was changing towards UDC lines of compound subject expression. Cutter was out of the race; though his classification had comparative merits for its day, it did not get established in use as DDC did. As Dewey well understood, "thrice armed is he who gets his blow in fust." Money to continue the scheme presumably came out of Cutter's estate; there is no mention of any foundation until a proposal for something of the sort with a large private endowment just before 1914. W. P. Cutter speaks rather bitterly of what he seems to think were broken promises and EC never survived 1914 and the War. [100] It was adopted on the grounds that it was more scientific than DDC, for example at Wisconsin University, and it was said in 1934 to be adequate for required amplification which avoided reclassification. In 1934 it had lasted 40 years, but in another ten the balance was against EC even where it had been used that long, and a decision was made to change to LC. [101]

Like the 35 base in the Athenaeum the progressive expansions were probably a time-wasting mistake as compared with successfully enlarged editions, as with DDC, and at some time a good abridged edition. DDC had six expanding full editions: in 1894, a second in 1912, a ninth in 1965. Clearly, Cutter failed as a competitor with Dewey in classification, and Dewey did not compete with him in alphabetical cataloging and lost out very largely to Cutter's form of this with his hopes for classified cataloging. Despite its competitive failure as shelf classification, Cutter's classification was remarkably influential on and through LoC's. That story is told in the next chapter.

Chapter 4

CUTTER AND CONGRESS: CATALOG AND CLASSIFICATION

When the new LoC had to make its choices there were of course choices, but was what was adopted nevertheless a foregone conclusion? It wasn't; many, for example, assumed DDC with a classified catalog; others, especially inside, wanted a classified catalog, but not DDC, and so on with other combinations. What seems as certain as can be is that the choice would not have been one of a combination without one element which already existed and was strongly supported. Cutter had begun with alphabetical cataloging and independent shelf classification, something he had become familiar with at Harvard and found satisfactory. The combination, then, was his, and the dictionary catalog with specific entry was also his. In retrospect, then, he was a major influence, the combination being his, the cataloging method being his, the classification not being his, but his a greater influence on it than Dewey's. Many other libraries had adopted his combination with DDC, before LC was really available. His early life and librarianship has been briefly covered at the beginning of the preceding chapter, and his classification has been considered. Now there is his subject cataloging or IR system to be considered. How did he get to it? Certainly, it was more than twenty years before there was much thought or talk of a new Congress catalog and classification in a new building at Washington.

4.1 Cutter's Rules and His Thesis, Antithesis, and Synthesis

Cutter's Rules for a Dictionary Catalog (of the kind later called combined as opposed to divided), in the last edition in his lifetime and the latest, the 4th edition, 1904, are available in a British Library Association reprint. In 173 pages and 369 numbered rules on author, title and subject entry and other things, only 20 pages (66-80, 122-128) and

33 rules (161-188, 339-343) are what he distinguished as subject entry rules, and these show less development and revision through his four editions than the others.

The rules average between two and three lines, some longer ones consisting of preliminary explanation rather than rules; but the rules have explanatory commentary in smaller type and of much greater length. The commentaries include examples, sometimes running to two or even four pages, on some of his most important principles, and perhaps prejudices are also stated in the commentary or notes. Little detailed reference is now made to them in America, in libraries, schools of librarianship or the literature. Many libraries and schools do not seem to have copies, but rely for a general idea or concept on subject heading lists and what are called "tracing notes" in published entries, notably LoC's. The general and somewhat vague concept of what Coates has called the American type of dictionary catalog[102] has been disputed in Britain by Coates and others; and there seems to be an idea that there was, a century ago, a concept of specificity in IR and subject entry, before Cutter, and of which his rules and principles are only a version. This is misleading.

There was alphabetico-classed which he knew well in its Harvard College version, and for which he at least established the name alphabetico-classed in place of such jargon names as the mixed or halfway system. Up to 1868 at least it could be called his thesis, but in the Athenaeum, to which he then went as librarian, Poole had begun a new catalog which he left inexperienced young men to carry on. One of the best of these, Lowell, was in charge until he died unexpectedly in 1870; when Cutter then had to take over the editorship he was appalled by what he considered the failure of Poole's title word entry applied to a large scholarly library and Poole's too loose and curtailed item description in entries of all kinds.[103]

This, in the terms of Hegelian logic and dialectic, was the antithesis of what would have been his thesis; but title word entry is generally specific because it follows natural language in this respect. Shingles in any one of three meanings are Shingles; they are not "Diseases - Shingles," or "Roofing - Shingles," or "Stones - Shingles," though of course with such homonyms there has to be definitive qualification. This was still his antithesis, not his first preference, but to avoid a fresh start and with consideration of time and money already spent, he began revision and produced an Hegelian synthesis, or integration of the later integrative levels theory, and one of the basic elements or parameters of his basic specific entry: his rule 172--"Enter books under the word which best expresses their subject, whether it occurs in the title or not." This is followed by 12 lines of small-type commentary and examples, including his naughty one, a late addition, that Beecher's Eden tableau is not the description of a Parisian music-hall, but treats of the events of Genesis. He was dealing with ambiguity of words in titles, of which both music hall and tableau were examples. The rule is loosely headed "Subject-word and subject." Subject word was current terminology for title words when the only known methods of IR were classification, called systematic; alphabetico-classed; and title word, called subject word. Cutter began his note by saying, "It is strange that the delusion ever should have arisen that 'a catalog must of necessity confine itself to titles'."

This seems an echo of what Edwards had said in 1859 of alphabetical catalogues or indexes on the plan of Watt's Bibliotheca Britannica: "of necessity such catalogues must deal rather with the phraseology of title pages rather than with the real subject matter of books." Cutter had to admit in his PLUSA chapter that the delusion had persisted, and it persisted much longer as a stick to beat the dog with, in such writers as Bradford in 1948, as a common assumption of catalog users, and among ignorant sellers of new-fangled systems right down to the present. Cutter finished with the brave words: "the title rules the title catalog; let it confine itself to that province." He did so confine it in his rules, but in them allowed title entry for anonymous works, which is reasonable and desirable, and also in Rule 152.b--"For other works, when the subject word is not the same as the name of a subject selected by the cataloger." At least partly on this ground it was introduced into LoC cataloging and has persisted in it.

4.2 What Is a Name, What's In a Name?

In ordinary general usage a name is a short adjectival phrase, a preposition-phrase of no more than two nouns and one preposition, or a conjunctival phrase of no more than two nouns with one conjunction, or just a noun--and the rose by any other name would smell as sweet. Dictionaries are indexed or arranged alphabetically by names as a means of finding meanings or definitions. Webster's New Collegiate has "VACUUM CLEANER: an electrical appliance for cleaning ... by suction," a definition or description or explanation which might be expanded into "an electric-motor-operated machine for dust removal by fan-induced suction." The name vacuum cleaner is a misnomer because the machine does not clean vacuums or create vacuums as a means of extracting dust, but that is the name these cleaners have come to be known by in English. It is what in some fancy jargon is called a surrogate or proxy for the subject, which can be used to index descriptions of items of information in entries which may also be called by the same jargon names. "Headings" and "entry word" are terms still in use. In one of the notes in which he laid down principles, Cutter said at the beginning of his rules for "Choice between different names":

> General rules, always applicable, for the choice of names of subjects can no more be given than rules without exception in grammar. Usage in both cases is the supreme arbiter--the usage in the present case, not of the cataloger but of the public in speaking of subjects.

Frequent identity of independently chosen headings with title words may have left the impression they were chosen as title words, and Cutter might have helped by insisting that any such identity was purely coincidental.

He did not entirely exclude some manipulation of names by catalogers. This came first in his long discussion of what he called compound-names, not meaning compound subjects, ending with what he admitted to be a vague rule of doubtful application: "175. Enter a compound subject-name by its first word, inverting the phrase only when some other word is decidedly more significant or is often used alone with the same meaning as the whole name." One way out of the difficulty with some names was to use a single noun such as ETHICS instead of an adjectival phrase synonym such as MORAL PHILOSOPHY. He gave ORIGIN OF SPECIES as an example in which the first word by itself was "of no account," so presumably this allowed inversion, species obviously being decidedly more significant. ARBITRATION, INDUSTRIAL would be an example of inversion on the second ground expressed in Rule 175. But he then went on with a long note in which he showed strong aversion to any inversion of adjective-noun phrases in which the noun may be regarded as a class name followed by a specifying adjective. Using strong

Cutter and Congress 77

language he said that "to adopt the noun (the class) as the heading is to violate the fundamental principle of the dictionary catalog," and that the common inversion rule that Schwartz proposed usually had the disadvantage that, as in "Parliamentary practice" and "Football practice," the adjective logically expresses an object and the noun only an aspect of it. Strangely, although he was an acknowledged master of French, in which the regular form is the inverted, as in Loi internationale, he did not say whether he would expect the French to alter what they regard with pride as good grammar and good logic. However, in English, the only language he considered, he also allowed some subheading in his rules for arrangement (340-343).

In his own Athenaeum he had some heading division and subdivision, such as "England - Law - History" and " - Law - Bibliography," but he thought of this as at least verging on classification, and perhaps out of place in his alphabetico-specific dictionary catalog. He also preferred putting even such subjects as Entomology under a country name with cross reference, or as a subheading, but has not been followed in this practice which is given doubtful justification in a note to his rules 164-5 on "Choice between subject and form," and in a final long note to his rule 343. His division or subheading was either systematic, as under countries and a few subjects such as WOMEN, or it was selective. He used DYES AND DYEING as a division for three items under COTTON, and gave them added entry under DYES AND DYEING; but this seems exceptional in his cataloging and is not covered in his rules. His catalog, however, came out in five volumes from 1874 to 1882 and did much to secure support for his specific entry, but there are some signs of development in his thinking about subjects in these volumes which are not matched by corresponding development in his rules as published in 1876, 1889, 1891, and 1904. His rule 77, "Enter a polytopical book under each distinct subject," in 1876 is duly changed in number in the fourth edition. The examples are the same as for coordinate subjects, such as Italy and Greece, England and France, and a handbook of drawing and engraving.

4.3 Cutter's Alphabetico-specific Entry
 and the Dictionary Catalog

In one of his useful discursive definitions before his rules he defined Specific entry as "registering a book under

a heading which expresses its special subject as distinguished
from entering it in a class which includes that subject." He
also made something of "individual" entry, but this arose out
of the contemporary situation in which libraries still had separate biography and history classes or sections, even in alphabetical catalogs, whereas Cutter wanted persons and places
under their particular names in the general arrangement.
He did not follow this up in his rules and it has been merged
in his specific entry, with support from logic, based on the
idea of no two things being alike.[104] What may be called his
basic specific entry rule is the first subject entry rule under
"1. Choice between different subjects, a. Between general
and specific." It is: "161. Enter a work under its subject
heading, not under the heading of a class which includes that
subject." This seems to need "special" before subject heading, but the examples clarify it: "Ex. Put Lady Cust's book
on The cat under Cat, not under Zoology or Mammals, or
Domestic animals"; and "put Garnier's Le fer under Iron, not
under Metals or Metallurgy.

What is to be noted is that for Cutter and his dictionary catalog it is the object of information which is specific,
not the information as it became in some British developments.
In his own catalog the title of Lady Cust's now immortal book
is The Cat: Its History and Diseases, but this limitation,
and the fact that neither Diseases nor History can be subordinated to the other does not seem to have worried him.
This rule of specific entry, he then said, "is the main distinction between the dictionary catalog and the alphabetico-
classed," having already said in his definitions that the dictionary catalog is differentiated from other alphabetical catalogs 1) by its giving specific entries in all cases and 2) by
its individual entry, and having gone on to point out that for
general books on a class or genus, the heading is specific
even in an alphabetico-classed catalog. But then, in his commentary on his basic rule, he went on honestly to admit a
serious difficulty, best stated in his words with his own examples. It must be stressed that this was said in his own
time and place, and without anyone metaphorically standing
on his shoulders, able to kick his teeth in.

> Some subjects have no name; they are spoken of
> only by a phrase or by several phrases not definite
> enough to be used as a heading. A book may be
> written on the movements of fluids in plants, a
> very definite object of investigation, but as yet
> nameless; it must be put under Botany (Physiolog-

ical). But if several works were written on it and it was called, let us say, Phythydraulics, it would have been seen that, under this rule, it no more ought to be under Botany than Circulation of the blood under Zoology. Thirty years ago 'Fertilization of flowers' could hardly have been used as a heading; but late writings have raised it to the status of a subject. There are thousands of possible matters of investigation, some of which are from time to time discussed, but before the catalog can profitably follow its 'specific' rule in regard to them they must attain a certain individuality as objects of inquiry, and be given some sort of <u>name</u>, otherwise we must assign them class-entry.

The specific subject or object principle and the name principle, with strict regard for what he called the usage of the public in speaking of subjects, could hardly be reconciled without some modification of the latter. He saw that the same subject could be named in different ways, one of his examples being "Floral fertilization, Flower fertilization, Fertilization of flowers; the first two, though not in any formal way, show an order of object and aspect and without very explicit statement." Cutter saw that aspects should come after an object and in the ALA <u>Subject Headings List</u>, 1st ed., 1895, he remained adamant, a minority of one in a committee of three, against the inversion History, Ancient; History, Medieval; History, Modern, because History was an aspect which should come after a period of history, which was an object although implied in an adjective. In his <u>Rules</u>, however, he said, if Fertilization of flowers was decidedly usage, then it should be used.

The object-aspect argument for Ancient history and so on, the argument against a class noun coming first, "to violate the fundamental principle of the dictionary catalog," and the decided usage argument seem at odds with each other, but Cutter does not seem to realize that this double or triple dealing with names, and the problem of descriptions which are not accepted names, brought his specific entry in an increasing proportion of cases into a state of almost utter confusion, if what he said at different points were brought together for reconciliation.

On the credit side, however, in talking of names or headings becoming distinct and established, he showed some anticipation of the idea later called "literary warrant." And

as will be seen, he seems to have had little contemporary
criticism, probably because his idea or principle of being
grammatical was one which had general scholarly appeal.
Also, while he saw something of the rise of subjects such
as the movement of fluids in plants with their term relations,
they had still not become seemingly important to most librarians and libraries, including the Library of Congress, which
as late as 1951 was preferring phrase inversions such as
"Plants, Protection of" to subheadings such as "Plants - Protection" because the former was nearer to the integrity of the
commonly used phrase, and was praising its paladin Haykin
for this kind of argument as practical guidance to its subject
headings, with little protest from dictionary catalogers generally.[105] This is anticipation here, but only to show that
Cutter must be seen in his historical context, though there
had to be modifications, slowly but surely. Neologisms such
as Phythydraulics were common solutions but depended on
adoption, and like many others, this one was not adopted;
the acronym which might have produced Mofip for Movement
of fluids in plants was in the future, and in Wilson's Agri-
cultural Index at least "Plants - Circulation" was found to
work.

4.4 Cross References and the Synoptical Table

Cutter called a catalog with cross references "syndetic, " and one without, "asyndetic"; syndetic he defined as
connective, "applied to that kind of dictionary catalog which
binds its entries together by means of cross references so
as to form a whole. " In his PLUSA chapter he praised
Poole's Catalog of the Boston Mercantile Library, mainly a
popular circulating library. He said of it that "each entry
was limited to one line. The imprints were given under each
entry whether author, title, or subject, but there were no
cross references. This is the first complete triple asyndetic dictionary catalog. From its economy of space, its
facility of use ... it has been a favorite type with town and
mercantile libraries. "[106] But this was the kind of cataloging he found in every respect deplorable for the scholarly,
mainly reference, and much larger Athenaeum library. Nevertheless, his comments did much to popularize the dictionary catalog, except that cross references were generally
thought necessary, as also was what was called a class subject table or synoptical table of subjects. Cutter included the
latter in a useful synopsis of "OBJECTS and MEANS of a
Catalog" in 1876 and he had apparently prepared a scheme for

Cutter and Congress 81

his rules, with a division under Subject entry into "A. Entries considered separately" and "B. Entries considered as parts of a whole," which were to include rules and guidance for the synoptic table. Apparently the balance of the scheme did not work out quite as intended, and he had some second thoughts. In his first edition, 1876, in the B Section he had only three rules and the third was: "87. Synoptical table of subjects: I mention its possibility here; I do not advise its construction because there is little chance that the result would compensate for the immense labor."

This disappeared from later editions and it has been forgotten and apparently little missed in dictionary catalogs. But Hulme in England criticized him strongly on this point, calling the labor a "bogey": this was in 1900.[107] Cutter's reply in his 4th edition was that he began such a table for the Athenaeum catalog; he adhered to his "immense labor" comment and said that his Committee, "eager to have done with the printing, voted not to include the table," and that his "observation since of the way in which catalogs are used makes me think that little practical utility would be lost." He suggested that classification tables and indexes such as those of Dewey's Decimal and his Expansive Classification could be studied for subject groupings. Although the idea persisted it certainly faded out among both compilers and users of dictionary catalogs throughout North America and in Australasia, where they have almost universal use in all kinds of library. Only British librarians want classified catalogs and bibliographies and assume their superiority.

This left Cutter with only two rules for cross references. By way of preface to these he said that "the systematic catalog undertakes to exhibit scientific arrangement ... in the belief that this will best aid those who would pursue any extensive or thorough study. The dictionary catalog sets out with another object ... but having attained that object--facility of reference--is at liberty to try to secure some of the advantages of classification and system in its own way." He went on to admit, with exaggeration, the "utterly disconnected particles" of the "alphabetical catalog," forgetting a useful comparison in one of his earlier notes, of the dictionary catalog showing at one view all the sides of each object, the classed catalog showing together the same side of many objects. The dictionary catalog has a single place for such manifold aspects of such subjects as Rabbits, Wool, Tobacco, though it does not in any aspect group Wool with Cotton, or Tobacco with Marihuana or Rabbits with Hares, and single place became for some a classification ideal. He concluded that by a well devised network of references, "the mob becomes an army ... the effective force of the catalog is immensely increased." But this too is little more than rhetoric and misleading metaphor. Cutter's two cross reference rules were:

> 187. Make references from general subjects to their various subordinate subjects and also to coordinate and illustrative subjects.
>
> 188. Make references occasionally from specific to general subjects.

There has been criticism of the "occasionally" only in the second rule, but as with his dropping of the synoptic table, experienced compilers and users of dictionary catalogs have agreed on this; to be effective, upward references have to be to many inclusive subjects and through a pyramid. Users seem to realise that, for example, they can turn to such headings as PLANETS and the SOLAR SYSTEM for information on MOONS; what they are weak on is the specific entry principle, being apt to wonder what "they" would put it under, whatever it is. In this respect, and because public libraries became places of remedial and adult education, downward references may have been overdone, but from such a downward reference as "Mathematics see also Algebra, Arithmetic, Geometry, Calculus," many learned something of the coverage of mathematics and some, with some surprise, that it includes their humble arithmetic.

Cutter in 1876, still with his monumental catalog to finish, beginning to turn to classification for his own library, with deadlines for his still useful chapter on catalogs in the PLUSA centenary report (35 pages with its statistics) and then for his Part II of his Rules, with the ALA foundation and conference and committees away in Philadelphia, was as one of the five leading men of the time, at least as much a doer as Dewey, if with less limelighting. He may have been cut short on his reference rules, but also he may have found that he had made too much of his distinction of his A and B sections. But his notes to his two rules, which cover only slightly over two pages, leave little else that really needs saying.

4.5 Dictionary Catalog, Specific Entry and Specificity

The dictionary catalog simply as a combined alphabetical catalog already existed before Cutter's catalog and his rules, in Crestadoro's index-catalogs and in Poole's public library catalogs. Cutter's dictionary catalog further refined it by extending his specific entry principle to individual entry for all subjects. There was continuing rivalry from title word catalogs, and of course from classified catalogs, but the dictionary catalog could be said to have triumphed in America and Australasia ideally because of Cutter's specific entry, and to an extent perhaps which required its adoption by LoC, though not without some concessions to classification. The latter, however, might well have otherwise been adopted for LoC's subject cataloging, with considerable effect on American and eventually worldwide cataloging. Involved, too, were ideas, even decisions, that LoC cataloging and copies of its cards should be generally available, and this is considered in later sections of this chapter. But first, what might have been the reasons for its triumph after 1876, and what continuing criticisms were there of specific entry in relation to emerging general ideas of specificity?

The rapid adoption of the card catalog in America was a factor because classification could not be displayed in this as it could in printed catalogs, where it was presented in a preliminary summary or in the tables to display to students a "map of knowledge." Specialisation was increasing and no longer meant just one of the sciences or even a group such as the biological or engineering; and a professor could no longer get an idea of the resources of other libraries from classified and printed catalogs. Poole's periodical indexing had shown the possibilities and convenience of direct specific indexing, to meet what became the majority demand--for specific information.

Shelf arrangement was classified but had at least rough indexing in the alphabetical catalog; faced with inadequate or no indexes in classified catalogs, one could, as Cutter said in his PLUSA chapter, turn to the dictionary catalog with specific entry. And not only does it, as he said at this point, enter items specifically on Zoology under Zoology, on Mammals under Mammalia, or Rabbits under Rabbits, but it provides entries for all aspects distinguished in the titles and possibly in subheadings. The scatter of such a subject as rabbits, or wheat or tobacco, under many aspects may be as much a defect of classification, with unwanted object grouping according to some likeness of little interest to an inquirer, he said, as the lack of such groupings as cereal crops in the dictionary catalog.

These factors encouraged opinions that alphabetical and specific arrangement in a catalog and classified shelf arrangement with open access for browsing were ideally complementary, especially in general libraries, schools at higher academic levels, public circulating, and even special libraries. The circular kind of argument that classification is scientific because it is classification lost in America the force it seemed to retain in Britain. If Jevons was right, what he called index classifications were just as much classifications as those based on subject, were related to a purpose as classifications must be, and were the only classifications based on common knowledge, that of word spelling and the fixed order of letters in the alphabet. Especially under the influence of evolution theories and of Richardson, librarians were not inclined to agree with Jevons that their classification might be a logical absurdity. They tended to accept their alphabetical cataloging as illogical and unscientific in its essence, but prgamatism was an influence; and it worked. On Dewey's own figures only 21,600 copies of his classification had been printed by the 9th edition, 1915. Cutter's Rules began with 5,000, then had a 2nd edition of 20,000, and another 10,000 copies in a third edition with reprints into 1903. There was then the fourth and last edition, and only the British Library Association reprint of this thereafter. Clearly Cutter's Rules were in demand at a critical period at least in North America. In 1885 there was the first of the three editions of the ALA list of subject headings, in 1909 the beginnings of publication of LoC headings, and in 1923 the first edition of Sears' list for small libraries. Increasingly, there were LoC cards with indications of headings. And there was a general but vague idea of specific entry, or just specificity, in the air.

The dictionary catalog with specific entry can be said to have been going strong at least as long as Dewey's classification, for a century and still with strength. In part, the reason for survival is the same for both: once in they are costly to change; but the dictionary catalog has had less change than classification. It has, however, had criticisms, and some of these may be traced with advantage before turning to LoC, which certainly maintained the dictionary catalog, but not without some impact on it.

Perhaps the best early appreciation, including some criticism, is Hulme's in Britain. Specific entry is, of course, as possible with a classification as with words at large, if its notation allows, and Hulme in 1902 was not distinguishing when he said that "specific entry is the classification of works as units under headings directly suggested by the ambit of these units. The warrant for the classes is purely literary."108-9 His term and the idea of literary warrant are usually only related to his well known writings of 1911-12 but they originated earlier. In 1900 he had criticized Cutter on two counts: the one already considered, on which Cutter replied--omission of a synoptic or class table of headings, and his substitution of a class heading in the particular example of "Movement of fluids in plants." Hulme argued that if Cutter could go down to "Botany, physiological," "until a properly attested baptismal certificate is forthcoming ... there can be no reason adduced against extension of the system to a point where specific entry is reached"--perhaps "Plants - Fluids - Movements." This method was more and more resorted to in LoC. But though Cutter was fudging somewhat with his "Botany (Physiological)," using the inversion he opposed, the fact remains that his "name in public usage" rule adhered strictly to phrases, as did his arrangement rule for what amounted to aspect division "when titles are numerous under a heading," although he still advocated avoiding subdivision, because he at least suspected what he had become even morbidly phobic about in his specific entry: any appearance or suggestion of classification. He and apparently his contemporaries were tied in their own knots, and particularly with the assumption, which must be taken a long way, that alphabetical indexing is a method requiring known names in a known order.

In 1942 Prevost aroused interest with her return to Schwartz's rule for adjectival phrase inversion, not merely for his reason of uniformity--which, as Cutter showed, would produce "Practice, Parliamentary," "System, Solar," "Juices, Gastric"; Prevost wanted nouns first, as strong words, followed by subheadings involving name changes, such as "International relations" into "Nations - Interrelations." This produces results which are sense as well as name changes and which get close to divided class entry. Although her approach is still cited as interesting she has not been followed. In England in 1953 Coates said that "Specific subject seems to have lost its former clarity. It is now possible for writers to discuss degress of specificity, and to question how specific a heading should be. There are, of course, no degrees of specificity. A term is either specific to a given subject content or not. Possibly coextensive subject cataloguing, a phrase favoured by Ranganathan, would better emphasise the accurate fitting of term to contents."[110]

Lilley in 1955 in America published a much cited paper called "How Specific is Specific."[111] He talked about supposition of some quality about a heading that "for all time and from every point of view makes it recognizable as specific rather than general." But then he said, "is there such a quality? Is not specificity always related to something? And are we always clear in our own minds what the something is, at any given moment, to which the specificity of a term is relative?" He searched for clues in Cutter, and quoted his rule 161: "Enter a work under its subject-heading, not under the heading of a class which includes that subject." This rule could have been better expressed but is made clear by the examples, to which Lilley does not refer. The rule refers to Lady Cust's book on The Cat, and Garnier's Le Fer. Lilley does not quote Cutter's definition of specific entry as registering a book under a heading which expresses its special subject. These examples were for Hulme what he meant by literary warrant. Lilley says there is at least implication that "the 'specific' and the 'class' are thought of as fixed categories." But where does he find this implication?

In his PLUSA chapter Cutter said quite clearly that "if a book treats of natural history, it is put under that heading; if it treats of zoology alone, under that," and so on through Mammals down to the Elephant. The writer has known dozens of dictionary catalogers who knew intuitively or explicitly that Cutter meant by his specific entry the use of a heading which is the name of the particular object of a book or other item of information; and the entry is specific by virtue of this relation. One soaks this up simply by reference work with a good dictionary catalog. The variation which Coates mentions above, with reference to Ranganathan, developed from him and was adopted in Britain; in it items are specific in relation to their information about the object of the information. As already noted, the fact that Lady Cust's book was limited to the history and diseases of cats didn't worry Cutter; he only saw it as specific in relation to the object, cats. If an item on rabbits is on a range of aspects then Rabbits is the specific heading; if it is on the extermination of rabbits by poisoning with cyanide then what might have been better called the coextensive heading is required for this alternative concept, something like "Rabbits - Extermination - Poisoning - Cyanide." This is not only later than Cutter and what Coates called the American type of dictionary catalog; it is contrary to Cutter's name principle and, rightly or wrongly, seemed to him to be classificatory. Lilley gets through to a solution, but unfortunately it is a class approach solution, requiring the would-be reader to decide which of 500 classes bottlewashing is likely to be in and then to look in it for what Lilley hoped would be clear and understandable subdivisions. Apart from not sounding too promising, it has nothing to do with Cutter's specific entry in the dictionary catalog.

Confusion unfortunately arises when Cutter's well established and original specific entry is called non-specific. Mills in Britain in 1967 called the American method of subject cataloging, "non-specific classes with a slight degree of multiple entry to boost the exhaustivity, as against the prevailing British method of single specific entry."[112] He admitted that this produces long class numbers, "so abhorred by many," and usually in <u>BNB</u> extended by words, because the coextension in notation or words, or the former extended by the latter, is required for chain indexing to "boost the exhaustivity." This practice is already disregarded after about only 20 years. In the following year, however, Mills took a more balanced view (cited by Angell of LoC and quoted by him), noting some advantages and disadvantages of both the British and the American methods.[113]

In what became Sears' <u>List of Subject Headings</u> for libraries of up to medium size, a new editor said in the 9th ed., 1965 that "a common criticism of any list concerns the degree of specificity in its headings. Specificity is relative and depends on the size of a library, its function, and its patrons." But these are not qualitative or quantitative constants from library to library; the only constant factor is specificity of items. For example, a small public or school library in a very thinly populated part of Australia might have a book or two on opals and their mining (and readers for them), but in many fields would probably have only fairly general books. This edition of Sears still has Frick's quite useful "Suggestions for the Beginner in Subject Heading Work," which are also useful for some who consider themselves advanced. These suggestions say that "appreciation of the principle of specific entry is fundamental." BRIDGES, it says in effect, is the specific heading for books on Bridges, not Engineering or Civil Engineering; and WATER BIRDS is not good

enough for Penguins. The list has "upward" references from
SUSPENSION BRIDGES and from VIADUCTS to BRIDGES,
though their listing as headings would take up little or no
more space. And the righthand columns of the list are blank
so that users can write in their own required and preferred
headings. Unfortunately many users put all items under the
most specific heading they can find, and do not use the blank
columns. This is following the DDC classifying rule which
Dewey himself stated as "Give every book most specific number which will contain it, " adding that "this varies in different libraries according to the number of figures used"--for
example, varying from 614 to 614.4738 for COMPULSORY
VACCINATION.

    Coates, in his <u>Subject Catalogues: Headings and
Structure</u> (1960), gave Cutter's basic rule without his examples or his definition and its examples, and after explaining
that subjects were fairly simple and separate in Cutter's time,
went on to say that "briefly there are two possible concep-
tions of specific entry. The one favoured by Cutter envisages
a set of stock subjects. " Coates continued with a metaphor
of ready-made clothing; but subjects which have what Cutter
called names hardly represent such a list of stock subjects,
and Coates does not cite one. His alternative conception is
"that of the subject-heading made to measure, the subject
co-extensive with the subject of the book. " This is loose
wording for coextensive with the information in summary.
And an "abstraction of the overall idea embodied in the subject content of a given literary unit" means, again, the information in the item on the subject object. If such summarization is not possible because the book has coordinate
subjects or coordinate aspects, such as "cats and dogs"
and/or "diseases and history, " then the book may require
several entries.

    Chain indexing could be used with classified summari-
zation. For purely verbal summarization and alphabetical
indexing Coates had to devise the method he introduced with
the <u>British Technology Index</u> in 1962.[114] But none of this
was even water in sight of the bridge in Cutter's time.
Coates tries finally to explain Cutter's failure with his name-
less subjects largely in terms which are sixty years after
Cutter, and based on ideas derived from Ranganathan which
are themselves questionable. Coates had some advantage of
hindsight whereas Cutter, of course, could have no foresight
of the ideas of Ranganathan and Coates.

4.6 Cutter Signs Off

Cutter signed off only a year before his death in 1903. He was fourteen years younger than Dewey when he died--66, as against Dewey's 80--but from 1856 until 1903 as the Forbes librarian and still working at the end on the 4th edition of his rules, he was continuously in librarianship and with an ever-growing reputation and recognition among his contemporaries. His last words in his final preface were:

> On seeing the great success of the Library of Congress cataloging, I doubted whether it was worthwhile to prepare ... this fourth edition ... but I reflected that it would be a considerable time before all libraries would use the cards of that library.... Still, I cannot help thinking that the golden age of cataloging is over, and the difficulties and discussions which have furnished an innocent pleasure to so many will interest them no more. Another lost art....

In part at least, when administrator librarians saw the possibilities not only of using LoC cards but also of having cataloging copied uncritically, there was less time out for discussions, at least on cataloging, but it took longer to reach that stage than Cutter perhaps expected. It can be said, even in 1976, that if you desire to see his monument, look around, at dictionary cataloging based on his ideas. Despite weaknesses and criticisms which are not always well informed, it serves at least as well as any other.

4.7 Library of Congress as National Library

The Library of Congress, of course, had a history before it became a national library. But here was a "national" library of a new kind--not the great national collection in a national capital and major center of population, like the British Museum Library in London and the Bibliothèque Nationale in Paris, but what may be distinguished as a national service library, working from an especially established national capital of small population, Washington. Of this kind it became the model, copied for example in Australia in its national library, which was not finally based on its federal parliamentary library, but in Australia's especially established national capital on the Washington model, in Canberra.

Had the first Librarian of the Smithsonian Institution in Washington had his way, the Smithsonian might well have become a national library and museum or museums, on the British Museum plan. Charles Coffin Jewett (1816-1868), a professor of literature who, in a common pattern, was librarian at Brown University, was uncommon in that he proved a good and innovating librarian, and he was made the Smithsonian's first librarian in 1848; but he reckoned without Joseph Henry, who had been made the Smithsonian's first secretary in 1846. Henry (1797-1879) was a physicist of note; he was not opposed to a national library and supported the idea of one in Congress, but won his point that the Smithsonian Institution was intended to be an active institution for the diffusion of scientific knowledge, and Jewett after 1854 became not a national librarian but a distinguished librarian of the Boston Public Library. Jewett also had another disappointment at the Smithsonian about 1850, with what Poole derisively called his mud catalog idea, as related earlier.

Henry collaborated with Spofford at LoC, who has been looked back on as a fill-in and even something of a figure of fun, but who has emerged more and more as probably the most successful promoter of LoC as a national library;[115] Henry got books transferred to it, increasing its barely 100,000 volumes by about 40 per cent and left acquisition by copyright deposit entirely to it. Disastrous fires in the LoC library in the Congressional building led first to an "iron" library, preceding the BML's though not on its external stack lines, and also promoted the idea of a separate building, which would, of course, have been necessary in any case for development. This building on the grand scale was first approved in 1886, and was opened without fanfare on November 1st, 1897. Under a great dome there was a great bare room, as Bodley had called that which had been Duke Humphrey's library when he took it over. Earlier in the same year, when his wife's illness prevented John Russell Young, a journalist and diplomat, going as ambassador to China, McKinley compensated him with the LoC Librarianship. At 56 Young might have been the first librarian of the new library for at least 14 years; he succeeded Spofford, who had been appointed in 1864 and now, at over 70, was reappointed to assist Young. Spofford remained when Young unexpectedly died as the result of slipping on an icy pavement on January 20th, 1899. George Herbert Putnam (1861-1955) finally succeeded on McKinley's appointment and with the required Senate approval on April 5th, 1899.

An unfortunate result of Young's short period of office has been that Putnam has been commonly reckoned as the first of the new national librarians, and much that was done or decided by officers appointed by Young has been credited to Putnam. He was not trained or experienced in library techniques down the line; son of a publisher, qualified to practice law, he became in succession librarian of the Minneapolis Athenaeum and the Minneapolis Public Library, then practiced law in Boston until he took over the Boston Public Library in a run-down period. He increased his reputation there and as a result of participation in ALA affairs was one of its representatives, with Dewey, before an 1896 Congressional committee, and supported Dewey in advocating card distribution. Dewey, as ALA secretary at the time, had supported Young's appointment as an administrator. The new building which Young briefly inherited cost $7,000,000; it was the largest in the world intended solely as a library, and the first annual vote for it provided for an increase of staff from 43 to 187.

4.8 National, But How or For What?

National the Library of Congress in its new building was to be, but how or for what? Spofford had promoted the name and the idea, but the name continued to be disputed, and LoC never seems to have become explicitly and by legislation, or even by resolutions of the legislature, a national library; it is only in fact that because functions which could be called national have been developed by, in and from the library, but it is still jealously regarded by the Congress as its library. This development began before 1897. When, after the destruction during the War of 1812, LoC was moved back into attic rooms in a new Congress building in 1818, and later was still better accommodated in a new building known as the Capitol, privileged use of it by outsiders as a Washington reference and research library had begun and was to continue.

No one, said Mearns, "took advantage of the opportunity to devise a definition. No acquisitions policy ... no imagination was anywhere discernible, save for the ingenuity of the architect."[116] At the time, the British Museum Library, which it was to emulate in important respects, was only getting into its stride, with Panizzi becoming its Principal Librarian in 1856. In 1864, in Harper's Weekly, LoC was not mentioned among American libraries for size or service; in 1861, when Spofford first became an assistant in it, its essentials were two rooms, seven people and 63,000 volumes. Spofford worked to develop it as a research and reference library.

Young, at least at first, was quite opposed to any lending, and even said that if he had his way, he would "make it as exclusive as the British Museum, limiting as far as possible the number of those who have access to its shelves." The BML was still the national library model, but Young was modifying his view up to the time of his unexpected death in January 1899, and really radical thinking and awareness that basic conditions were quite different from those of the BML seems to have begun at the top with Putnam. In an article for public information in the widely read Atlantic Monthly in February 1900 he made the usual still valid comparisons, to the advantage of the BML: LoC was rendering effective service as a reference library for the District of Columbia, "but such a service scarcely justifies a seven million dollar plant, maintained at an expenditure of over a quarter of a million dollars." But this he saw as "an opportunity, presented to no other library, not even to any other national library." He supported card distribution and, what might have been his own idea, deposit copies of the growing card catalog, taking LoC aid in IR out of Washington, into the nation. He must have thought cataloging and classifying policies and practices had to be radically revised; but thinking about this had begun under Young, and what is most relevant here is the IR thinking--by whom, with what influences and conclusions--and all this involved a staffing question with which Young had to struggle before Putnam.

The patronage system was not as peculiar as some seem to think. In Great Britain the Colonial Office, for example, had a Patronage Office in the 1830s, dealing with job solicitation; but perhaps more attention was paid to the qualifications of those who had influential patronage. For example, Fortescue, who eventually established the BML Subject Index, was a sailor nominated by a BML Trustee, his uncle and an archbishop, but he had to pass some entrance tests. LoC suffered under congressional patronage, and the usual ideas prevailed, that any more or less educated literary failure was eminently qualified for librarianship. About 150 new positions were to be filled, and the existing staff, with the exception of reappointed Spofford, included hardly any known merit on the strictly library side, and especially in IR techniques. Young got presidential approval for the appointment of some really experienced people in cataloging and classifying, but even then there was a limitation of regional preference--to the west.

A. J. Rudolph is chiefly remembered for a patent catalog involving a kind of endless chain or belt of printed cards, which did not succeed, but while he was assistant at the Newberry Library under Poole's successor, Cheney, Rudolph was selected as LoC head cataloger. He finally did not accept and was in disfavor because of his criticism of conditions at LoC. The head cataloger then came indirectly from the Newberry through the Wisconsin University Library; he was Hanson, and as assistant to him came Charles Martel, directly from the Newberry. As Hanson himself said later, there were better qualified men and women in the east, but the Western states limitation was satisfied perhaps more fortunately than it might have been by Hanson and Martel, whose reputations have stood up. They laid foundations--good, bad or indifferent--for an increasingly widespread IR service, or in older terms, a national and even international cataloging and classifying service, which did serve especially in general libraries, though it might have served better.

4.9 Options and Choices

Options presented themselves and choices had to be made, with or without possibilities of change, when the new, and first separate LoC building was approaching completion in 1896-97. In terms of cataloging and classifying, three men were mainly concerned in LoC: the librarian, Young, and the new, more or less experienced, expert, qualified head cataloger and his assistant, both out of one library and both influenced by one man, Poole.

The simplest option was that concerning the physical form of the catalog--the card catalog option--but even this was complicated. As already discussed in another connection, ideas of centrally published and distributed cards go back at least to 1876, when Dewey both advocated Battezatti's Italian system for publishers' slips for booksellers and also misrepresented it as a classification fruitful in ideas for his own. An ALA committee considered publishers but also thought of LoC as possible publishers of cards for library use. Twenty years later LoC was a real possibility; advocacy of this course was presented, on behalf of the ALA, by both Dewey and Putnam at the 1896 Library Committee inquiry

preparatory to the new building's opening in 1897, and ideas
of service to libraries by LoC had already emerged.

But preparation of cards for possible use in a wide
range of libraries, with some suggestions on them about
main and added entry headings, is one thing; <u>using</u> the cards
and the directions of one particular library, <u>of</u> a special kind
(reference and research) and unique in size, is another.
Somewhere along the line this economical idea had emerged,
but within LoC there still had to be some thinking about for
what and for whom its cataloging had to be designed. By
1897 there were Hanson[117] and Martel to advise, and Young,
soon to be succeeded by Putnam, to make the final determination. LoC was not going to run a bureau something like
<u>BNB</u> in England about fifty years later, primarily to produce
a national bibliography, with cataloging use of the work a kind
of by-product. BML had not accepted this idea and probably
it was not thought of in LoC. A card catalog for LoC was
decided on, eventually using the unit card approach, facilitating off-printing of the cards for libraries which thought they
could use them. Then, for LoC itself and for other libraries,
the <u>kind</u> of catalog became the important question, and here
too there were options.

The basic alternatives were alphabetical and classified.
There had of course to be classification for shelf arrangement, and this could be what already existed--a many times
transformed version of D'Alembert's version of Bacon--with
perhaps more change. Hanson had entered on duty on September 1, 1897, and was able to get his old Newberry colleague Charles Martel appointed to assist him as from December 1st, 1897. He reported in the same month to Young,
"against any revamping of the old system." Spofford, however, who was not in favor of elaborate classification, had
been against change in reporting to the 1896 committee, expressing himself in favor of what he called a subjective system, not governed by any Procrustean system of classification.[118] He may have influenced Young, who postponed consideration of classification, while Hanson and Martel wanted
to get on with it, if only for shelf arrangement. Instead, Young
wanted thirty years of uncataloged and unbound material taken
out of the Capitol building and cataloged by the following
March. LaMontagne used the word "cataloging" in this context, making Hanson and Martel's task appear to be greater
and more detailed overtime task than it seems to have been.
It appears from Hanson that he and Martel sorted and arranged the material for shelflisting under the existing system,

and that the actual listing was done by some of the better
subordinate staff which was still coming in under Congressional patronage. The eventual outcome shows that time and
labor expended on this cataloging or shelf listing, which later
had to be included in the total revision, was wasted. For
cataloging in a new system both Hanson and Martel favored
classification related to a new shelf classification, but whereas Martel remained adamant about this, convinced that nothing else was suitable for a reference and research library,
Hanson showed himself prepared to compromise on alphabetico-classed cataloging, and not to be thoroughgoing even
on this, as things developed.

On cataloging there were outside pressures, particularly from the ALA, which was watchful. W. C. Lane, who
succeeded Cutter in 1893 at the Boston Athenaeum, and later
of the Harvard University Library, then made a survey for
the ALA which seemed to show majority preference for a
dictionary catalog, more or less according to Cutter's Rules.
The combined if conflicting influences of Jewett, Poole and
Cutter seem to have influenced opinion in favor of alphabetico-specific subject cataloging, though there were uncertainties
about it. Further canvassing of opinion in 1900 confirmed
this consensus and undermined claims for DC. In LoC itself, if Hanson had been more positive, if Spofford in whatever position he held had not been an anti-classification man,
the American battle of the catalogs might have gone differently, and through the influence of its services LoC might
have made America as much a classified catalog country as
Great Britain, where the battle in the public libraries at
about that time went in that direction--though certainly not
for the same reasons.

4.10 LoC's New Subject Cataloging

LoC's new subject cataloging was welcomed by Cutter
in the year of his death, 1903. But there had not been much
development by then. In discussion in 1908 on a conference
paper on cataloging and reference work relations, uneasiness
was expressed about the suitability of LoC cataloging, especially for small libraries, and preference was expressed
for "index headings" and less "roundabout catalog headings,"
implying criticism of alphabetico-classed tendencies. This
led to the reading in 1909 of a frank, information paper by
Hanson.[119] There is talk in this paper of dictionary cataloging and specific entry, but little if any mention of Cutter's
Rules.

Later, in 1943, a Chief of the Subject Cataloging Division, Haykin, author in 1951 of <u>The Library of Congress Subject Headings, a Practical Guide,</u> said in the Introduction to the LoC <u>SHL</u> that, "at the time the Library's dictionary catalogs were begun ... there was no solid body of doctrine upon which it could be based... whatever measure of logic and consistency has been achieved ... is due to the continuity of oral tradition which stems from ... Hanson ... Martel ... and their associates." Surely Cutter's Rules were something of a body of doctrine providing some "theoretical basis for a system of headings." Haykin went even further and said that "there was not, to begin with, a scheme or skeleton list of headings to which additions could be made systematically."

Hanson and Martel, or Haykin after them, might have been expected to have studied, and altered to their own satisfaction, Cutter's Rules, but there doesn't appear to be any published evidence of anything of the kind. There was, however, an SHL (the first of its kind) published by the ALA in 1895, "to be considered as an appendix to Cutter's <u>Rules for a Dictionary Catalogue,</u> ed. 3," and Hanson did say <u>in 1909</u> that it was "decided to adopt it as a basis for subject headings with the understanding, however, that considerable modifiction and specialization would have to be resorted to." Other lists used, in addition, included a Harvard list by Lane, that of the Public Library of NSW, by Anderson, published first in 1896 without knowledge of the 1895 ALA list, and also the BML Subject Index which Fortescue had established.

In answer to criticism at the 1908 ALA Conference, Hanson admitted an undeniably strong tendency in LoC cataloging to bring related subjects together, "by means of inversion of headings ... even by subordination of one subject to another," and to "establish a compromise between the dictionary and the alphabetico-classed catalog ... without a too serious violation of the dictionary principle." This seems to echo Cutter's view that adjectival phrase inversion could be violation of the fundamental principle of the dictionary catalog; on points like this it would have been better to have made explicit alterations to Cutter's principles. Hanson's interest was in the class entry question; he seems to have made nothing of the specification limitations in Cutter's adherence to established and distinct subject names, but as late as 1951 Haykin was to make much of this as sacrosanct, though it became a major difficulty in LoC headings. Hanson assumed that LoC use would be more and more restricted to "the student and the investigator ... best served by having related topics brought together." This was and continued to be a class entry argument while a man embracing botany or physics could be a specialist or expert in such subjects, but it lost much of its force as experts became those who knew and read more and more about less and less. In 1951 Haykin found that "in most instances, a reader either seeks material on a particular topic, or desires a treatise on a broad subject," both being served by specific entry.

For Hanson in 1909, specific entry of minute subjects would mean the "ultimate dispersion of the literature on one and the same topic under various headings." On this basis he approved upward see references to headings without subdivision, admitting that this meant searching through all entries under the heading referred to. This went on with such examples as "Milk substitutes see Food substitutes," and "Dry cleaning see Cleaning," but with the later addition of "Dry cleaning machines," this resulting in subject dispersal, not the intended reverse. Catalog revision could be a remedy, but one thing not foreseen was that while the card catalog, to begin with, saves catalog revision and reprinting by its intercalation capability, wholesale or piecemeal revision of a really big one such as LoC's would soon become prohibitive in cost. Martel was so sure that a specific entry catalog would break down and that a fully classified catalog would come into its own that what was called a card shelflist was maintained until 1940. This, LaMontagne said, was, with added entries, a classified catalog; then it became the only shelflist when the working one, known as the Sheet shelflist, was discontinued. 120

In its genesis, development and results as IR for its own and other libraries, LoC's 20th century subject cataloging needs further consideration, though necessarily in brief form here. How and in what ways did it depart from Cutter --on such questions as title or subject word entry used to supplement or substitute for independent headings; on usage-- meaning subject names established and distinct; on specific entry to the total exclusion of class entry in any form; on modification and punctuation of headings; on the order of object and aspect in compound subjects; on the alphabetical arrangement of headings, and in other consequential ways? In general terms, what did its catalogers do about logic and consistency in headings?

4.11 Logic and Consistency

Logic and consistency, said Haykin, in whatever measure it was achieved, could be attributed to Hanson, Martel, and their associates. This verdict was made when Haykin was Chief of the Subject Cataloging Division in 1943, and in the SHL Introduction (4th ed.), but such expressions as "in whatever measure" have to be weighed carefully as qualification by Haykin. He went on to say that "the failures ... are, of course, due to the fact that headings were adopted in turn as needed, and that many minds participated in ... choice and establishment. A growing awareness of the need of a statement ... has tended to correct deviations ... and ... led to gradual improvement." He himself wrote the statement he said was needed: Library of Congress Subject Headings, a Practical Guide, published and acclaimed in 1951. But the evidence of the successive SHL editions is of decreasing logic and consistency. Haykin said more than others in explanation of the list, but a successor did say in the Introduction to the 6th edition, 1957, that "the list is the product of evolutionary forces, among them the growth of the Library's collections, semantic changes, and varying theories of subject heading practice over the years. As a consequence the list is, at any point in time, accurate reflection of practice but not a complete embodiment of theory"; nice words but meaning what? The list at any time, of course, shows practice at that time, but from what times does it date? With what conflicts?

A comparison of lists from the 4th ed., 1943 to the 7th, 1966, shows a decline in new adjectival phrase headings in the inverted form which Hanson favored but which Cutter rejected as class entry. But the older inverted headings are still in; ARTIFICIAL FUR is the newer heading, but the older one, WOOL, ARTIFICIAL is still in for current use; similarly, so is LEATHER, ARTIFICIAL. New heading forms in conformity with new theory present little difficulty, but revision of entries under old forms according to discarded theory do. Another method of bringing related subjects together was process or aspect, with objects in subordination, as with PHOTOGRAPHY OF ANIMALS through to PHOTOGRAPHY OF YOUTH and PHOTOGRAPHY OF WOMEN, but, however, WEDDING PHOTOGRAPHY. For COOKERY there was a new punctuation for COOKERY (APPLES) through to COOKERY (WINES). Another example of the prepositional phrase form was FOLKLORE OF AGRICULTURE through to FOLKLORE OF WOMEN, but with a change being introduced in the aspect-object relation with cross references such as FOLK-LORE OF CATS see CATS (IN RELIGION, FOLKLORE, ETC.). The filing order of this reversal had to be determined, and the result was its placing after dash aspect divisions of the subject, and before inverted phrases, which were followed by uninverted phrases: thus, CATS - TRAINING; CATS (IN RELIGION, FOLKLORE, ETC.); CATS, FOSSIL; CAT'S CRADLE; CATS IN ART; CATS IN LITERATURE.

The ALA was not enthusiastic about the form, or the filing; in 1956 LoC, in its own filing rules, agreed that the filing should have been after inverted headings and stated that a revision would be made "as soon as resources permit." But there was also this general comment: that to "change the filing order of millions of cards ... is a task which can be accomplished only over a period of years," and ten years later, in the 7th ed. of the list, the particular order is unchanged. This exemplified what may be called the nemesis of the card catalog, the great defect of its only advantage; card entry intercalation gets over the old printed catalog problem of supplementing and reprinting, but changes much smaller than would be required by extensive LoC overhaul of headings and/or arrangement become practically impossible. And many libraries, having followed LoC, would not have welcomed changes in its headings or filing, any more than many who have adopted a classification welcome changes in it.

"Logic" and "logical" in their popular use do not differ much in meaning from "consistency" and "consistent," and in their original use have had little more than spurious applications to IR. LoC's growing inconsistencies have only been touched upon above. Cutter's ideas of syntactical usages in headings were clung to, but were compromised by punctuation to aid what Hanson called synthetic arrangement, which was effected further by aspect-object term orders, inversion and punctuation, and by simple dash division for aspect division. This, however, was loosely taken to mean class entry in some proper logical sense, even Haykin reluctantly admitting that the appearance was not always the reality; in fact, it was rarely if ever so. What becomes apparent is that there is no halfway house between systematically, consistently, uniformly structured compound headings and inadequate, inconsistently modified syntactical vocabulary. Two or three other developments of inconsistency may next be usefully considered, before considering the growth of informed realization and protest, and admission, even if still reluctant, from within LoC.

4.12 Title Entry

Title or subject word entry, supplementary or substitute, seems to have been countenanced by Cutter, despite his rule 172 for subject entry--"under the best word whether in the title or not," and the concluding sentence of his note, that "the title rules the title catalog; let it confine itself to that province." Under title entry he spoke of subject word reference, meaning title word entry without imprint and with a cross reference to a full entry, usually author. He said, "52. Make a subject word reference - a. for all anonymous works... b. for other works when the subject word is not the same as the name of the subject selected by the cataloger." He had in mind especially title word entry under rejected synonyms. There was, however, a confused proliferation of title word entry--at best supplementary to entry assigned, whether in the title or not--in LoC cataloging and in American cataloging generally; and in Great Britain the writer found that an Association examination requirement was satisfied by assignment of title words for books to serve either as indexing for a single entry classified catalog, or for a shelflist, or for a dictionary catalog; nothing was said about subject heading lists and their uses.

In America in 1941, Lubetzky described what was going on in a <u>Library Quarterly</u> article called "Titles: Fifth Column of the Catalog." Lubetzky said that "there is an elaborate code to regulate the author entry, and manuals to guide in use of the subject entry; but the title entry, which constitutes one fourth to one fifth of the catalog, is left to the unlimited discretion of the individual cataloger." He omitted any reference to LoC and did not attempt to explain the growth of what he very fully exemplified, together with its unfortunate consequences. His examples included true title inversions, word selection from the title and other sources (extending into the text), and "finally, for a climax, the cataloger will not flinch on occasion from contributing a title of his own."

Confused thinking about terminology has led most dictionary catalogers not to think of cataloging a class of books on the same subject under the same term, or at least with cross references, but of cataloging or indexing books separately. As a result, only one of several books on essentially the same subject may be given so-called title entry, distinguished in LoC tracing notes as "II Title," and so on, even to III and IV. But to what Lubetzky called "the catalog trudger," a book under one of these entries can appear to be the only one on a subject on which in fact there are several others, these appearing under one or more true subject headings. Even two books with the same title words may not both have the same entry. In LoC one called Rise and Decline of the Cold War has a true title entry beginning with RISE, and a subject entry under HISTORY, MODERN - 1945; another called A New History of the Cold War has the same subject entry, a true title entry, and in addition, "II Title: The Cold War." Catalogers often think they are helping a reader to find a particular book, and there has also been a curious tradition that, without advice or instruction, readers should find books in catalogs under whatever they may mistakenly expect. What is often forgotten is that what may be kind-heartedly thought of as possibly helping one person may certainly mislead a lot of others.

Hanson, in 1909, recognized that what some librarians wanted, when they complained about "roundabout" subject entries the year before, was subject word entry, and he thought the needs of libraries favoring this might be "best served by adding ... an indication of subject words." This consideration may have led later to the additional so-called "like" entries, but they also became a means of making up for deficiencies in allowed proper headings and of avoiding the procedure required to get new headings even considered, thus avoiding, too, the effect this might have on a cataloger's total output. In libraries receiving cards these entries may also have been a way of making up for supposed deficiencies, and even of substituting simple subject word entry or derivative cataloging for assigned headings. No research has been attempted here to find out how LoC cards were used, but tracing notes can of course be crossed out and others substituted on a unit card used as a main entry.

Using the ALA list for the internal LoC subject headings file was abandoned and the printing of LoC's own list begun in 1909. There was some distribution, reluctantly, on demand. This was when a 3rd and last edition of the ALA list was pending in 1911. Sears' list began in 1923 and flourished, in a way showing conflicting demand; the LoC list has had seven editions, 1909-14 to 1966, and Sears' nine from 1923 to 1965. Neither, of course, includes title word entry arising out of particular titles. Conflict of opinion by users comes out early in two ALA conference papers in 1912, and especially in that by the ALA list editor, Mary Briggs, which cited opinions of LoC card users, particularly in public li-

braries. The other paper was by Mary McNair, who edited
the LoC list for some time. Her paper also disposes of the
idea of references derived from the classification, an idea
about dictionary cataloging dear to many who know more about
classification than cataloging. McNair shows that while general principles were followed, the approach was pragmatic,
and that many references were not yet in because there weren't
yet entries to which to refer. References cannot be made to
headings without entries any more than in a classified catalog
index there can be subjects with class numbers if there are
no corresponding entries in the catalog under these numbers.
The difference is that between, on the one hand, a library list
or file of its headings in use, and on the other, a general
list somewhat like classification tables.

There has been and may still be confusion or conflict
about the differences in function of cross references and entries. The SHL which LoC first used--the ALA list, 1st ed.,
--suggested this when it said that reference would not be
made from one heading to another "unless the book cataloged
actually illustrates the subject from which reference is made."
But single entries cannot determine references, which must
cover as many items as are under the related headings. In
Sears' list it has been said, in its useful "Suggestions for
Beginners," that a book discussing both inventions and patents
will be entered under both, but that the reference "Inventions
see also Patents" must not be made if only the same book is
found under the heading to which reference is made. The
reference is then clearly not what it has sometimes been--
merely a space saving device for reference from Tennyson
to Dickens to avoid entry of an item about both under both.

Susan Akers, in her Simple Library Cataloging (3rd
ed., Chicago, 1944), saw the difficulty of several books under
both BALLET and PANTOMIME when not all of the books under either heading would contain any information on the other
subject. With cross reference both ways, however, as could
be expected, the reader could look at all items under one or
the other heading, and finding information even in one item
under, say, PANTOMIME which was mainly on BALLET,
would be satisfied. Cutter saw the difficulty of which book,
but thought it met by, for example, "Gothic architecture see
also Spain - Architecture (Street)," identifying the book by
Street under the heading referred to. The only proper answer, however, seems to be that the references only indicate
related subjects, and the cataloger and the user must accept
this. Downward references such as "Mathematics see also

Algebra" only refer from a general to a more specific subject and heading, and references are not usually made upward. What have been called collateral references may be made both ways if books are about collaterally related subjects. LIBRARIES and SCHOOL LIBRARIES are not collateral headings; SCHOOL LIBRARIES and CHILDREN'S LIBRARIES are, because they have the common factor of child use. From the start there seems to have been understanding in LoC that cross references were only to be determined by subject relation, not by the chances of item content. Coates argued, as others did, that references should be systematic, with derivation from a classification, but from the start McNair in LoC found it desirable to develop them on a more pragmatic and selective basis, rather than in a rigidly hierarchical way on purely theoretical grounds.

4.13 Punctuation and Arrangement of Headings

Punctuation and arrangement of headings may be related. Cutter assumed alphabetical arrangement of words and phrases as his basic indexing device, known names in known order, as in "Cat; Cat breeding; Cataracts; Catholic Church; Cato Street Conspiracy; Cats ... Ceremonies; Cetacea," but in columns down pages. For his divisions (only of numerous entries under a heading) he assumed subordinate headings, not dashes and subheadings in line with headings. This dividing of entries by aspects, as in "Women - Biography; - Clubs; - Crime; - Diseases; - Dress," may also represent compound or composite subjects when in horizontal linear form, especially at the top of cards. But Cutter did not see this as a way out of his "Movement of fluids in Plants" difficulty, nor did LoC, at least in the early days, with its continuing "Plants, Motion of fluids in," though it did get through to some headings such as "Aeroplanes - Turbojet engines - Air intakes."

An alternative to what has been called Word-by-Word alphabetical filing has been Letter-by-Letter through words and phrases, as in Cat; Cataract; Catastrophes; Cat breeding; Cat feeding; Cats. It has been useful in some reference book arrangement, because spelling or compounding does not need to be known in such examples as New Town and Newtown, which in Letter-by-Letter would file together, not with Newtown following New Zealand. But for IR purposes, letter-by-letter breaks down with such sequences as Art education; Artichokes; Artillery; Art, Primitive; Arts and crafts; Art societies.

LoC, unable to update, did not proceed to flexible and consistent subheading for composite subjects; for example, it has DIAMOND SMUGGLING, not "Diamonds - Smuggling," along with nearby DIAMONDS, ARTIFICIAL and DIAMONDS, INDUSTRIAL. But with names which have both singular and plural forms there can be wide separation; for example, with CAT see CATS, Cat breeds are about 18 columns away from CATS with its subheadings and phrase. This must separate results even in the subject heading list, not to mention the catalog itself, with its millions of entries facing the man or woman Lubetzky aptly called the "catalog trudger." LoC should have put its house in better order before it attempted the improvement on Word-by-Word which has been called Logical, and which depends on punctuation--consistent punctuation--for useful grouping. The prospects for them were hardly improved by their results. Here are examples of Letter-by-Letter and Word-by-Word with COAL. The comma is only used for sense in inversions and does not affect order in these two arrangements, the difference being apparent in Logical:

Letter-by-Letter	Word-by-Word	Logical
Coal	Coal	Coal
Coal analysis	Coal analysis	Coal - Analysis
Coal, Anthracite	Coal, Anthracite	Coal - Carbonization
Coal, Bituminous	Coal, Bituminous	Coal - Gasification
Coal, Cannel	Coal, Cannel	Coal - Liquefaction
Coal carbonization	Coal carbonization	Coal - Research
Coal gasification	Coal gasification	Coal - Testing
Coaling	Coal, Lignite	Coal, Anthracite
Coalition Governments	Coal liquefaction	Coal, Bituminous
Coal, Lignite	Coal money	Coal, Cannel
Coal liquefaction	Coal, Pulverized	Coal, Lignite
Coal money	Coal research	Coal, Pulverized
Coalport porcelain	Coal testing	Coal money
Coal, Pulverized	Coaling	Coaling
Coal research	Coalition governments	Coalition governments
Coal testing	Coalport porcelain	Coalport porcelain

Here is the LoC headings and arrangement:

Cutter and Congress

Coal	Coal, Lignite
Coal - Analysis	, Pulverized
- Carbonization	Coal gasification
- Gasification <u>see</u> Coal gasification	Coal liquefaction
- Liquefaction <u>see</u> Coal liquefaction	Coal money
- Testing	Coal research
Coal, Anthracite	Coaling
, Bituminous	Coalition governments
, Cannel	Coalport porcelain

This, of course, is abstraction, without entries; without the movement up or down from drawer to drawer, if not from cabinet to cabinet, complicated by the cross reference and turning over of cards; without the likely title word headings with entries somewhere further on; and with the further complication of entries for numerous places whose names begin with COAL, and corporate entries for a few organizations whose names begin with Coal. Some of the reasons are fair enough; on balance the achievement has been magnificent, and, of course, like vintage cars, it has been well preserved and maintained. The intention here is not to condemn, hardly even to criticize, but simply to show the state of the art.

4.14 Attack and Defense

Attack and Defense here are of the subject cataloging that was Cutter and became LoC. Following Lubetzky's attack on title word entries in 1941, Prevost's in 1946, also in Library Quarterly, has been related to Schwartz's "none rule" for adjectival phrase inversion with root and branch rejection by Cutter in his rules. It has been widely cited and was not merely a rule for uniformity for its own sake; for example, she not only proposed LAW, INTERNATIONAL, but also such changes in usage as NATIONS - INTERRELATIONS for INTERNATIONAL RELATIONS. Prevost wanted aspects of subjects brought together, by means of placing the "strong" noun term first, and she leaned towards alphabetico-classed entry, as in EDUCATION - COEDUCATION. She had probably never heard of Kaiser's systematic indexing and "Concrete-Process" separation, which went even to the length of turning BIBLIOGRAPHY into BOOKS - DESCRIPTION and EDUCATION into CHILDREN - INSTRUCTION. Two criticisms of her are that she ignored Cutter's point that subject or object can be in the adjective and aspect in the noun, and that she did not go far enough in systematic structuring of subject names, while denying the proposition that headings should be whatever untutored readers expect. There was also defense out of loyalty to and regard for the authority of LoC, on the lines that it must have good reasons for its anomalies even if the speaker could not give them. At the same time there was increasing demand for some detailed official statement, and this was apparently foreshadowed by Haykin in his introduction to the 4th edition of the LoC list and finally written by him and published in 1951 as <u>Library of Congress Subject Headings, A Practical Guide.</u> It was acclaimed, and he was honored, but it was not the answer to the needs of outside users of the LoC headings as given on offprints of its own catalog cards.

Haykin's book is only on subject headings, without title word supplementation, and was intended primarily for internal trainee use. Multiple word forms, with and without dash and comma punctuation, are discussed, but parenthetical qualification is not examined. In 1969 Dunkin[121] dismissed the book as little more than an attempt at rationalization of accumulated inconsistencies, and Haykin himself admitted that he had presented desired change rather than actual usage. He limited specificity to what might suit the reader, and thought "Gallows very near the limit of desirable specificity," but said nothing about the idea of item specificity being the determinant. He did not question inverted adjectival phrases for subject grouping, but did not like prepositional phrase inversions, preferring, for example, PLANTS, PROTECTION OF, "to preserve the integrity of the commonly used phrase," rather than PLANTS - PROTECTION. Readers, however, might well think the latter nearer ordinary usage, and the list has over a dozen such headings including PLANTS - MIGRATION and PLANTS - REPRODUCTION. But he opposed the dash division as a heading of the "alphabetico-classed type," only belatedly admitting (p. 36) that many headings "resemble alphabetico-classed headings in their outward form only." To call it, as he does, the alphabetico-classed form is prejudicial in view of its very mixed use in LoC, and reinforces a common misunderstanding that the form in itself is alphabetico-classed entry, whereas it is generally much less so than the comma divisions of inverted adjectival phrases.

He explained LoC arrangements as "word-by-word" but with a mixture of "non-alphabetic" filing, restricting the meaning of alphabetic to suit his argument. This filing with dash subheadings, he admits, avoids such mixtures as COLOR, COLOR PHOTOGRAPHY, COLORADO RIVER, COLOR ANALYSIS, which he would otherwise have preferred in the subheading form.

The Introduction to the 7th ed. of the LoC list in 1966 said that "the choice and form of headings and references ... have been guided for many years" by the principles and practices Haykin set forth, but this is not borne out by comparisons. In a note under "Research," a major example of his, after listing phrases from "Advertising research" down to "Wildlife research," it is said that there is also a subdivision, "Research under subjects," for items which do not lend themselves to the phrase form of heading, but the collection of about 177 examples and their analysis does not show consistency. Apparently this kind of homework had not been done by LoC itself.

As a study of subject cataloging derived from LoC cataloging, Haykin's at first much acclaimed practical guide proves of little practical, or even theoretical, use. But he was in a difficult position as an LoC officer and as the retiring Chief of the Division, apparently under some pressure to do something; and LoC was apparently not prepared to call in outside opinion. Haykin's study remains of some historical interest, as a contemporary state-of-the-art contribution in 1951. An updated contribution is that of Richard Angell, a successor as Chief of the Technical Processes Research Office. It is called "Library of Congress Headings--Review and Forecast" (1971), and was cleared by the Library for contribution to a symposium on <u>Subject Retrieval in the Seventies</u>, which also includes a paper by Wellisch that exemplifies what had become standard criticism of the headings. Of course, there had been by then much more water under the bridge and writing on the wall. Coordinate indexing had only begun to emerge clearly about 1950, and the next twenty years were the most radically fruitful since 1876 and 1896. Angell's paper is also much less equivocal, is direct and clear in exposition, more impartial, and without Haykin's peculiar style of thought and expression.

4.15 <u>LC</u>

LC is the accepted abbreviation for the Library of Congress classification, to be distinguished from LoC as one for the library. As already shown, it was to be a classification

complementing a dictionary catalog, not, as Martel would
have preferred, one also used for a classified catalog. LC,
at least as seen from Great Britain, was not likely to be an
outstanding classification, even for LoC's own use, and certainly not likely to become competitive with, or replace others such as DDC, EC, or BC in large general libraries, especially those of universities. In the last decade of the 19th
century LC became one of several emerging classifications,
including Brown's in England, and that of the Royal Society's
International Catalogue of Scientific Literature, the rival of
what became the UDC of FID. There were also the emerged
DDC and EC in America, and Hartwig's Halle University
classification in Germany. The principal makers of LC were
aware of all of these, and at first concentrated on the last
three as possible ready-made classifications. At that time
there was no intention of devising another new classification,
there being at least a possibility, strongly supported by Spofford, of "revamping" one that it could already call its own:
the classification it already had which dated back to the Library of the Philadelphia Company and to one after 1814
built round Jefferson's library, and which was vaguely the inverted Baconian of D'Alembert in its order. The experience
of Hanson and Martel in having to catch up on arrears of
cataloging or shelflisting, using this scheme early in 1898,
convinced them that nothing could be made of it which would
be satisfactory either for the new present or the future.

Of DDC, EC, and Hartwig's schemes, the first was
rejected by Martel on grounds that advocates considered its
great advantages; it had a notation which was decimal and
hierarchical, to which the classification was fitted, not the
reverse; it did not allow of new subject intercalation, except
by subsectioning--the decimal or radix fraction extensions of
which so much was made; and Dewey would not agree to alterations. As LaMontagne said, he could hardly have done
so in his own interest or that of the already comparatively
numerous libraries which had adopted it, because had he accepted changes proposed by LoC, then "the D.C. would no
longer have been the D.C."

Cutter was prepared to make alterations, but Hanson
had had three or four years experience of using EC as Head
Cataloger at Wisconsin University. While there he had drafted
an alternative influenced by his previous experience under
Poole in the Newberry, and, as LaMontagne said, this was
probably the basis of an "Outline" which he and Martel submitted to Putnam on April 21, 1900, little more than a fort-

night after Putnam became librarian in succession to Young on April 5. EC, of course, was still a classification with an hierarchically used notation, though it was much better based and allowed gaps for interpolation as well as extension, and this Cutter claimed as an advantage.

Poole was certainly more primitive, of an earlier generation, though certainly aware in middle age of Dewey and Cutter. He was born in 1821, 16 years before Cutter and 30 years before Dewey. Hanson was born in Norway in 1864, and after some teaching, academic studies and baseball, chose, in preference to a combination of college teaching and baseball coaching, a job in the new Newberry under Poole. There, beginning in 1890, he learned librarianship by experience, and in 1893 went as head cataloger to the University of Wisconsin, and then on to LoC in September 1897, with the considerable advantage of having worked in two libraries. Martel, born in Switzerland, did not have this kind of experience when he joined LoC in December 1897; he had remained at Newberry where, Poole having died in 1894, he did have the advantage of working under new men--Cheney as chief and Rudolph as deputy. Poole's influence on LC through Hanson and Martel was clearly fortuitous, but it was also clearly considerable.

At Newberry Poole collected more than 150,000 volumes and pamphlets, and so was beginning to think in hundreds of thousands. In writing a chapter for PLUSA in 1876 he had talked of libraries growing from ten to fifty thousand. One of his shelf-marking systems then used mnemonic letters for subjects, with running numbers for books in each subject, but with blocks reserved for subclasses. He admitted that these reserved areas would be the product of guesswork, but acknowledged the common idea that in time there would have to be "an entire and radical rearrangement." Printed catalogs in volume form accompanied this scheme, and provided for librarians a "might-as-well" excuse for radical changes. Poole started in this way in the Newberry; Hanson and others had to break numbers for books into classes running mnemonically from A - Archaeology to U - Useful Arts, and allot subdivisions. For help they turned to DC's tables, apparently without Poole knowing; in the process, Hanson and probably Martel got a knowledge of DDC.

At LoC thousands had become hundreds of thousands, and obviously cataloging and classifying had to be more lasting. Nevertheless Hanson and Martel either mulled over their recollections of Poole and the Newberry and/or tried out his methods again. Hanson mentioned this in his memorandum to Putnam, but reported that the mnemonic or significant class idea had little value and that the following numbers should be applied to subclasses and further subdivisions, not to books, which could be distinguished by Cutter's alphanumerical numbers. From his references to Brown and the ICSL, the need to leave gaps seemed to be assumed. What became the central feature of the LC notation had emerged, and it and its auxiliary devices can now be considered in more detail, with reference to some criticisms and appreciations.

4.16 LC's Classification and Notation

LC's class order was not scientific in the sense Richardson established for a time, of conforming to some assumed scientific and evolutionary order of the sciences. Richardson was among the formidable list of American librarians finally consulted in 1900, a list that must still impress. At the time he was delivering his influential lectures on Classification Theoretical and Practical (which were much more the former than the latter) but apparently he made little impression on those who made and received decisions. The classification was not made up as its creators went along, as some students have said, but it could be said to have preceded notation, not followed notation as in DDC. There has to be a plan for classification, but it can be fluid, as the LC scheme has been over more than half a century.

The basic plan was not for a departmentalized library, but for an integrated, universal collection excluding nothing. It called for a scheme with separate classes and subclasses, based on the widest literary warrant--that of the growing LoC--that had been applied to any classification, worked on by a wide range of experts; even so, it did not include all the detail necessary for two other national libraries which later emerged, those of medicine and agriculture.

The classes were not subjected to such uniformities as dividing according to history, and then according to geography, such subjects as constitutional law; these were really sacrifice of classification to notation and what Dewey called number building in his DC. Spofford is generally supposed to have opposed minute classification and decimal systems. The numbers, as distinct from the letters, are not uniform three-figure numbers beginning with 000. Nor was there any tempting "waste not, want not" final 0, and no final 1-9 to be used for uniform form numbers first in the main classes. One result was that a proportion of nearly ten per cent of the one-, two- and three-figure numbers in the 1 to 9999 sequence was of more use and of more advantage than numbers of even length; they were not even required for hierarchical use, with the numbers treated as decimal fractions, as in UDC. The numbers up to four figures were treated in LC as whole numbers. But one conclusion jumped to by critics who were only familiar with DDC was that LC had no uniform numbers because it has no uniform 01-09, with mnemonic uniformity in meaning, in its main classes. It does have form subdivisions which are uniform in class subclasses, and even some called "floating" for use where considered satisfactory in any subclass.

Another criticism leveled against LC by those who assumed DDC as the norm has been that LC has no general index, but there is no completed version of LC which could have successive editions like DDC, with all of its main tables in one volume. However, in the SHL, class numbers are given for subjects with corresponding LC classes; for example, nine numbers are given for Horses in different aspects and two for Horses (in religion, folklore, etc.); and the 7th ed. of the SHL is 4,296 columns in 1,432 pages, compared with 2,066 columns in 1,032 pages of the Index in the 18th ed. of DDC. Auxiliary tables for particular classes in LC may be called intricate, and for space saving there are even some "divide like" or "arrange like" notes.

More sophisticated criticism of LC has been that it does not allow number combinations for "co-extensive" subjects or synthesized numbers for compound subjects. But this is to make comparisons with what only began to emerge clearly with UDC about 1908; it was being rejected about 1899, at least for general use, by Cutter and even by Dewey. But UDC's colon compounding, to allow permutable entry with main class numbers, would be possible with LC numbers. For example, QH431:QL955:QL703 could be used as an equivalent of a UDC number used for the Science Museum, London, by Bradford--575.17:591.3:599--as a permutable number for a book called <u>Genes in Mammalian Development.</u>

Clearly, Martel wanted a classification for a catalog, which he maintained as the card shelflist with added entries; but this thinking, like Cutter's for his dictionary catalog, hardly went beyond multiple entry for items on distinct but related subjects, such as the history of France and England compared, or Drawing and Engraving. With their punctuation the two numbers given above are of equal length. LC's numbers were criticized for their length; they usually included two letters and, for most items, four figures. But DDC's numbers also increased in length, especially in the 600 class; for example, its 621.4834 for specific types of nuclear reactors, without specification. LC's TK9203, Nuclear reactors, provides for special types, A-Z, notationally specified alphanumerically; e.g., TK9203.B6 - Boiling water reactors to TK9203.S65 - Solid fuel reactors. Even with this degree of specification LC's number is only two characters more than DDC's.

With what is an admittedly extreme case, this illustrates what gaps could mean in LC. In 1948 it had a gap of 401 numbers in TK, Electrical engineering and industries, and under Atomic power it used 9001 for Periodicals and societies and 9145 for General works. By 1964 it still had far more blanks than used numbers in the series; for example, after nuclear reactors, it still had, for propulsion, 9231 to 9349. Many have not generally understood LC gaps were really gaps, not just occasional blanks. Besides using its alphanumerical subject extensions, also, it had used two decimal fraction extensions to get in "Patents" and "Nuclear engineering as a profession" at appropriate points. Dewey himself talked about alphabetical subarrangement as an alternative, and use of the UDC colon, but neither notation was developed, and in the 18th edition his editors in effect broke away from Dewey and, among other things, opposed alphanumerical subarrangement and UDC punctuation. Mineralogy, QE 35-399 in LC, has 49 three-figure numbers; there is extension decimally and alphabetically. DDC's Mineralogy, 549, seems to be about in the same in detail in the 18th ed. Every number in DDC has to be an extension of one three-figure number, 549, and every LC number begins with combinations of two letters; but average number length slightly favors LC, and the advantage would seem to remain with it in any further expansions of both schemes, although there may not be much further advantage to be obtained from LC's gaps and their distribution.

Alphabetical subdivision can only be terminal, otherwise it would cut across classification. Some purists have shown almost religious fervor in objecting to any mixture or association, but many supposedly classificatory sequences are only arbitrary or random numerical sequences, dependent finally on alphabetical indexing. Maltby admits that alphabetical subdivision "can be used to good effect within the classification," but hardly mixed with it, "when there is no obvious systematic order to be adopted." This explains decimal extension of a number in LC for a classification of minerals, with alphabetical arrangements of particularly known and named minerals and of those besides diamonds which happen to be "precious stones."

Ranganathan remained one of the declining number of critics of LC, saying misleadingly in 1949 that it "uses only the primitive device of leaving gaps between integral numbers." This followed his questionable assertion of what Dewey first intended. Ranganathan said LC rejected Dewey's powerful devices "on grounds of ephemeral expediency," but it is clear that, rightly or wrongly, the devices of hierarchical notation were rejected on principle.

LC was adopted by the National Library in Wales, drawing attention to it in Britain. It received more detailed and favorable consideration, and Savage adopted it for the Edinburgh Public Libraries, saying it was "as near perfection as he could imagine." In his articles or chapters in 1911-12, which preceded Savage's praise, Hulme said his conclusion was "that the Congress schedules are such as will admit of the exact classification of the bulk of the world's literature to date at the lowest possible cost; and that in this respect the class headings ... have reached the theoretical high-water mark of efficiency indicated in the preceding chapters." This high-water mark he found in what he called "literary warrant," the term which Savage helped to revive. Hulme then turned to the latest edition of DDC, the 7th in 1911, criticizing it as having classes with insufficient literary warrant for library classification and cataloging of books. "If the paramount claims of book classes to the exclusive use of the notation marks be not asserted in good time," he said, "the field will be found to be occupied by the snippet literature with definitions of details for which no literature in book form is likely to be forthcoming; and the new book classes on their arrival will fare badly."

Hulme mentioned the emerging Brussels Expansion of DDC, which was to become UDC, as a bibliographical classification, for analytical or index entries, and concluded that "There are two rational types of book classification, based respectively upon concrete and analytic entry." The former type he saw ideally represented by LC classification and LoC cataloging; the latter, the analytical, he saw as "the registration of literature reduced to some lower unit than that which it originally issued, " and concluded that "we shall be safe in describing such a system as possessing a higher extension of classification and notation, " or of alphabetical indexing, "than that of a book system pure and simple. " Then he returned to DDC (7th ed.), stating that it fell between the two stools and was "ill-advised and calculated to prejudice its earlier well-deserved reputation. " Of the Brussels extensionists Dewey admired, Hulme said: "under their system exact classification can be carried out, but at a prohibitive cost from the standpoint of the shelf classifier. " He probably saw himself striving to classify a perhaps inadequate Patent Office collection with equally inadequate resources.

In what may be called the premises of his argument, Hulme may have fallen into error. Relying on the logician Mill, he accepted (what seems to be true) that for the mind, subject-matter "is almost indefinitely divisible"; but he rejected this basis for subject distinction for our purpose--that is, bibliographical or IR purposes--because it would lead "to a universal index of minutely divided subject headings ... a scheme revived from time to time by indexing enthusiasts, but which for library purposes may be safely dismissed as an economic absurdity. " He may have been referring to Campbell's "universal index matters, " but Campbell's interest in 1896 was in national and international bibliography. All he seems to have meant by "universal index" was a general, international, index of the subjects of books--what Panizzi called an index of matters, meaning one of books by subject, indicated by title words in Watt's style. For such subject indexing of a catalog of the BML the warrant was to be as much literary, according to the library's collection, as was the warrant for the LoC's LC. Periodical articles are still units, although analytical, and these were being indexed first by Poole by his permutative entry method and then by the Wilson indexes, which followed LoC's subject cataloging methods, which in turn were based on Cutter's, but with some improvements.

LC was a departure from a pattern which Dewey had established with DDC, of the general classification published for general use, in a one-volume package. Both DDC and LC were made in a library, mainly by people employed by it or a governing institution, but no one made the Congress classification his own as Dewey had the Amherst classification.

Cutter and Congress

It is a doubtful proposition that he who makes a better mousetrap will have a path beaten to his door, unless he advertises. LoC did not offer or advertise its classification for sale at a price, but it did incidentally advertise it on its advertised catalog cards, and did link its cataloging with its classifying. It was, of course, talked about, written about, as a classification for a great national library, but it was also, in effect, related to the operations of other libraries, and they beat a path to its door.

4.17 Congress Cards: The Package Deal

Congress cards gave LC numbers as well as subject headings, some time before DDC numbers were graciously added. LC had no handy overall index, though its SHL became a substitute; but what was gradually realized was that, among other possible advantages, if LC could be used in a library, Congress cards would give the required class numbers, as it gave subject headings, with no need for checking indexes or tables or lists--and, as Cutter said of cataloging, classifying would be another lost art. Its cards and their availability has been the distinctive feature of LoC as a national, and even international, library, and of the new model which it established.

As already shown in Dewey's double play with the unknown Battezzati's "system," there was interest in card printing by publishers as early as 1876; 20 years later the idea came prominently before the LoC Library Committee Inquiry into the new library to be. What may have been unexpected or not realized in its full effects was LoC's insistence on processing its books for itself, first and last, with card distribution only as a by-product or spin-off.

Hanson mentioned cooperative work in 1909, saying that he referred to the distribution of printed cards, but the cooperative work which was developed was with a few specialist or very large libraries whose holdings did not duplicate LoC's, not with the great majority of those who took or were likely to take the cards. There was talk, as Hanson shows, of additional subject word cataloging to meet "the needs of libraries that favor strict adherence to subject word entry," using the back of the card. But a confusion of detail for catalog users was left on the front, probably because printing on both sides would have added to cost. What would have helped readers would have been a heavy line under the entry, the latter being limited to no more than 1-1/2 vertical inches. The cards were only longer than that to facilitate filing and use, not for the proliferation of bibliographical description. Under the suggested line, above the notes of headings and class numbers that came to be known as tracing notes, there could then have been the italic heading, for office use only.

At the time, Hanson said, over 1,200 libraries were subscribing to the cards, with a 16 per cent annual increase. He wanted to think that this was mainly because subscribers valued the "suggestions" later known as tracing notes of subject headings; but with his honesty the best he could say was that "if it is safe to conclude that ... success ... has depended largely on this ... then it may be well said that the time and money spent on a dictionary catalog has been well expended," though he still thought it a question "whether the Library itself might not have been better served by a subject catalog according to the alphabetico-classed plan." The latter, of course, would not have precluded unit cards or tracing notes.

Unit cards cannot be properly used with a fully classified or systematic catalog unless it has a complementary author catalog which uses the same descriptive cataloging-- that is, one which does not just provide author name and title indexing of a classified catalog. Also, in a classified catalog there still has to be subject indexing of the classification, for which unit entry cards cannot be used. Author and subject indexing of a classified catalog are an economy with printed page catalogs, and had once been seen as the only alternatives. With the arrival of the card catalog, however, this writer was told, the reason for establishing a dictionary catalog in the Holborn Library in London, instead of the much more common classified catalog with an index, was that maximum use could be made of unit cards, which could be mechanically duplicated; the reason given was not the indexing merits of the dictionary catalog.

This shows that what Hanson was tempted to conclude, and what sells unit cards, is much more complicated. With LoC cards one got for his money: first, a blank card, well cut (though apparently LoC did not start with perfection), with, printed on it, descriptive cataloging (for which at least for many years no charge was made) which has been generally more acceptable and more in accordance with internationally accepted rules than subject cataloging; but there were also subject headings which were at least suggestive, and there were class numbers so that the cards could be used in shelflists. With cards, even handwritten ones, there was no longer a need to abridge added entries as in printed catalogs, though this was persisted in for various reasons--supposed economy in copying labor, established practice--possibilities which faded out with the establishment of the card catalog, which eventually became copy also for the printed catalog.

Cataloging was, as Cutter implied, as much a hobby as a professional occupation, and catalogers were resistant to change, but librarianship became thought of more in administrative and economic terms, and chief librarians were less and less catalogers and classifiers in the Cutter tradition, even though their head catalogers became queen consorts. There were problems in the supply of books and cards for them from different sources, problems of getting and matching cards with books without delays, but later developments have meant that entries could be found in bibliographies even as books were ordered, and equipment for duplicating cards in libraries from one typed copy proliferated and improved.

Then there was the idea of cataloging in the book itself, which is not recent: Jevons referred to a suggestion that books should include slips which an owner might head and file as he wished. There was a proposal in the English Cyclopaedia, 1854-62, that the BML, using a "manifold writer" to triplicate slips for control in printing its author catalog, could make copies for several slip catalogs in the library. A century later libraries and booksellers were making their own copies of LoC cards and entries, and writing or typing indicated headings and class numbers on unit cards has been reduced to no more than an uncritical clerical operation--copy cataloging as distinguished from what was already being distinguished as original cataloging.

If there is less and less to be done, less and less fundamental teaching in schools of librarianship, then the art decays, and may decline even at the center. Though reluctantly, almost all general libraries gave up their own indexing of periodicals. If one accepts, for example, Wilson indexing becoming taken for granted, why not then first search for books in bibliographies and then merely check for actual holdings in an author catalog? Periodical indexing, of course, has the control and uniformity of indexing the contents of given periodicals; the book problem is different, and bibliographies, at least as they are, tend to be specialized and diverse in method. In some ways and to some extent a National Bibliography on the lines of BNB may be an answer, and cards for catalogs have been reproduced from it. But libraries and cataloging are not limited to basically British books, or to books in the English language; especially in technology, BNB would have been weak but for British editions of American books included in it, and one of the advantages of LoC cataloging and classifying has been that while it has included American books, it has not been limited to them.

There seems no doubt that the package deal helped to make LC a preferred classification for larger general libraries, especially university libraries, and not only in America. The classification, indeed, seems to have proved more acceptable than the subject headings; these, however, may be more readily scrutinized and altered if desired. Informed opinion has been expressed that LC certainly becomes superior to DDC when collections get over a million in general libraries, in which UDC has hardly proved a rival. There was at first British and probably American criticism, too, of the card entries as standardization, but there is no doubt that they raised standards of appearance and of bibliographical accuracy; with few exceptions, the only British cataloging comparable, at least in appearance, was in printed catalogs. With all of its inconsistencies and outdated heading forms, dictionary cataloging and indexing on the LoC pattern, dating back to Cutter, has and still does account in library catalogs and periodical indexes for an enormous amount of information retrieval from books and periodicals, as distinguished from the new report literature, which began about 1950 to produce a revolution in IR methods for some purposes.

Chapter 5

BRITISH BATTLES OF THE CATALOGS

"Battle of the catalogs," said Sayers, dignified a controversy among British librarians, almost exclusively public librarians, who were allied to the advocacy of the classified catalog in place of Crestadoro's alphabetical index-catalogs and who advocated open in place of closed access lending libraries or departments, because these required classification. The name magnified rather than dignified, Sayers said;[122] but it is a convenient metaphor for controversy. At the same time, just at the end of the 19th century, there was the battle within the new LoC over its cataloging; the service idea of a national library (to include catalog service) had been accepted and the question to be decided was what the libraries to be served wanted. The kind of cataloging they had more or less decided on was dictionary cataloging. A national library was already established in Britain but, almost by determination rather than default, was not to be the kind of service library for which America provided a model. It was certainly above the battle of the catalogs, at least until well into the 1970s.

The controversy is hardly worth much detail here. The leading attackers or stirrers were Jast of Croydon and Brown, first of Clerkenwell, then Islington, all in London. Jast was an advocate of DDC but not with any very clear ideas of how it should be used. The poverty of the public libraries, dictated by the Penny Rate, was a grievous factor, and Jast and Brown both talked rather vaguely of class lists rather than integrated classification. Brown, however, was the most effective advocate and demonstrator of open access, and the only British librarian who produced a classification of his own. Six references are given in the notes to this section to The Library, not yet superseded by the LAR, one to the proceedings of the second International Library Conference in London, 1897, and one to a useful retrospective article in LAR by Jast in 1903, in which he shows that as usual the battle or war was won in less time than the reconstruction it effected was to take. There are short lives of both Jast and Brown by Munford, [123] who has also written a life of Edwards and a useful book on the Penny Rate and its effects. [124] Jast and Brown took the usual line of comparing bad alphabetical with good classified examples, and under counterattack claimed that they were only trying to be provocative to help the cause. However, Brown as a classification maker is worth some separate consideration. But first there is to be considered what Sayers called "progress and calamity."

5.1 Progress and Calamity: Edwards, Jevons and the Indicator

Sayers "progress" was based on Edwards, and his undoubted advocacy of municipal libraries and his preference for classification. But Sayers had to admit that there was little connection between this and what came later. And he does not say that Edwards had to leave Manchester without establishing his classification there and let in Crestadoro with his alphabetical cataloging and indexing, which became established generally. He said only that Edwards towered above his contemporaries both in his knowledge of book classification and in his recognition of its potentialities, and that a few broad groupings constituted the average arrangement of books in the public libraries. Again, this says nothing about what seems to have been fairly broad adoption of the dictionary catalog, which Crestadoro called an index catalog. But Edwards had few followers, Sayers said, for nearly forty years, and then a couple of calamities fell upon libraries.

W. S. Jevons, "the most popular logician of his day ... declared roundly that the classification of books by subject was a logical absurdity."[125] Brown, Sayers thinks, later refuted this, but the essence seems to be that the strict classification of logic, which was the context Jevons was thinking in, and the loose division and arrangement of subjects which libraries have unfortunately called classification are two different things for different purposes. This was Sayers' first "calamity," and Jevons' statement was undoubtedly used by opponents of classification.

More important was Sayers' other "calamity," the indicator. With closed access, books were hidden from view or at least were not accessible behind a counter, in what Crestadoro called an inventorial or acquisition order, with

British Battles of the Catalogs 121

acquisition or accession numbers usually given in an indexcatalog of the Crestadoro type. Library collections were not large and an indicator was invented, the essence of which was numbers which one way 'round in one color showed that books were in, and the other way 'round that they were out. Manipulation of this saved a counter assistant from going back to the shelves to check whether a book was in or out, and even from checking loan records. One result of the indicator was a vested interest in closed access. The Library Association, said Sayers, actually commended the indicator to library authorities--the greatest blunder in its history, putting progress back thirty years. Sayers also said that the difference between the American and the English librarian was that the latter showed "an intense occupation with the mere machinery of libraries." The real difference, however, seems to have been that between the library "economy" (in one of two senses of the word) of the two countries.

5.2 James Duff Brown, 1862-1914

Brown was born in Edinburgh and, leaving school at 13, rose from shop assistant to bookkeeping and commercial traveling. He was musical and came from a family which was musical above the average, and eventually wrote on and compiled a bibliography on the subject. His biographer suggests that the superiority of Scottish education compensated for his brief formal education, but he never caught up as much as some others, such as Savage in Scotland and Jast in London, by self-education. He was, in fact, still short of 13 when he was apprenticed to bookselling and publishing, and he might have remained in that field had his family not gone to Glasgow in 1876. There, he found himself in a less congenial city and bookshop, in which, however, he learned to appreciate smutty stories, for which he later had something of a reputation. He probably read in the newly established Mitchell library and got an assistantship there late in his sixteenth year, to escape the bookshop if not the "vile stories."

Events showed that he had found a vocation suited to his interest in techniques, and presumably having answered an advertisement, he was interviewed by a member of the Clerkenwell committee, an advanced-thinking layman named Fincham. Brown, at the age of 25, was appointed at a salary range of £150 to £250. Later, with ten years' experience and the authorship of a paper to his credit, and with Fincham as a continuing friend and supporter, he had the opportunity in 1893 of going to America with a grant of £15 towards expenses. Unfortunately, he seems to have gone determined to see what was wrong with America, not what might be right.

There was then more liaison between British and American librarianship than there was to be later. Brown accepted some American achievements but attributed them to economic advantage, and thought American libraries did comparatively less than the British with their resources. There was controversy in LJ where schools of librarianship were advanced as one American achievement, to which Brown replied that he made a present of the idea with all his heart, saying "may its operations not ... flood the universal globe with a 'monstrous regiment of women,' which neither trumpet blasts, nor acts of legislature will ever keep in check." Yet he was not hostile to women, believing that they should have equal opportunities; what he was hostile about, probably because of his own beginnings, was special qualifications and corresponding exclusions. 126   He thought the Americans produced standardization, apparently not realizing that the highly centralized LA examinations and certification which he helped to establish could produce even more standardization, uniformity and brainwashing in some directions--especially classification, taught first from his own textbooks and then from Sayers'. In 1899 Brown went to Islington for a better salary and remained there until his death at 51. Before this, in 1912, he had resigned irrevocably from the LA, suspecting tendencies (which certainly existed) toward a closed profession, through qualification control and a professional register. In a letter he advised the newly formed New Zealand association to beware. 127

Brown worked first with Quinn of Chelsea on classification for open access, not with results which were comparable to either Dewey's or Cutter's. His "Adjustable Classification" came out in 1898 in a useful book he wrote; more detailed than the first edition of DDC, it did not, however, equal Dewey's second edition, and by then Jast may have seen the 2nd through 4th editions of DDC. Hanson, working towards LC, however, referred favorably to Brown's scheme in a report to Putnam in 1899. The culmination of Brown's classification efforts is his now dead Subject Classification, first published in 1906. It had a 2nd edition in the year of death, 1914, and a third, revised by his nephew, J. D. Stewart, who became in effect a co-editor of the 2nd edition during Brown's last years. Stewart was acting Chief Librarian of Islington in 1913 and got out his revision (the 3rd ed.) in 1939.

SC, more than any other of the classifications which had something of a life, could be said to have been a bundle of somewhat conflicting peculiarities. The keyword to it was science, in one or more senses as Brown understood it; for him, such terms as traditional, customary, arbitrary, conventional were critical of classification. He had a scientific or philosophic base, more or less evolutionary on Richardson's lines, his order being Matter and Force, Life, Mind, Record. The first two produced the physical sciences, the second the biological, the third the philosophical and social, leaving language and imaginative literature, history and geography as Record; but he confused the order of his basic causes in nature with the order of the related sciences in knowledge and writing. His notation was somewhat akin to LC's with one class letter and numerical sequences running up to three figures, and, like LC's, was not used hierarchically; LC might have been an influence on Brown. Certainly unlike LC, his subject classifying was single place, with a scientific place for music, and this has been his most criticized and cited example. But he had two escapes. One was his Categorical Table, which seemed primarily a form and aspect table, but employing nearly a thousand numbers (with a point) as extensions of his main class numbers. He also had some general numbers such as H900 for "Recreative arts," so that H900.260 could be used for music; and main class numbers could be combined, as in I223E600, which is a general gardening number combined with the single botany place for roses in aspects. Brown said he used the adjective categorical for his somewhat miscellaneous table "in the absence of a better portmanteau word," but according to all dictionary definitions of category and portmanteau, category is not a portmanteau word, such as brunch, which combines breakfast and lunch.

As a British product Brown's SC was welcomed by librarians who were still under the influence of Richardson; they saw it as scientific and scholarly and an answer to DDC. Sayers went on saying that Brown "occupied a place in British librarianship equivalent to that held by Dewey in America."[128] But finally, in classification Brown did not hold a place, even in Britain, equal to that attained by DDC, and certainly by the 1970s Sayers' claim is not viable. Brown's primary objective, however--the classified catalog, for which he was endeavoring to provide what he thought would be a simple, practical classification--was gradually achieved, aided by his forthright <u>Manual of Library Economy</u> (1st ed., 1903), which Sayers piously carried on, though his editing

removed its vigor and nettle-grasping with too much "on the
other hand" balancing. What emerged was something like
Crestadoro's indexing applied to single-entry catalogs. This
must first be distinguished from Brown's single-place classifying, but as developed it can be best studied in Sharp's Cataloging, a Textbook for Use in Libraries (1st ed., 1935 to
4th ed., 1948) and in what Brown and others considered a
good example of the classified catalog, the Glasgow Public
Libraries Union Catalog in book form.

Henry A. Sharp, of the Croydon Public Libraries,
must be distinguished from John R. Sharp, the author of
Some Fundamentals of Information Retrieval and of the indexing system he called SLIC, Selective Listing in Combination,
1965, an indexing system for special libraries. H. A. Sharp's
book was the counterpart of Margaret Mann's Introduction to
Cataloging and the Classification of Books (Chicago, ALA,
1930 and 1943). The latter was mainly for the dictionary
cataloging but gave a simple formula for a classified catalog,
using LoC cards: it was a classified catalog with multiple
entry, such as Martel would have preferred for LoC, and
with a complementary catalog, for author-title entry, also
using LoC cards, with which the classification of the classified catalog could not be used. Sharp did not cite Mann on
this, and while his book was useful for the LA examinations,
it still showed confusion of thinking about the classified catalog which had emerged--as, indeed, did the LA examinations
themselves.

5.3 Glasgow, Sharp and Cranshaw

Glasgow began with a reputation for dictionary catalogs,
according to the accepted British definition, which was also
Cutter's primary definition: one with author, title and subject entries in one arrangement. But Glasgow's catalog had
little regard for Cutter's own version of specific subject entry; it had headings which were perhaps coincidental with
title words but which were independent of them in assignment.
Brown, in 1912 and 1916, said that the modern dictionary
catalog as now understood was anticipated by the index to the
catalog of the Signet Library, Edinburgh, prepared by George
Sandys in 1803; but if this was an index to a catalog it certainly wasn't a catalog, and Brown said nothing about its
headings. Brown included in his book a facsimile of a page
of a Glasgow Public Libraries catalog, apparently about 1900;
up to a point it is specific, but "The Color question" under

British Battles of the Catalogs 125

"Man" is hardly specific, and this was after the appearance of Cutter. In 1910 the Woodside District Library in Glasgow issued an index catalog which might be called dictionary; though without cross references, its inclusion of a classified table of headings, using DDC, is interesting, but then the headings seem to follow this table.[129] Apparently, however, at some point the Glasgow Public Libraries went over to the classified catalog of the prevailing kind.

Sharp[130] thought a lively article in The Library Assistant in 1937, "The Public and the Catalogue, Dictionary or Classified?" by James Cranshaw, not all on the classified side, and incidentally, felt that it praised Glasgow as being better than Dewey at indexing. But first, Sharp gave a good account of the dictionary catalog, summarizing Cutter's subject entry rules, and saying that "whatever added and analytical entries are appropriate to dictionary cataloging are equally so to a classified one," though not necessarily in the same place in the same form. In his chapter on "Catalogue Indexes" Sharp said there is no entry that finds a place in the scheme of a dictionary catalog which cannot also (and should) find a place in a classified catalog, whether via actual catalog entry or via some sort of indexing entry.

Cranshaw, quoted or summarized by Sharp, said that the classified catalog could be made "of greater assistance to readers in the wider analytical construction of its index. But this is not often attempted." He went on to say, in effect, that the indexing used--DDC's specific subject and class indexing--was not good enough because DDC's indexing wasn't. He obviously hadn't read Brown because he was back to the confusion over the function of DDC's relative indexing. Cranshaw said that "one has only to check up the Union Catalogue of additions to the Glasgow libraries (which is one of the few classified catalogs with an adequate index) to realise the shortcomings of Dewey's relative index. Dewey's index has nine places for Psychology; Glasgow, dealing with actual books, has twenty-nine." He continued with other examples and concluded that "Dewey's relative index is not relative enough.... Dewey does his best in successive editions; but he is always limping painfully behind the field."[131] Whether Cranshaw knew or not that Dewey the man had been dead for six years by 1937 is not clear; what is clear is that he had completely missed what Brown had realized, that whatever relative meant, the index to the DDC tables is not an index of actual books, as indexes like that of the Glasgow classified catalog are. Sharp, not altogether clear himself, said that "perhaps Mr. Cranshaw has rather overstated the case against Dewey's own index ... actually, much of the detailed indexing in the Glasgow catalog is due to a useful idea of making the index serve to some extent the function of added entries" --which is what Cranshaw meant by analytical entry. But where was the economy and efficiency in this?

Brown recognized the importance of identifying items in classes, and settled for doing this from book titles, but only in shelf arrangement; that is, in classification as distinguished from cataloging. For actual items and entries in classified arrangements there has to be first identification of classes and then of items in them. An alphabetical catalog serves as a class index because it gives items class numbers; though it doesn't do it very well because it gives different numbers for the same subject in different aspects. Looking over a few entries, however, for example under Horses, a reader can get a good idea that a number to be tried for browsing is 636.1; and perhaps at least 50 per cent of the uses of an alphabetical catalog or of an index giving class numbers is for direction to classes on open access shelves, where selection is then made.

Sharp, though doing much better than most in what he attempted on classified catalog indexes as he found them, was not quite clear. First and last, he felt, their advantage was the saving of added entries, and though he did not say so, as far as possible they should stick to single entry. He gave two examples: an item called The Mind and the Film: a Treatise on Psychological Factors of the Film and one called Borderland of Music and Psychology. The first, he said, is classified at 791.4, but is indexed also at Psychology; by which he means that the index, under FILM, has at least two numbers--150 for Psychology and 791.4 for Films as Public Entertainment. The second, in the index under MUSIC, has at least 150 for Psychology, and 781.1 for Aspects and Relations of Music. Sharp goes on to say that "the reasoning that has prompted this idea seems reasonable and sound. For nine people who would want either item for its film or music interest, one would want them for their psychological interest perhaps." This is Sharp trying to justify the class choices for single entry: Films 791.4, Music 781.1. But why single entry, except for reasons of economy? And how in the indexing does an inquirer know which numbers are which, and which single entries will be chosen? Apparently, as with a dictionary catalog, he finds 791.4 predominant for films, and 780 for music; but what about the odd man out

with the psychological interest? How does he know which
number to turn to so that he can scan titles for the key
words, "psychological" and "psychology?" And why didn't
either Sharp or Cranshaw make clear the title keyword essence of this classified catalog indexing?

Apparently with some difficulty, Sharp had understood
the central point of Cutter's "Subject word and Subject" rule
--"a book's title does not invariably determine its subject
heading"--but apparently both Sharp and Cranshaw, and most
of their readers, assumed title word indexing in the classified
catalog; in his four editions from 1935 to 1948 Sharp was not
prompted to any amplification or extenuation. The Glasgow
catalogers themselves claimed that they "usually" made added
entries for multiple-subject items, and there was some increase in this practice as time went on. An example given
was a book called Folklore and Psychology by Marett, which
was really a collection of essays in the related fields of
social anthropology, social psychology and religion; but the
title was relied on, and as "Folklore" could hardly be spanned
by a single class name, there was a double entry under both
Folklore and Psychology. Just inside the limit was a book
called Fairs, Circuses and Music Halls, by M. W. Disher,
which was given a single entry under 791, Public Entertainment, but as well as the usual index reference to this number
references were also given under each specific subject.

What then happens to the nine-to-one argument? In
another example, 940.5342 is the number assigned to an
item on Mass Observation, but this is a 1939-45 war number,
and 64 entries have to be scanned to find the first one with
"Mass Observation" in it, and 40 more have to be scanned
for nothing. This remained the state of the British art of
classified cataloging and the outcome of the 1890s battle until the 1950s, when BNB and Ranganathan's chain indexing
came on the scene.

5.4 An International Battle

An international battle was proceeding at the same
time, and in London, as the one in Washington and the Library of Congress and the one in British public libraries.
Two American representatives were in the international battle, one of them Billings of the U.S. Surgeon General's library. British public librarians were not in it, and most
perhaps not aware of it or its significance; it was a battle

they were below, not even level with. In this battle the basic
interest here is in the classification of the International Catalogue of Scientific Literature (ICSL), begun in 1901 and
ended together with its classification along with Cutter's, in
1914; and in the classification of the Repertoire Bibliographique Universal (RBU), in Brussels, beginning with DDC as it
was in its 1894 edition but being modified into UDC and still
going strong toward the end of the 20th century, although RBU
also came to an end with the 1914-18 War. The complicated
story of attempts at international bibliography by international
bodies is fairly well summarized in a History of Some Attempts to Organize Bibliography Internationally, by Kathrine
O. Murra (1950), in 26 pages and with 78 references to the
literature. But some brief summary of the opposition to the
ICSL classification and the beginnings of UDC is relevant
here.

Bradford, the promoter of UDC in Great Britain, said
in 1948 that about 1900 everything was going well with the
developments originating with La Fontaine and Otlet in Bel-
gium--an International Conference on Bibliography in Brussels
in 1894, the adoption of the Dewey system or DDC for a
standard bibliographical classification, and the establishment
of the Institut International de Bibliographie (IIB), later the
Fédération International de Documentation (FID), and the development of DC into UDC--when the worst of adversities,
even calamities, befell in 1901, "with the appearance of a
bibliography, restricted to pure science only ... this was
the result of an International Conference held in London, under the auspices of the Royal Society in 1896."[132] This suggests that something unexpected happened in 1901, but shadows
had been cast earlier in conferences in 1896 and 1898, and
in a report of a Royal Society of London Committee to the
1898 conference specifically on an International Catalogue of
Scientific Literature with "Schedules of Classification." There
had been manifestations of a desire to start with the new century; and there had been developments well before 1896.

In 1831, when Panizzi was appointed to an assistantship in the BM's Department of Printed Books, the Royal
Society had a members' amateur classified catalog of its own
library; in 1832 Panizzi was employed, in addition to his BM
work, to do what amounted to an updated catalog for the Royal Society, but with the same classification. He alleged serious inhospitalities in the classification and also criticized classified catalogs. Panizzi was subjected to members' criticism
of what he did, and thought his professional status was not

properly recognized and that he was not adequately paid according to agreement. The work and the controversy went on until 1839, and is supposed to have left Panizzi prejudiced against scientists.

In 1858 the Royal Society decided on a Catalogue of Scientific Papers, with international coverage but not international in promotion or management. It began in manuscript in 1860, with slips or cards in quadruplicate, and with ideas of author, serial and subject (classified) arrangement. The first two should have been possible from the slips; the third would need classification and notation, perhaps intended to be based on their own because the classification eventually proposed by the ICSL committee in 1898 suspiciously resembles it. Later, the government agreed to pay for the printing of an author catalog from the slips, with an alphabetical index of subjects. Title word indexing may have been assumed, though nothing came of it, and decennial continuation of the author catalog went on, apparently guaranteed to 1900, with the aid of a £2,000 gift by Ludwig Mond. This and other benefactions did not break him, but some who were interested in the IIB developments gave almost all of their private fortunes, and this dependence on private charity was a weakness on both sides. However, in England Ludwig Mond's support renewed hope of a subject index, and spawned a committee which debated classified or alphabetical arrangement for the Catalogue of Scientific Papers, and began talking what became the ICSL. 133

Britain and America, and some other countries, were not at the 1895 conference in Brussels, which Murra said "was not international in the sense desired because planning and issuance of invitations came too late to permit wide participation." Nevertheless, the conference established an Institut International de Bibliographie, sanctioned further adaptation of the Dewey system, recommended it for classifying bibliographies throughout the world, authorized preparation of a Repertoire Bibliographique Universel, and finally agreed on the nature of the International Office of Bibliography. A few days later the Belgian government created that office and assigned to it the preparation of the universal catalog. This seems quite a lot in a hurry for little Belgium to have done in the way of international organization, without representation of the two major nations in political and even bibliographical terms. Learning of these events, the Royal Society of London, really Britain's national academy of science, with a charter from Charles II, sent over its Senior Secretary to make further inquiries. He returned to report that "all must admire the energy and enterprise which has thus been displayed in Belgium." This was then the Belgium of Leopold II (1835-1909), who made the Congo Free State in Africa practically his own private property, until criticism at home and abroad forced him to hand it over to the state in 1908. "At the same time," said the Senior Secretary, "the magnitude of the work and the importance of the interests involved are such that it appears most desirable that the action which the Royal Society has already taken for an International Conference should be persevered in, so that decisions may be arrived at which may ensure, if possible, complete success." There may be a question of who had stolen a march on whom, and one certainly arises as to whether the Royal Society was fitted for leadership toward "complete success" and why leadership and decision was handed to it by the Conference, on the important and controversial question of classification. Murra did not explore these particular questions, on which there is some evidence in the conference proceedings.

The Conference agreed upon the desirability of compilation and publication, "by means of some international organization," of "a complete Catalogue of Scientific Literature, arranged according both to subject matter and to authors' names." The international organization was to consist of an International Council and a Central and Regional Bureaux, to collect material for a catalogue to be issued by the Central Bureau in the form of slips or cards, and "in book form from time to time, the entries being classified according to the rules to be hereafter determined." And these "rules"--what they should be and how, when and by whom they should be determined--became the most debated and most delicate issue of the conference.

On one side, DDC was pressed as a classification by La Fontaine, Otlet, and de Wulf, all members of the IIB (which had been inspired by La Fontaine and Otlet) and all three comprising the Belgian delegation. On the other side were those who vaguely did not want a minute classification, with complexity of item marking (by which they meant notation), and those who definitely did not want DDC. But it was DDC, not the emerging UDC, and DDC identified with its 5th ed., 1894, which was the one adopted at the Brussels conference. The most outspoken and best informed delegate about it and Dewey was Billings from America, his fellow delegate Newcomb, of the U.S. Nautical Almanac, apparently leaving this matter to him. Billings identified DDC with shelf arrangement, as it had been, even though Dewey claimed it was devised for cataloging. Billings also questioned the significance of its adoptions in America; new small libraries, he said, were adopting it, largely because Dewey's students became their librarians and because the Library Bureau, in which Dewey was interested, provided equipment. He showed his own preference for direct alphabetical indexing, even suggesting alphabetical subarrangement within the classes constituted by the sciences. He quoted a letter he had received from Dewey to the effect that his classification and notation had to be adopted as he had published them, because otherwise learned men would always be seeking and making alterations--as they did later, turning DDC into UDC. Billings made telling points, though some were not much more than debating points. A resolution was arrived at, that "whatever system ... be ultimately adopted ... it is impossible to accept the Dewey system en bloc"; to this there was a foreshadowed amendment that "in its present form" be substituted for "en bloc." That this resolution would be divisive in either form was clear; overnight an agreement was reached for a resolution that "the conference, being unable to accept any of the systems of classification recently proposed, remits the study of classification to the Committee of Organization." No other systems seem to have been formally considered by those voting and the resolution was unanimously carried, with the Belgian delegates recorded as abstaining. The committee, however, became one of the Royal Society, and for more or less legal reasons it became the publisher of the catalog, advancing money for costs with the aid of a Government grant of ₤1,000 a year for five years, intended to at least cover any losses. In addition, Dr. Ludwig Mond contributed ₤19,836.17s. 6d, from 1901 to his death in 1909, and even then the Society had eventually, in 1935, to write off ₤14,000 in bad debts.

In the Report of the Royal Society's committee on classification its members are not named, and nothing is said of what could be called professional or expert advice being sought or taken. The classification schedules, the notation system, and so on seemed to be all their own work; it was tentative, they said, for trial purposes, but it fixed the catalogue in its fundamentals. And what the Committee presented in less than a year seems to be what had been in mind all along for twentieth century continuation of their 19th century Catalogue of Scientific Papers; indeed, it was traceable back even further, to their own library classification of 1832-39 which had been disputed so bitterly with Panizzi.

There is room for more research on this matter.
One question is, of course, the classification, represented
only in sets of the ICSL in libraries, not in any readily available, published schedules.   Another is why, in effect, the
project became one of the Royal Society, not one of the Central Bureau, so called, and operating from London? The
answer probably lies in the inability and/or reluctance of
delegates to the Conference to commit their own governments
or any of their national institutions, and their willingness to
have a counterbalance to Belgium's IIB, IOB and RBU provided by another organization in another country.   And this is
what it was; the Catalogue had international cover, it had international committees and bureaux to help it in garnering
what it catalogued, but in publication and underwriting it was
not even national in a governmental sense, but an institutional
activity with limited government assistance, considerable private assistance such as Mond's, and subscriptions which began at £18 a year for all the seventeen class lists, A-R, and
proportionate amounts for these separately.

5.5   RBU and ICSL

RBU, the Repertoire Bibliographique Universel, and
ICSL, the International Catalogue of Scientific Literature, did
not continue after 1914, but as Murra said, there is danger
of attributing to the 1914-18 war "results ... at most only
hastened by it.... Investigations ... after the war ... show
that if the organization had continued along the path it was
following it would probably have collapsed of its own weaknesses."[134] RBU, as over ten million cards, seems to have
had some survival, but apparently not in any service, or in
any duplicated and decentralized form; ICLS in fourteen volumes has survived as a bibliography of science covering fourteen years in many libraries all over the world, in its original form and in one or more reprints.   Why then was it not
continued, even after a break?

Murra said that "it did not render prompt service and
could not do so with the existing set-up," which involved waiting for entries from its Regional Bureaux; and it provided
"subject indexing when abstracting was wanted." Murra noted
that even a President of the Royal Society said in 1920 that
he preferred abstracting journals for his own work, and that
the ICLS, "because of its form ... was difficult to use," and
the "financial responsibility was inequitably distributed." Subject indexing and abstracting, however, are not usually an

British Battles of the Catalogs 133

either/or, and lack of verbal abstracting has been generally agreed to have been a weakness. Also, the association of pure and applied science or technology was growing apace. Even so, other factors need consideration. One is the limited demand and purchasing power at the time compared with half a century later when new universities, for example in Australia, with the original edition still readily available could buy ICSL and other reprints at prices around the thousand-dollar mark; also, the selling any of the 17 parts separately may have unbalanced more than aided its early financing. But finally, of its kind and for its purpose was it difficult to use, compared with various indexes which emerged with some use of UDC or, at the other extreme, the classified catalogs which became established in British public libraries about the same time, which have been examined in this chapter and which their own authorities, such as H. S. Sharp, could not adequately explain?

ICSL was in 17 separate classes, A to R, but they were not the crude class lists being advocated by Brown, Jast and others for public libraries. Each was a complete annual bibliography for a particular science, self-contained but taking its classification from a general one for pure science. Each part consisted of its appropriate schedules or tables, those of Class A for Mathematics and so on, with indexes in four languages which were emphatically only indexes to the schedules, unmixed with any indexing of titles in the classified catalog, complemented by an alphabetical author catalog. In a few minutes any educated librarian or library user could understand ICSL at least as well as dozens of other bibliographies that he might have to consult for references, especially because of the complementary author and subject catalogs, the inclusion of classification, and the simplicity of the notation compared with UDC's or even DDC's. The indexing of the tables probably owed something to DC, but the indexing for the Mathematics class seems to be a mixture of generic and specific entry. There is nothing under "Double Gamma" or "Gamma," but there are several divisions under "Functions" and numbers under "Elliptic functions" and under "Integrals of algebraic functions"; a mathematician would do as well with it as with many other indexes.

5.6 <u>UDC, Otlet and Special Libraries</u>

UDC came into yet another battle, that in which the special libraries in industry formed their own association,

ASLIB, triumphing over the LA representatives of technical and commercial departments of public libraries, including some of the larger public libraries like Manchester and Sheffield. Jast and Savage fought for government aid for these public library departments but it went to industry and its organizations. While UDC was rejected for the Royal Society's ICSL, it was at least sponsored by newly-formed ASLIB, and was used in many special libraries, aided by the advocacy of Bradford, Pollard and Lancaster Jones, all of the Science Museum. More detail on this will be found in the references. [135]

UDC comes into this study because of its English language use, but there is also its universal, multilingual use, which was supremely Otlet's motive in developing it. Its notation appealed because it was in almost universal use, as the alphabets derived from the Greek and with much in common were not. Otlet also rejected alphabetical arrangements as far as possible on the worn simplistic ground that they scattered subjects. He was inspired and sustained by a philosophy of collectivism, worldwide, universal, "mondial" and "universel" being keywords for him. Donkers-Duyvis, the first secretary of his organization and a collaborator, said that he rejected all particularism to advance collectivism in all its forms, and that analysis for him was only preparation for synthesis--and for him, the final synthesis was "l'idée mondiale." Comte had this idea of a final synthesis of social and physical sciences, with his own classification of the sciences, so for Otlet the basis of the projected work would be the classification of the totality of things, "la classification universelle," which gives the intended meaning of universal in Universal Decimal Classification. Philosophically, metaphysically, mystically, it would be the golden key hidden in the tree of knowledge which would open the door to the vast treasury of human thought. [136]

Prosaically, it was only one more general classification, as Dewey's was, but Otlet saw DC in his own way, and wanted to retain it in his own classification or to have it march with his. As early as 1895 he began applying his ideas of analysis and synthesis and universality to complex subject numbering, and to effecting a union of particularism or specialization and universality at a practical level of bibliography. He said,

> In short, the decimal classification should be at the same time a classification and a bibliographical no-

tation. As a classification it should provide classes in which ideas are subordinated one to another successively in different ways, according to the principal or secondary rank given to them. As a bibliographical notation it should be really a universal system capable of expressing by figures, grouped in factors self-contained and permanent in meaning, all the shades of ideologico-bibliographical analysis. These factors will express the limitation of the principal idea by an auxiliary idea, which will sometimes be another principal idea taken as a whole from any part of the classification, sometimes a bibliographical category of general application, such as the auxiliary table of time, of place, of language, etc., sometimes even the nomenclature of the subject.

Varying the combination of these factors with each other will do away with the making of entirely new classification numbers each time it is desirable to classify the same entries from different points of view. So the encyclopaedic needs of the universal bibliographical catalogue and those of the special bibliographies will be reconciled. 137

Even in 1899 Dewey seemed unaware of, or not in agreement with, thinking at its more or less higher levels, when he said classification could not represent "the best philosophical statement of the interrelations of human knowledge uptodate."138 But "uptodate" is a keyword in his thinking then about library (meaning book) classification on shelves; he went on to say "the expense and confusion of change would be prohibitive." In his DC introduction he stressed differences between bibliographic and general use, but while going some distance toward welcoming what he called bibliographic modifications of DC, he added, "when its remarkably rapid work precluded even adequate criticism, it was authorized to publish its tables and assured that American revision would vary from them as little as practicable...." His editors in the 18th edition, however, disallowed use of bibliographic modifications, and said that "differences have appeared ... due in part to the more complex requirements of a bibliographic classification; but even with the substantial revisions now being undertaken by the UDC, the foundations of the two remain recognizably the same." They are, in fact, much closer than DDC and Harris's inverted Baconian, especially in notation, but classifications can have common origins or one can be closely based on another, and still become two separate classifications, as DC and UDC have done, in their use and in their users.

Otlet's concern about DDC was not only classificatory; in the field he had chosen for the application of his world idea, DDC represented America. The 1914-18 war and the following Bolshevik revolution did not help an international pacifist conception of DDC, and his centralist ideas had to give way to federalism expressed by UDC and the cooperation of those using it, and in this transition the name Documentation took the place of Bibliography. This represents a distinction between the mere listing of books and their physical storage in libraries. Both <u>bibli</u>- and <u>libri</u>- mean books in a traditional sense, and in French <u>bibliographie</u> and <u>bibliothèque</u> have the same Greek root; but documentation was a neutral word without commitment to books and librarianship. The differences between documentation and librarianship in its cataloging and classifying aspects were exaggerated, however.

About the same time in America, and then in Great Britain, a new kind of librarianship and even a new kind of library was emerging. These were special subject librarians and special libraries, especially in commercial and technical fields. General public libraries sought to specialize in business, especially in America in downtown branches and in some cities such as Pittsburgh with heavy industrial needs. But industry began to look after itself, forming libraries different from those of existing medical and law associations and those of institutions such as the Smithsonian in Washington, which saw itself as somewhat akin to the Royal Society in London. In Great Britain a collective and national governmental interest was aroused in scientific and technical research by the 1914-1918 war. Since public libraries were, in a sense, all in one national scheme under a national library act, though they depended on local government finance, a few public librarians such as Savage in Glasgow and Jast in Manchester saw the possibility of getting central government aid for business and technical sections in public libraries, and a Library Association Committee was set up to pursue this. In the majority of public libraries, however, the tradition was mainly cultural, with perhaps some aid for the industrious mechanic in the manual arts and recreation for the tired seamstress. Too, it would have been difficult in all but the larger central libraries to assist a variety of industries from the same library.

An Advisory Council for Scientific and Industrial Research was set up in 1916, and in 1918 it established research organizations which would be controlled by industries through their associations, assisted through the Department of Scientific and Industrial Research by a Treasury Grant. In 1924 a conference of interested parties in effect established the Association of Special Libraries and Information Bureaux (ASLIB), then helped by a grant from the United Kingdom Carnegie Trust.

Had this conflict gone in favor of public libraries with business or technical departments, what would they have done about classification? The fullest study of special libraries and services, with comparison of developments in America and Great Britain, is that by Johns--Special Libraries, Development of the Concept, Their Organization and Their Services, 1968. In this she refers to a group visit to Brussels in 1921, reported by Berwick Sayers.[139] He was impressed by the Palais Mondial, apparently a Crystal Palace sort of building and, like it, left over from an international exhibition. It housed IIB, the IOB and so on, and other international organizations; and Sayers came back full of enthusiasm for a British branch. In discussion of this group's LA conference report, however, there was considerable dampening down. Jast, who had been with the group, said the idea of making a start, any sort of start, underlay many of the principal activities of the Institute, with "vaulting ambition overleaping itself," and that "one great disadvantage of that card expedient is that it is second-hand bibliography; it is not made on first-hand examination of the book." Hulme, who had been admiring of UDC in his cautious estimate in 1912, and critical of the 7th edition of DC, in 1921 supported Jast's criticism of the RBU classified cataloging as largely title word descriptions translated into the UDC notation, without any revision with the actual items in hand. Because of this kind of criticism in the LA, and because DC had become well established in public libraries and Hulme had his own classification in the Patent Office Library, it does not seem likely that UDC would have made much headway in either, even for special collections. But the new and favored special libraries were different in more ways than one.

UDC's first complete publication of its tables is reckoned as that called Manuel du Repertoire Bibliographique Universelle, in 1907, the first edition being in French. The classification was called Classification Décimale Universelle, from which came the English name, Universal Decimal Classification. Under the title "Dewey Expanded," Henry V. Hopwood, Senior Assistant at the Patent Office Library, had a 15-page review article in LAR in 1907, a good account of what he saw as the system, meaning its class marking or notation. It seemed certain, he said, that UDC, "whether we use it ourselves or not, will be so widely employed that we shall all, sooner or later, have to make acquaintance with it."140 For some this was their first acquaintance with UDC, and even their last; others hardly nodded, but Hopwood's article did begin influences in UDC's favor among emerging special libraries.

One line of influence was through the developments which led to Aslib; another was the influence of men associated with the Science Museum Library in Kensington, especially Professor Pollard, and librarians Bradford and Lancaster Jones. They were prominent in the British Society for International Bibliography (BSIB), which was established in 1927 with Pollard as its first President and Bradford as its first Secretary. In association with Aslib it became the British National Committee of FID, and "did very much to popularise the use of UDC in Great Britain," according to Ditmars. Lancaster Jones died in 1945, and Pollard and Bradford in 1948, and Ditmars wrote an article on them entitled "A Chapter Closes."141

In her "Coordination of Information" survey Ditmars said, incidentally, that lack of success in any large-scale plan very possibly "arises from the fact that those who have preached its necessity have too often coupled with their plan propaganda for one or other technique," and sight has been lost of the end while arguing about means. Of the Science Museum trio she said that none of them "had ever received professional training as librarians and their interest in bibliography was practical, not academic." For Bradford, she said, "documentation and the UDC were synonymous." This goes far to support the explanation of the supposed difference --that documentation was librarianship done by academics. In her obituary of Bradford, Ditmars said that in his life as a librarian two ideas were dominant: "the superiority of UDC over all alphabetical systems ... and, as an inevitable corollary, the necessity of supporting the International Federation of Documentation as the world centre for cooperation in documentation." Perhaps unfairly brought together, these remarks may be relevant in more ways than Ditmars realized.

Of the Science Museum trio Bradford had the most

British Battles of the Catalogs 139

achievement, or the greatest reputation, mainly because of a book called <u>Documentation</u>, first published in 1948 and reprinted in 1953 with a laudatory introduction by two distinguished Americans, Shera and Egan. Before considering this book, it may be necessary to say more about UDC, since it is not as generally well known as some think, even in Great Britain where in its particular field of special libraries it has had far wider adoption than in America.

5.7 <u>UDC in English and Bradford</u>

UDC follows DC in its main class and subclass order, though Otlet would probably have preferred Comte's classification of the sciences, physical and social. UDC has ten main classes with 0-9 as notation extended hierarchically. Whether with knowledge of Dewey's first 1873 proposals of entirely decimal fraction numbers or not, decimal fractions were adopted in UDC and were apparently found more acceptable by its users than by DC's. This means that there aren't whole numbers extended decimally, so that length of number has no effect on order and there is no making up of numbers to any minimum length with noughts as in DC. The initial decimal point of arithmetic is omitted. There may be some "divide likes," taking over from DDC as in 1894 or even later, but number combination is either by direction or at classifier discretion, whereas DC "divide likes" are emphatically only according to editorial direction. Basically, the results may be the same; for example, in both schemes there is plant species division of 635.9, "Ornamental horticulture," by numbers from the Botany class.

DDC's form numbers--later standard subdivisions-- began with his "waste not, want not" use of terminal zero digits in three-figure numbers, but with all their extensions the numbers remain in one arithmetical series. In UDC, truly auxiliary tables were developed with their own "signs of association" derived from grammatical and algebraic punctuation. At least ten "Tables of auxiliaries" have been listed, with their signs, but this general listing is misleading. There are "Common Auxiliaries" for subjects with geographic and/ or chronological limitations of treatment, with addition of Language for document specification, and Race and Nationality. There is a "Form of Presentation Table," a development of DC's original form numbers, letter extension representing numbers. There are what are called "Common Auxiliaries of Point of View," which could be called aspect auxiliaries.

And there are "Special Auxiliaries," also called "analytic," varying from class to class and in the signs of association--.0 and a hyphen--with complications for which any reader is best referred to an English edition of UDC.

This leaves in the auxiliary listing the "Relations Sign" and its table, which is misleading, because its table is the whole "main" classification, and what is involved is the relation or combination of main class numbers, by direction or at discretion, and the possibility of permutation. This has already been exemplified by the use of 575.17:591.3: 599 in the Science Museum Library, to show that this, the most commonly used UDC device, could be used with LC and other classifications. As a result of the colon sign; it has been called colon compounding. The points after three figures are not decimal points, only points to help in reading long numbers, like the comma used commonly in numbers like 1,000,000. This point before 0, however, has other meanings.

Otlet wrote in 1895 about varying the combinations of factors, to do away with the making of entirely new classification numbers "each time it is desirable to classify the same entries from different points of view. So the encyclopaedic needs of the universal bibliographical catalog and those of special bibliographies will be reconciled." At that time Otlet may not have anticipated the device, and two purposes are implied: 1) the use of one number in special bibliography and one in another; 2) combination permutation for added entry in the same bibliography, special or general, while preserving the synthesis of elements at each place. The latter has been the commoner use of the device, because subject relation and term compounding can still be necessary in a special field as well as in the broad one of a really general library.

What has to be realized, though, is that to allow permutation of main class numbers, any one of which can be the primary filing number, use of the colon has become mandatory to replace numbers in the true auxiliary tables, because these, by definition, are subordinate extensions. Main class number meanings are changed; for example, the auxiliary table number for history as a form of presentation of any subject is (091), but :94 has been used with subjects to allow of permutation, though it means modern European history. The result is a muddle of subarrangement. The Point of View table offers some relief, but it is doubtful that it was ever intended for any wide range of subject documentation, and it has to be eked out by the other common auxiliaries and the colon.

Otlet never seems to have realized that notation has to be adjusted to arrangement, not the reverse. In development, the internal arrangement of elements in compounds, called horizontal, and overall arrangement, called vertical, seem to have been a problem. The latter is, of course, from general to particular within the same generalization, with a fresh start for a related generalization, using a consecutive number. The former is from subject specification (related to documentation), through limitations of treatment, to aspects, space and time limitations of treatment, and even documentary form distinctions. Merely following this out as expressed by notation, however, doesn't help if its use is muddled and at cross-purposes. Ditmars' remarks, quoted above, on one-eyed planners and on Bradford's obsessions, may seem applicable to Otlet.

UDC is international in its numbers, but accepts A/Z subarrangement, so was perhaps not much more international than ICSL, with its mixed single-letter and four-number notation. By being multilingual in its classification tables and their indexing, ICSL also met a problem not at first solved to any extent by multilingual editions by FID. A user must usually have the meanings of what are code numbers in a language with which he is familiar, and needs indexing in the same language. The word "internationally" is used ambiguously when applied to codes which are obviously not natural languages.

Whatever Bradford's weaknesses, he had enthusiasm and the ability to get things done at an organizational level. Apparently he was mainly instrumental in getting the British Standards Institution (BSI) to declare UDC a standard for classification with little or none of the canvassing of opinion that seems to be required to secure BSI's acceptance of sizes in such things as screw threads, and moreover BSI set up an office to prepare UDC for publication. A first complete English edition, numbered as a 4th International edition, began appearing in parts in 1943; the first part was introductory, other parts issued from 1943 to 1958 were for Maths and Physics; Chemistry; Geology and Biology; Electrical engineering; Mining and Military engineering; Metallurgy; Rubbers, Plastic, etc.; Building; the last five apparently becoming part of a "one volume ed. of UDC 5 in preparation." In 1948 an

abridged English edition was published; this included some
philosophizing about DC-UDC to prove it was not Baconian,
which was either written by Bradford or in his style; this
was omitted from the Abridged English edition, 3rd revised,
1961, the one used for reference here. The parts of the
complete edition which have been given priority show where
the major interest in UDC lay.

Samuel Clement Bradford was born in London in 1878,
and as a chemist went into the Science Museum in 1899. He
was in the Museum's library from 1901 until his retirement
in 1938 at the age of sixty, but he continued his work in the
cause right up to his death on November 13, 1948. He said
in a Preface, dated July 1947, to his Documentation, published in 1948, that he had been urged to write an English
book on the subject. It was based, he said, in the main on
BSIB writings. It seems mainly adaptation and summarization and in two important chapters: chapter 2, on Alphabetical subject indexing, and chapter 4, on the preparation of
subject indexes to volumes of periodicals, depends on papers
by Pollard and Bradford in Aslib Conference Proceedings,
1930 and 1932. The Shera-Egan introduction to the 1953 reprint of Bradford's work is not particularly on documentation
or Bradford; its central thesis is that librarianship and documentation are basically the same, but that the former drifted
away with the identification of public libraries with education,
especially remedial and of the masses; classification as the
best instrument of documentation seems to be assumed without any explicit criticism or comparison. Documentation was
the new word, however, even if it had little or no difference
in meaning, and Bradford did a lot to popularize it.

In his first chapter he defined documentation as "the
art of collecting, classifying and making readily available the
records of all kinds of intellectual activity." He went on to
trace the history of classification, with reference to what he
describes as Edwards' criticism of alphabetical catalogs,
which necessarily dealt with title pages rather than real subject matter, but Bradford does not make it clear that, like
Bradford himself, Edwards had little or no knowledge of subject cataloging after Watts, and Bradford made no reference
to any American authorities.

In his second chapter, still on alphabetical subject indexing and its inadequacy, he quoted Pope, that "words are
like leaves, and where they most abound / Much fruit of
sense beneath is rarely found." Going back to his and Pol-

British Battles of the Catalogs 143

lard's reference in 1930 to the LA's Subject Index to Periodicals for 1972--a deplorable example of single-entry title word indexing with cross references for added entries, which they then called a good example of alphabetical indexing-- Bradford refers to entries under "Cells" for both living and geometrical cells, without distinction, and their statement that this was reminiscent of "the librarian's classical error of entering 'Lead Kindly Light' with Lead Pipes." This is a classical error of Bradford's and Pollard's too, inasmuch as the indexing they reluctantly admitted their classification needed could include similar alphabetical juxtapositions.

In his third chapter Bradford said, "We turn from the complexities of alphabetical arrangement, to give the simple scientific classification of subjects, and all the disadvantages of the former method immediately disappear"; but this has been written the other way around, especially with UDC in mind. Bradford went on to say that, of course, there were many classifications, but "fortunately ... only one" which is satisfactory, referring, naturally, to UDC. So ... out with alphabetical indexing and all classifications except UDC!

Bradford seems to have been first to apply Boolean logic to synthetic classification, as it was also later applied to synthetic alphabetical indexing. However, he gives "1, " as denoting the all-including class--the final universe of discourse of genus generalissimum--as the reason why the Decimal Classification "is used to signify the whole of knowledge." This might be a rationalization of decimal fraction numbering, but hardly a reason for what Bradford is claiming.

5.8 Bradford's Criticisms and Later

Bradford first accepted but then rejected Otlet's idea of UDC as having a document specification function as well as a classifying one. In Part 1 of volume 1 of the incomplete edition of UDC in English, in 1943, Bradford either wrote or approved a statement that all available detail would be needed for the documentary specification of periodical articles. But by 1948, and in the first English abridged edition, he had realized that what he distinguished as codification of subject classification was the function of the notation, and not bibliographical specification for its own sake. He said that 526.9:336.211.1(431 "1972" (027) = 3, for a Guide to Prussian Cadastral Surveying in 1927 in German, was justly described as "not classification, but idle jesting."

At the same time he had got as far as recognizing that the Special Auxiliaries which applied over a range of classes were "a small logical defect" in UDC, perhaps derived from DC's original form divisions. This, he said, was because they are subordinate extensions of main class numbers, and could be said to "hide information." Had he not used concealed classification as a criticism of alphabetical indexing, he might have said that they concealed classification.

In the English Abridged UDC (3rd ed. revised, 1961) an example given is .052 for spinning as an extension of 677, textile manufacture numbers. Thus, 677.052 becomes the number for textile spinning generally, and 677.21.052 for cotton spinning in particular; but this presents a problem, a solution of which might be to use both 677.21.052 for cotton spinning and 677.052:677.21 for general textile spinning with a special extension. There is a problem of "distributed relatives," which it is said may be brought together in an index; for example "Spinning machines 677.052; Cotton 677.21.052; Flax 677.11.052," and so on. This has been called bringing together scattered information, but as Cutter pointed out much earlier, cross reference and indexing, however justified as economy, do not bring the actual information together, or the item entries for it. Colon compounding of main classes is a way out, allowing multiple catalog entry by reversals or permutations, but even with some forcing of the meaning of numbers there is not always a satisfactory main class equivalent of a subordinate auxiliary. A general effect, at best, is that the main class order is not always suited to the required subdivision of a main class number, and in the close classification of a special subject such as "paper" Bradford admitted the result could be a muddle "of raw materials, organization and heat processes."

He then turned to the Point of View table, consisting of .001-.008 for areas of administrative interest. For the paper industry, 676.007 could be for manpower and personnel problems, and there could be further specializing by colon compounding; for example, 676.007:331.8 for hours of work. This has an advantage over direct main compounding, as 676.331.8, by introducing a collecting point or categorization, but there is an increase in number length of three digits; and this "out of the frying pan into the fire" result is achieved by most of this UDC improvisation.

Leaning back again on poor old Dewey, as editors of DC have done, Bradford attributed excessive number length to original poor distribution of the notation in DC, but said not a word about the shortness of the decimal base, this being one of the most sacred of UDC sacred cows, linking its appeal to the metric system. Bradford admitted the possibility of literal and mixed notation, referring to its use in scales of notation in arithmetic; his concern, however, was not so much the length of base for subject notation, but the "signs of association," as they were called, of the different conjoined tables, which were and remained mathematical and grammatical punctuation signs with no generally known order. In addition, there was not just "a small logical defect," as in the subordination of the subordinate auxiliary tables, but also a "serious error" in the order of the auxiliary and analytical signs, which of course means an error in the order of what they signify in compounds. Bradford therefore altered the order and, at the same time, met a classification requirement of known signs in a known order by using small letters instead of the existing signs in an arbitrary order.

UDC use, however, had gone too far for alterations to be made lightly; like other classifications, it was stuck with what it had. Otlet had a confusing lot of counsel, entirely or almost entirely presented by amateurs like himself, but he above all was the begetter. He had the same organizing and proselytizing abilities as his disciple, Bradford, but he never reached down to a fundamental understanding of IR needs. In the use of classification, which he assumed too readily to have superior virtue in itself, he fell into the common loose thinking about notation simply as enumerative coding which somehow in itself was a kind of language, whereas it can only represent both the classifying decisions of a user and the language used to express them, which has to come out in indexing.

Bradford rejected suggestions that, with additions, UDC could be used as an international language in the strict syntactical sense. But with Pollard he did argue that "Decimal numbers frequently are more accurate representations of the information in the original papers than the abstracts." Abstracting is, of course, not always perfect use of natural language, but to assert that UDC or any other classification notation has proven more flexible than the natural languages is absurd. Bradford, nevertheless, with all his admissions of conflicting makeshifts in UDC as a semantic instrument, could still assert that it "had been gradually developed and perfected, with the collaboration of leading experts in different countries."

*

UDC was accepted in Great Britain for cataloging of special libraries, mainly in physical science and technology, and for some bibliographies, far more than in other English-speaking countries, although for a while UDC was influential in Australasia. In 1972, in a symposium on Subject Retrieval in the Seventies, Lloyd, with a long association with UDC and the Classification Department of FID, seemed to accept criticism of it as a prehistoric monster, but wrote of possibilities of its adaptation as "an international switching language," meaning roughly one which could be used in the international exchange of information; and others have spoken of such a tool, with or without reference to, or any preference for, UDC. 142

Without going far into this question, a lot of careful consideration is needed, beginning with use of the term "language" for what are only codes for expression of language for a particular purpose, as in the case of UDC classification and specification of documents. Another question is national differences in what began with one system whose international application was a basic assumption or proposition. Lloyd said that "he believed that there was no longer any possibility for managing at one centre like FID or anywhere else, the enormous 'prehistoric monster' known as the full edition of UDC." And there are national differences of more than one kind. For example, in Russia and other communist countries there is dispute about politically ideological classifiction of items with UDC, while other countries have taken it for granted that classification was completely free from such ideological considerations.

Also, not enough may be known about differences in national editions in UDC, or in rules for their use. A startling example of this appeared in Great Britain in 1963, in a Guide to the Universal Decimal Classification (UDC), issued as British Standard 1000C:1963 and as FID No. 345. It was issued by the British Standards Institution in London, the British sponsors and publishers of UDC, but no reference is made to BS 1000A, the Abridged English Edition of UDC, 3rd edition revised, 1961, though its General Introduction is, in effect, superseded by 1000C as a guide to the use of UDC. The earlier guide assumed multiple entry with colon compounding of main class numbers, and reversal or permutation of the compounds, and only in its subsidiary consideration of "hidden information" through the use of subordinate auxiliary numbers, discussed above, is the use of indexing as a remedy proposed, and this does not mean Ranganathan's "chain indexing" of single numbers. In the new guide, single entry is assumed, though many users of UDC favor a method of multiple entry--and not without reason, since it is prescribed in UDC editions up to BS 1000A and is assumed by such authorities as Bradford.

A basic argument for single entry with chain indexing is that multiple entry of a compound subject with even only three elements in the compound could mean six entries; for four elements twenty-four entries; for five, a hundred and twenty, and so on. But permutation in IR systems has usually, if not always, been selective, going no further than some method which makes each of the terms the entry term --which for three terms means no more than three entries-- and with some complication, chain indexing is a method of selecting and limiting permutation based on classification. In the UDC Guide, UDC is adapted to facet classification with chain indexing as DC was in BNB from about 1950 to about 1970, at which time a selective permutation method of indexing, independent of classification number construction, was substituted.

It may be worth noting at this point that UDC was a classification with a method of application for one or more purposes, as stated by Otlet when he spoke of varying combinations of factors to avoid making new numbers for varying points of view so that "the encyclopaedic needs of the universal bibliographical catalog and those of special bibliographies will be reconciled." This has seemed exceptional insofar as classification arrangements--the "order of the sciences" and so on--have been a major interest of makers and users. This was not true of Dewey, who was not interested in philosophical classifications although he adopted a version of one, and he prescribed the use of his tables and their index for cataloging. For cataloging, however, DDC was used, as described at the beginning of this chapter, to suit the economies of printed catalogs and open access, with an established method of title word indexing adapted to the indexing of single-entry shelflist catalogs, while in America it became almost solely a method of shelf arrangement, with independent dictionary cataloging. Cutter intended his EC to be used this way, but in Great Britain it may have been used in some cases in much the same way as DDC. Brown's SC had its arrangement philosophy, and its single place theory for subjects (not to be confused with single entry), though Brown seems to have assumed the latter being applied title word indexing in it popular cataloging use.

5.9 Bradford and Pollard: 1930, 1932

Bradford's reputation and influence were generally established by his opportune publication of the book called Documentation in 1948; the time was right and the title right, at least until "Information Retrieval" became a rival. In a Preface he said it was based in the main on earlier writings. These are listed in the bibliography of his writings on documentation compiled by Ditmars for the 1953 reprint, which is misleadingly called by its publishers a second edition. Bradford did not say in 1948 that the information in the book was not updated and that important parts dated back to papers of 1930 and 1932, published in proceedings of annual ASLIB Conferences, a great forum for Bradford's and Pollard's advocacy of UDC. These parts are on the essentials of the mechanism of UDC and the possibilities for subject bibliography apart from library catalogs. The first paper was presented in 1930 as by Pollard and Bradford, as a proof of "The Inadequacy of the Alphabetical Subject Catalog," and the second, "Systematic Subject Indexes in Periodical Volumes," was proposed by Pollard and Bradford as a remedy. In 1948, while quoting from both these papers in the second and fourth chapters of his Documentation, Bradford greatly summarized them and made no reference to Pollard.

Bradford and Pollard cited bad examples as good of their kind, but almost entirely ignored American work, not mentioning either Cutter or Billings. They made much of what they called reliance on concealed classification in alphabetical subject cataloging and indexing; from varying descriptions, without any named examples, they seem to have been referring to the subject heading list and especially its downward cross references. This list, they said, was before the index maker but not the user of the index, and it was supplemented by title word indexing. Some later writers have taken "concealed classification" to mean the synoptic table which was to be published in a catalog for users but was rejected by Cutter. Bradford and Pollard also argued that alphabetical indexing must be inherently inadequate because it could only consist of verbal representations of simple notions or ideas, not of any compounding of these, whereas these compounds could be represented by extended and/or compounded UDC numbers. These syntheses can, of course, be represented in words, but may be dismissed as complicated phraseology rather than subject names, somewhat as Cutter argued. Bradford and Pollard dismiss verbal representation of complex notions, in either natural syntactical forms or in specially, structured forms on some consistent logical base and arranged alphabetically. They even went so far as to assert that alphabetical indexes are in reality fit only to deal with single words. But this left them in a dilemma:

> ... the utter futility of the Alphabetical Subject Index without a corresponding scheme of classification becomes apparent ... [but] a good classification must always be accompanied by an alphabetical index of terms.... Such an alphabetical index of the relative type used in conjunction with a universal classification scheme ... is an aid of first class importance....

A classified catalog follows a scheme of classification, and either its "relative" index or its classification, in whatever sense this word is meant, may serve as an index to simple notations in the arrangement of the catalog. The problem Bradford and Pollard considered was that of periodical volumes, principally of abstracts, which may or may not be classified according to a scheme such as UDC, and not in one unified sequence of entries. How could they be supplied with a classification of their items to complement an otherwise inadequate simple term index? The Alphabetical Decimal Reference Index referred to class numbers; for example, "Engines, Diesel - 621.436"; then, turning to the Classified Decimal Reference Index, there would be for a given abstracting journal, "621.436 - Diesel engines, I, 191, 238," etc., these final references being to volume and serial item numbers. This would be followed by all number extensions and compoundings, such as, in the example given, "621.436-142 Double-acting Diesels"; "621.436-185.4 High Speed Diesels"; "621.436.003 Diesels, economics"; "621.436.011 Mechanical studies," etc., etc. The point was stressed that verbal equivalents of what the numbers stand for were given, but clearly these were not such complicated phraseology that they could not be used in direct alphabetical indexing, and if all were given with "Diesel" as the first term, they would all come together in direct alphabetical indexing.

Bradford and Pollard's chief examples of use of the method were in Power and Fuel Bulletin, but this, while giving UDC numbers with its abstracts, did not arrange them by these numbers, and in any case it ceased publication. The other example, Plant Breeding Abstracts, used a UDC arrangement with UDC numbers and indirect indexing, but eventually, while retaining UDC classification, it dropped all use of it in both indexing and contents listing, and used direct reference to serial item numbers in its alphabetical indexing. For example, an item numbered 1012 and called "Gene induced mutation of an heritable cytoplasmic factor producing male sterility in maize" had seven indexing entries beginning with "Cytoplasmic inheritance 1012" and ending with "Sterility 1019," in general alphabetical order.

In 1948 Bradford still wrote as though the scheme in which he had been associated with Pollard had come into general use. More than any other classification before it, UDC had the appearance of science, which appealed to scientists. This was its great selling point, rather than real merit. There were, of course, the appeal of classification as somehow scientific in itself, and that of mathematical notation, though the latter had critics, including Bradford himself.

Chapter 6

BLISS AND RANGANATHAN

Bliss and Ranganathan became rival prophets for Great Britain about the same time, the early 1950s; in 1951, Palmer and Wells, in their Fundamentals of Library Classification which superseded Sayers' books as an LA textbook, while they dedicated the book to Sayers and Ranganathan, said in their preface that it was largely founded on Dr. Ranganathan's researches; they also paid prefatory homage to the unparalleled work of Henry Evelyn Bliss on the subject of helpful order. Bliss was already well and favorably known before 1950; for example, there was an ecstatic essay on Bliss by the Director of the London University School of Librarianship in 1949.143 Ranganathan had first published his Colon Classification in India in 1933, but it was only with his adoption of the facet-focus-phase terminology and the emergence of his generalized facet analysis theory with his 4th edition in 1952 that he became widely known and accepted.

Bliss became known as a theorist with his Organization of Knowledge and the System of the Sciences, 1929; his Organization of Knowledge in Libraries, first edition, 1933, and second in 1939; and his System of Bibliographic Classification, 1935, in one volume. In 1940 he published volume 2 of Bibliographic Classification extended by systematic auxiliary schedules for composite specification and notation, General introduction and classes, A-G; in 1947, Classes H-K were issued, and in 1953, Classes L-Z, with a further general introduction and a General Index. He presented no generalized theory or practice of classification with notation, such as Ranganathan's facet analysis, but his classification was far more detailed and adequate for general use than Ranganathan's Colon Classification, the one-volume Indian editions of which were obviously inadequate even for small public library or school library use in Great Britain, quite apart from the fact that Ranganathan did not give ready-made numbers. There was immediate advocacy of Bliss' BC, whereas, while Palmer and Wells had laid some foundations,

151

Ranganathan got his first big push from the memorandum of the Classification Research Group, published in LAR in July 1955 and called "The Need for a Faceted Classification as the Basis of all Methods of Information Retrieval,"[144] although the Group did not agree on Ranganathan's five fundamental categories of facets laid down in his Colon Classification.

6.1 Bliss, Chronology and Biography

Bliss, like many other authors, was always vaguely thought of as middle aged; in 1950, however, Ranganathan was 57 and Bliss 80. The relevant questions, though, are what age he was at time of writing, and the age and sources of his ideas. Bliss (1870-1955) was about 80 when he made a second effort to explain his classification, and as published in 1953 was pathetically trying to put Ranganathan's new terminology into his own terms, saying of focus that it was "out of focus for this classifier's old eyes." In a Preface he said, "half a century had trudged onward ... since this work was projected." We may be reminded of Lorado Taft's statuary representing veiled time and trudging humanity, with Austin Dobson's unexpected lines, "It is not time but we go slowly by."

Bliss' ideas, derived from Richardson's, were influenced through him by Comte, who also influenced Otlet, though only in his social philosophy. Otlet wanted a universal classification but he was satisfied to take this from DC and to add his synthesis, so that by varying combinations of notation "the encyclopaedic needs of the universal bibliographical catalog and those of special bibliographies will be reconciled." Although Bliss felt obliged to supply a comparable synthesis which he called "composite specification and notation," his first and last interest was an "order of the sciences" philosophy of classification; he was trying to put into practice what Richardson had theorized about.

In 1967 Ranganathan said he had read Bliss's two "organization" books (over 700 pages) in less than two hours before midnight, and was moved to write his Prolegomena (1st ed., 1937),[145] but there is little indication that he got anything from Bliss, and certainly not ideas about an order of classes in classification, about which he said little or nothing through the three editions of his Prolegomena (1937 to 1967) or anywhere else. His interest, and his originality, was in what may be called an algebraic approach to a basic synthesis of elements in compound subjects, whereas both Otlet and Bliss grafted their synthesis on to enumerative classification, as Ranganathan called it, with numbers for subjects perhaps already with implied facet combination.[146]

These ideological differences are important, and the two main elements in Bliss's philosophy to be applied to classification were expressed in one paragraph in 1940 in which he said, first, that "the point of view of this system is the central view of humanity, whether subjectively or objectively regarded. This combines the so-called naturalistic view with the humanistic view."[147] This might imply agnosticism, if not atheism, although at least as he aged he was appalled by what was soon to be called permissive society; but in 1940 he stressed both purpose and divinity in nature as required by organization of knowledge, "both teleological and developmental in a destiny that is evidentially Divine and Universal." His second point, which caught on more, was that "comprehensive and coherent, this system is mainly consistent with the systems of science and education established in the consensus of scientists and educators and embodied, tho imperfectly, in their institutions, curricula and programs."

Born in 1870, Bliss became a student in the College of the City of New York, where he received his Ph.D. According to Sayers, he became a librarian on the college library staff in 1891 and by 1910 had apparently become Chief Librarian, that is, at the age of forty. In that year he published an article in LJ called "A Modern Classification for Libraries, with Simple Notation, Mnemonics, and Alternatives."[148] It reads like a summary of his later thinking, except for the compromise with documentation and UDC he made in his composite specification in 1940, when he was seventy. A major problem for Bliss was to avoid following the established American classifications--DC, EC and LC--while plausibility claiming improvements. He said in 1910 that he spent the summer of 1903 in Northampton, Mass., studying Cutter's EC in the Forbes Library, with the idea of simplifying it. One of its good points, he thought, was its numerical Local list, "but the thing was overdone." It relieved the literal notation, however.

Apparently getting nowhere with the much older Cutter, whose classification seemed then more successful than it eventually proved to be, Bliss decided on a classification of his own. After some years of work on it he was able to install it about 1908 in the college library of 50,000 volumes; he thought the same schedules would suffice for collections up to six times as large. In his 1910 paper in LJ he stressed economy of notation achieved by length of base, but also by limiting specificity. He criticized LC for specifying boathouse architecture as NA 6920, yet designating a shorter notation, RK 660, for materials for false teeth plates, remarking ironically that "this is too much for humanity"--but perhaps he still had his own teeth at the time. DC he criticized for 833.82 applied to the still distinguished German novelist Gustav Freytag.

Already Bliss was using his term "consensus," and saying that a fundamental order of the sciences was the special problem of a classification for libraries, but for the solution of it modern evolutionary philosophy had developed a rational base. This was in 1910. He had probably attended Richardson's lectures, and in a bibliographical note on them in 1933 he said that "the order of sciences that is indicated ... entitle it to its place among the very few that have nearly solved that part of the problem";[149] at the same time he thought Brown's SC did in part "crudely represent the established order of the sciences"; he thought classing a subject or object to its nearest place in science was good, "if not carried to extremes."[150] What seems to be the basic proposition of both Richardson and Bliss for Bibliographic Classification is that there is an objective, real order of the sciences, meaning of all subject classes, which is being revealed by science. The contrary view is that the grouping, and thus the ordering, of subjects--of things as subjects of literature--can be varied subjectively, to suit different purposes or simply preferences and opinions.

6.2 Consensus and Classification

The idea of his consensus as being some kind of poll of informed opinion on the fundamental order, expressed by scientists and educators in their institutions, curricula and programs, appealed to many, but Sayers questioned it in rather a confused way. It was, he said, no more than what was being done, or should be done, to arrange according to the methods of workers in educational and scientific occupations, but should it not be in some accord with the literature, and the needs of those using it? Irwin cut the Gordian knot more simply, saying that "the consensus will admittedly vary in different countries and different periods"[151] as it did in

the ancient great cyclopaedia, the circle or system of the
arts and sciences, the seven liberal arts, the trivia and the
quadrivia, down to the curricula of modern times. This is
just what Richardson and Bliss did not admit; a permanent
consensus and a corresponding order were emerging and Bliss
was setting this out as far as discovery allowed. A consensus ascertained by some kind of polling on his classification
should have established how far scientists and educators
thought it conformed with their curricula, but there is no
evidence that Bliss attempted such a poll, and it is not clear
in any case that it should be limited to scientists and educators. There is the general or average reader; would he
accept what runs through DDC's 700, 800, 900 classes as
not being a useful sequence of broadly entertaining, recreative reading about recreative things, especially in the 700
class, and think--as apparently Bliss did--that putting Language quite apart from Literature (as Harris did according
to his Hegelian philosophy) was wrong?

Bliss had to admit about the indoor amusements which
he put with the aesthetic arts that in them "the purely aesthetic element is less patent." He did not seem to doubt
that the outdoor sports he classed with hygiene--in his broad
human or anthropological class which includes medicine--
were scientifically classed, but this ignores the fact that the
basic motivation in these sports is participants and spectators. And this still leaves his "QU - Recreation, Social and
cultural aspects," in Q which has no all-embracing name but
a heading made up of five terms: "Social Welfare, Amelioration, Women, Socialism and Internationalism." In part he
explains them as being "residual," a term he applies to his
"U - Useful arts."152

Though criticizing Brown for overdoing the classing
of subjects with sciences of which they might, in a sense,
be applications, as music is of sound, Bliss went as far as
he could with this idea himself. But many useful arts or
technologies have not been products of applied science, and
with interdisciplinary problems increasing in both the sciences
and technologies, both his and Brown's ideas on these lines
may now seem too simple.

Table I in vol. 1 is a one-page "Concise synopsis of
the order of the sciences" in four columns, intended to show
Bliss' ideas of philosophical integration and interrelation.
Table II is an expansion of this over two pages, though of
course the actual classification in use has to be linear.

From his Introduction and his Organization books it then has to be understood that he relates Philosophy and Science as being scientific in method, whereas earlier classifications had associated Philosophy and Religion as speculative, with conflicting "isms," religion being distinguished by assumptions of divine revelation and knowledge of a supernatural. SCIENCE in Bliss' scheme extends through physical and social sciences, including political history and ending with religion, theology and ethics, political science and economics. HISTORY, in his synopsis, embraces all historical treatment of subjects; it is not just politico-social history. And his TECHNOLOGY AND THE ARTS embraces all technological or useful arts, whether classified with a science or separately treated as Useful Arts, and the fine arts, with, as indicated above, some vaguely aesthetic amusements. Irwin thought this synoptic integration and relation even beautiful to contemplate, though he thought the classification had to be tried out in use, as if it could not be examined in its schedules.[153] If it had been properly examined with some expert advice it might not have been installed in two Australian university libraries, mainly because academics thought they liked it, and then have to be later rooted out at far greater expense than was involved in putting it in.

Table III shows the main notational classes in one vertical arrangement, and the schedules show hierarchical breakdown, which he called "gradation by speciality," and seems to have assumed in both the classification and the notation; but, more than in other classifications, specific subjects in BC are named in classes without specific notation, which was one of his notational economies. After "anterior numeral classes" which include such subjects as bibliography and librarianship and book publishing and selling, his PHILOSOPHY, including General Science and Logic and Mathematics in A, is extended through to G for Zoology. Volume 2 is called "H-K Human Sciences," but he uses human and anthropological synonymously, including Medicine and Hygiene down to K Social Sciences, including Sociology, Ethnology and Anthropogeography. Vol. 3 then includes "L-O History, Social, Political and Economic," with O embracing all of Australasia, the Pacific Islands, Africa and Asia.

He saw Theology as being or having been the Queen of the Sciences, in the old sense of philosophies. As well as supernatural and divine, he also saw it as human or anthropological, "so closely related to human interests that allocation to the humanities in the broadest sense is more consistent with the principles on which this classification is based, especially the principle of collocation." Probably no other class gave him more worry or more uncertainty about its placing. Whether he became aware of resemblance or not, he had a basic threefold division of Philosophy and/or Science, which could include Religion, a History class and an Arts class, and which had some likeness to Harris's version of the inverted Baconian classification, which Dewey fitted into his cramped notation. Bliss covered Harris briefly but fairly well in his 1933 book, but saw him, as in the Bacon-influenced schools, as preceding the influences of Comte and Spencer. Basic divisions of a philosophical kind do not show up in a notation such as Bliss' or Dewey's.

6.3 Bliss's Notation, Cataloging, Indexing

Bliss in 1910 saw economy as dependent on notation, achieved partly through distribution or apportionment and partly via limited specification. He criticized DC and LC in this respect.

In his 1910 version he used as notation 25 letters, A-Y, and nine numerals, 1-9, and seemed to regard these as a total base of 34. He did not use them as a single base, however, as the Dewey-Cutter 35-base was used; the letters for main classes and the numerals for auxiliary tables were complementary, as in LC, though not used in the same way. With some allowances made, he reckoned on "a practical capacity of over 20,000." With his "Composite specification and notation," introduced in 1940, however, he had to extend his notation, distinguishing uses of the same capital letters with a comma. For example UARV is a straight class number for "Tobacco culture and products," but UARV,V would be "Tobacco, varieties," and UAUA,V would be "Citrous fruits, varieties."

A. C. Foskett, who can be called impartial, said in his Subject Approach to Information (2d ed., 1971) that the "notation of BC is good, provided that only the basic symbols shown for enumerated subjects are used, though even here one has to enter the proviso that brevity is often simply a reflection of lack of detail"--that is, in notation. Verbal distinctions are common under class names; there are, for example, ten and an "etc." listed under "HLI Boating." TKG is given as a simple class number for "Sensationalism in advertising, Obtrusiveness, Exaggeration, Vulgarity, Ugliness";

and under this there is "Sexuality, Sex, Voluptuousness, Nudity in advertisements, Poster girls, Girlhood, Pulchritude in Advertisements." Of these, Sexuality, Nudity, Pulchritude are listed in the General Index under Advertising, with only the notation TKG. Foskett said that with the synthetic devices, notation and filing become unsatisfactory; he thought the base was badly distributed to begin with, that far too much was given to History and far too little to Science and Technology. This is a complicated question insofar as Bliss might have used something like his small letter geographical divisions--as Cutter did his local list--and saved his capital letters; it is clear, however, Foskett says, that notation length will begin to exceed Bliss' economic limit of three or four digits. Bliss gives as composite notation examples TNVac, CP,N or TNPac,CP,V for "Ocean ships of the Canadian Pacific Transport System"; each consisting of ten elements including commas. "Short notation," such as Dewey's original three-figure whole numbers in 1876, may be called famous last words of classification makers.

Bliss never got around to saying much about classified cataloging techniques; while advocating classified cataloging he took the usual refuge in criticisms of alphabetical cataloging, with hypercritical and exaggerating emphasis on ambiguities, homonymity and synonymity in words, in which he had a prolix, pedantic interest. As Foskett said, "although he recognized the need for some forms of synthesis (composite specification), Bliss was hostile to the idea of complete analysis and the thesis put forward by Ranganathan." It is doubtful that he ever got through to understanding facet analysis; it was with UDC that he felt himself obliged to compete. He produced such compositions as TDM, UAUAbgv or the reverse, UAUAbgv, TDM, which were obvious permutations, but while he spoke of different viewpoints he did not produce any explanation of reversal for multiple entries or entries in different bibliographies, as Otlet and his British editors did. Foskett said "his scheme may thus be regarded as the last of the great enumerative classifications, despite its provision of systematic schedules."

In 1960 Coates, in his Subject Catalogues, Headings and Structure, attributed Dewey's relative indexing, its showing of class or generic inclusions of specific subjects and its "black" or boldface type for numbers with extensions in the tables for further specification of the subject, to Dewey's search for economy, in comparison with Bliss's inconsistent showing of specific divisions under generic headings in his index. Coates

Bliss and Ranganathan 159

conveys the impression that Bliss is superior compared with Dewey, the stumbling forerunner of Ranganathan. He cites a chemistry example, and the advertising example already cited, with more than a column of subheadings under advertising; there are actually sixty-two, with references only to 24 three-letter numbers.

The introduction to the General Index of BC shows a man becoming obsessed with the growing excesses (as he saw them) of a permissive society, and a man who has lost his grasp of the IR essentials; but he was then eighty or more. Foskett refers to omissions, one being Sermons; but History also isn't in the Index. Under "Race, Races," there are 52 subheadings, not one of them referring to racing in any kind of sport. Britten is included as a contemporary British composer, and Handel and Haydn are in, but not Elgar (1857-1934), who was a household word while Bliss still lived, if only in his "Land of Hope and Glory." Foskett's kindly conclusion was that "to be an adequate tool the index would probably have to be completely revised and recast; at present it is too erratic to be reliable."

If the real needs of IR by the classified catalog method are considered, and forgetting questions even on the philosophy, Foskett as a textbook writer didn't leave Bliss many feathers to fly with. Sayers, on the other hand, opened his account of Bliss (with unconscious ambiguity) with the statement that "woven into the texture of this book"--his Manual of Classification--"are many yarns from the loom of the most scholarly of American classifiers."[154] Sayers, however, had begun with his canons in 1908 by pinning his faith on Dr. Richardson, so he and Bliss had much in common.

On his side Bliss coined a phrase which has gained some currency, along with his term "consensus." In his 1933 book he said that "the opinion that imperfect or confusing classifications can be rendered efficient by means of a correlative alphabetic index to their notations, the writer has called 'the subject-index' illusion." Altogether, he referred to what he meant and to the name no less than eight times, but he did not explain that this indexing has been used for economy in classified cataloging by single entry methods, with indexing substitutes for multiple entry and collocation in catalogs ranging from crude title word indexing to more or less sophisticated chain indexing and subject term permutation indexing for composite subjects. Perhaps the unkindest cut of all is that his classification has been adapted to facet structure with chain indexing by Mills, who performed the same service for UDC and also became the editor of BC.

6.4 BC's Reception and Adoption

In Great Britain and beyond the seas Bliss certainly had a good reception, the ground having been prepared for it by his early books, the common knowledge of Richardson's earlier ideas, and much more interest in classification than existed in the US. There were, however, misunderstandings and many wrong assumptions about what H. W. Wilson's actions and intentions in relation to Bliss were. H. W. Wilson the man (1868-1954) was another Bowker in his support of libraries, the ALA and bibliography. In the tradition of Poole, he had worked his way through college, then he and a fellow student ran a college book business, which he subsequently developed into a great index publishing and general publishing business. He happened to tell the writer about 1948 that he finally embarked on the publication of Bliss's classification because he thought Bliss should have a hearing. This was in character for Wilson, but though he had staff who could have edited and carried on BC, he did not enter into any relation with it such as the Library Bureau had with DC, holding the copyright of DC for a time as one of its assets.

In July 1953, D. J. Campbell, Librarian of the Institute of Cancer Research in London, and C. B. Freeman, Librarian of the Institute of Education, University College of Hull, wrote advocating BC in the Australian Library Journal. Their idea was user cooperation, and they said that the H. W. Wilson Company had expressed a willingness to issue an occasional bulletin of news, provided that at least twenty or thirty librarians were willing to purchase it at cost. A British group provided copy and the Wilson Company stencil-duplicated it from 1944 to 1966. By then H. W. Wilson had been dead a dozen years and the classification (1940-53) out of print, but the British group continued with an occasional bulletin.

Campbell and Freeman in 1953 listed 42 libraries which were using Bliss; of these, 26 were in Great Britain, one or two in Australia, one in India, eight in New Zealand, three in the British Colonies and Protectorates, one in the United States--Bliss's own library--one in the Argentine and one in Norway. At the most only about five general libraries were listed, all of them academic; the rest were what may

Bliss and Ranganathan 161

be called departmental special libraries, in medicine and education. New Zealand shows eight, four of them in schools; BC was strongly supported by Harris of the Dunedin Public Library, but no public library was listed. Two drop-outs and 17 more adoptions were listed in the ALJ in April 1954. In 1967 a British survey reviewed in the Journal of Documentation (JoD) by Mills indicated that of libraries replying to a questionnaire, 542 used DDC, 18 UDC, 16 BC, and 45 "others."[155] Maltby, the editor of Sayers' Manual of Classification (4th ed., 1967) reported that the original City College of New York and "at least one special library" in America were using BC, and estimated that the scheme was being used in about 100 in all, mostly college and special libraries in Britain and the Commonwealth. Australia had two--the new graduate national library and the older University of Tasmania--but both have felt obliged to face the greatly increased cost of replacing it, and both in different ways are in favor of the LC package deal; both used BC only for shelf arrangement.

School library use increased, mainly in Great Britain, and the British Bliss Classification Working Party produced an Abridged BC for school use in 1967, and reprinted it with corrections in 1969. With assistance from generous donations, Butterworth's in Great Britain expected to bring out a new full edition about 1974 by photo-offset, which in Great Britain was to cost about £50 for three volumes. It was being edited by Mills, apparently at the North London Polytechnic. Mills seems to have adapted it to facet single entry, as he did UDC, and this and other improvements might not be what was in Bliss's own mind. Opinion generally seems to be that BC will suffer a lingering but certain death, as did Brown's SC in England, and EC in America.

6.5 Ranganathan and Bliss, and Ranganathan's Beginnings

Ranganathan and Bliss are dealt with together in this chapter because they happened to come into competition with each other as well as with earlier classification makers, in Great Britain and about the same time. Sayers said in 1957, in a Preface to Ranganathan's Prolegomena (2d ed.), that Ranganathan acknowledged influence by Bliss. But in 1961 Ranganathan said that Bliss had written to him in 1933 about "the theory of library classification" forming the basis of the Colon Classification (1st ed., 1933)--presumably meaning theory in the Bliss sense--and that he had replied that he had no such prior theory.[156] There is no evidence in the results that Ranganathan was influenced by Bliss in either classification or notation; for one thing, his CC, though developed and radically changed in terminology, was not radically changed otherwise in six editions from 1933 to 1963.

Bliss's BC, on the basis of its adoptions, could hardly be called successful, but it was far more so than Ranganathan's Colon Classification (CC), which had no adoptions in Great Britain. Bliss had become interested in problems involving classification order in relation to general philosophy, and thought that in his BC he had the answer to these problems. He stands or falls by library use of his BC for shelf arrangement and classified cataloging. But in Ranganathan there seems to have been for the first time a man whose fame and success in IR in Great Britain is not identified with a particular classification, even though he produced one. America's Richardson also achieved fame and influence in Britain but he never produced his own classification.

Ranganathan generated a general theory and practice of what he called "facet analysis," and a theory of classification in relation to cataloging, and the indexing of classified catalogs and bibliographies by what he called "chain procedure." In 1949 he related this to what he called a "symbiosis," a living together of classification and cataloging, but with classification the dominant ecological associate. His facet analysis in special classifications was far more successful than Bliss's BC, and this and his chain procedure were adapted to several classifications, including UDC and BC. There has therefore to be a measure of comparison between Bliss and Ranganathan different from that between him and authors of earlier classifications from DC to UDC, though the latter looks more influential on Ranganathan than any other. One difficulty is that Ranganathan was very sparing in any acknowledgments, though obviously he read widely; it is only in the 3rd edition of his Prolegomena that he shows acceptance of the idea that scholarly work should be accompanied by bibliographical references. However, first to be considered is his biographical background, his entry into librarianship, the influences on him, and his own on others.

Shiyali Ramarita Ranganathan was born in India in 1892 and died there in September 1972, his reputation already past its zenith. There was no more than a three-column obituary in LAR by one of the original faithful, Palmer, when a whole issue devoted to him might have been expected. According to Sayers Ranganathan became assistant professor of mathematics in the Presidency College, Madras, with presumably a doctorate on the way, but then was nominated in 1923 to be librarian of Madras University Library. One may wonder at this kind of transition--exemplified by Bradford and Ranganathan and others--from professions of great distinction to what hardly seems an advance upward. However, Ranganathan went first to the BML to study until the Director suggested to him the University of London School of Librarianship. There, Sayers said, he found the only subjects taught upon his own level to be library administration and classification, taught by Sayers, who advised him to read library economy, to work for a month in a public library, and then, with that experience, to visit different types of libraries. It hardly seems the best preparation for a university librarian. However, Ranganathan was back in India by 1924, thinking out his Colon Classification, the name he gave to the scheme's first edition in 1933 and retained through its fifth in 1957. He was a great believer in terminology. In the 2d edition of his Prolegomena (1957) he said:

> A vast specialised terminology has already come into vogue. More will be coming in future in spite of phlegmatic and rhetorical protests from old guard take-it-easy librarians. These come from those with little experience of the exacting demands of intensive reference service. These also come from those holding classification to be little more than shelf-marking. Thought on the discipline of classification must march on in spite of them. New terminology will continue to precipitate in its wake.

In fact this precipitation of terminology may have turned more people away from a study of his theory and practice than anything else.

By 1952 and the 4th edition of his CC, he had developed his own terminology in an amazing amount of writing, and he there introduced the expression "facet analysis." This may be regarded as the name of his generalized theory and it has had more influence than his CC; had he not become committed to the earlier name, it is quite likely that he would have called his classification "facet."

He said in June 1936 that he had read the entire range of 740 pages of Bliss's two Organization of Knowledge books, endeavoring to put himself to sleep between ten and midnight; instead, his own Prolegomena to Library Classification (1st ed., 1937) was "precipitated." His mind "was pressed through these pages in so intimate and critical way that ed. 1 of my own book emerged clear-cut as from a mould. All that remained was to fill in details and provide illustrations."[157] He did not give Bliss's careful citation of sources and only in the 3rd edition of his Prolegomena (1967) did he append a list of 183 "Bibliographical references."

He began by making much of the inspiration of a "Meccano" engineering model building set he had seen in a shop window in 1923, and in the 5th edition of CC in 1957 he said, under "0.3 Analytico-Synthetic Classification, 0.31 Meccano analogy": "In the Colon Classification, ready-made Class numbers are not assigned to topics. The schedule ... may be said to consist of certain standard unit-schedules ... correspond[ing] to the standard pieces in a Meccano apparatus ... so also by combining the numbers in the different unit-schedules in assigned permutations and combinations the Class numbers for all possible subjects can be constructed ... the function of the Colon (:) and other connecting symbols is like that of the nuts and bolts in a Meccano set. It is therefore an Analytico-Synthetic scheme."

A basic limitation, however, was that in some classes this was hardly possible; as, for example, in his first object class, for parts of the body in medicine and plants in agriculture. Thus, with this and several other subjects, such as mathematics and physics and even geology and useful arts, he had at least to begin with traditional classification--which he called "canonical." He must also have come to realize that while paper-saving (as against time-saving) with ready-made numbers might have advantages in India, it had no appeal in some other countries, least of all America, where classifiers expected all the divide-like numbers made by directions in DDC to be indexed. Also, the Greek letters with which Ranganathan expanded his defective notation were hardly suited to any western typewriter use. Above all, he finally realized the general inadequacy of CC's unit schedules, and in the 5th edition he proposed a reorganization in which his CC as it had been would only be volume 1, a "Basic" classification only "sufficient for the classification of Macro Thought embodied in books taken in general libraries such as public libraries and libraries of schools, colleges and universities"--though it would not have been considered adequate for any of these in Britain or America. Volume 2 was then to be "more elaborate schedules necessary for the Depth Classification embodied in articles in learned periodicals." It was to come out in fascicules, but none have been seen.

6.6 The Colon Classification and Chain Procedure

Ranganathan's Colon Classification is a particular classification, in six editions beginning in 1933, and with a major change of terminology in the 4th edition. The latter included facet analysis, which may be called his generalized theory and which became accepted general theory in Britain. In the line of DDC, UDC, EC, LC, SC and BC, CC is the seventh general classification actually with some library application to be considered here. It was a radical development though not without some forebears, and, reminiscent of the adulation of DDC and of Dewey as genius and saint, Ranganathan appeared to some to be another Einstein. But his sources, like Dewey's, are not easily traceable in the literature.

He began with only the colon but later added the other punctuation marks of English writing. He habitually thought and expressed himself in analogies and metaphors, many of them Indian. It has to be realized, for example, that his "Wall-Picture" principle for facet sequence or citation order of terms in compound subject headings refers to murals on walls, not pictures in frames or on easels.

Ranganathan had certainly studied Dewey as his favorite pin-up boy from the past, and said his "great contribution was the finding of an ordinal number to represent the subject matter of each book."[158] In his context this means no more than the use of a decimal, hierarchical system for relation location according to subject, but he further stated that Dewey began to represent "specific subjects by ordinal numbers, but was thwarted by opposition." This needs considerable qualification, because Dewey no more intended what became known as the coextensive number or heading for each item than did Cutter; Dewey did not compromise by giving up "the attempt to establish a one-one correspondence between subjects and class numbers," and in this respect he did not mislead later classificationists, who accepted Dewey's idea of one or more specific subjects for limited numbers.

The UDC users of DDC had the new ideas. Ranganathan, reading and talking with Sayers and getting around in England in 1923, could hardly have been unaware of UDC. In it, the main class numbers have been misleadingly listed as one of its tables, along with the tables by which these main class numbers are extended or compounded by use of the colon sign. Ranganathan's great innovation was treating all tables and hierarchical parts of some tables as what he called facets--for example, Anatomy, Physiology and Pathology in Medicine. What he called facets required some determination of orders of association or sequence in different classes; this was to provide for what has been called horizontal order within numbers, and not to have the contrasted vertical order of number determined by arbitrarily arranged "signs of association," as they are called in UDC, consisting of a mixture of punctuation and mathematical signs.

His first breakthrough was the colon sign with a minimal ordinal value so that, for example, within L - Medicine, L:411 would be "Hypertrophy as a general complaint" and in the general order of the classification in use would precede L37:411; in this L37 is "Arteries as Organs of the body" and :411 is "Atrophy." This implied settlement of a question of permutations. Given trains of what he first called characteristics, and later foci in facets, and these ideas, there are possibilities of permutation and so some determination of order required; even with only two characteristics, two permutations are possible, and with four this becomes 24. Ranganathan presented a preferred order in his usual style, inventing five rock-bottom, "Fundamental Categories of Facets," which he called "Personality"--an unfortunate name which was puzzling even to himself--"Matter, Energy, Space and Time," with the acronym PMEST. It may be easiest to think of Personality as simply a specific object; "Dolls, Celluloid, Moulding, Japan, 20th century" is an example of PMEST shorn of the pseudo-scientific look. Celluloid, which is matter in this example, in another subject could be Personality (P). In the Medicine class P becomes the Organs of the Body, there is no Matter, and Energy (E) becomes Problem or Cause and Cure. In Agriculture, Plants called cultivars become P, and E covers cultivation. An example of P and E, or Organ and Problem, in Medicine is L27219:415 for "Vermiform appendix inflammation" or appendicitis, and L27219:415:77 for appendectomy. These are "manifestations" of the fundamental facets which some writers and readers seemed to think Ranganathan's "researches" had actually revealed in nature, but he himself finally said they belonged only to the classificationary discipline, having nothing to do with Metaphysics and Physics.[159]

The classification, meaning the facets and their foci or isolates and so on in the various classes such as L - Medicine, had in some way--its own way--to be indexed. This meant not giving ready-made numbers, and the L class was unusual in the number of "illustrative" numbers given in the Schedules of Classification (which were Part 2) as well as in Part 1, which presented the general rules and definitions and the formula for each class with some explanation and exemplification. The index gave formulae for specific subjects or a lead, although in the 5th edition ready-made numbers seem to have increased--for example Aneurism - L37:4711 and Angina Pectoria - L34:411. Further extension for treatment required reference to the facet information, rules and formulae. One of Ranganathan's early ideas, apparently influenced by medical terminology, was that of getting at "fundamental constituent terms" to reduce "derived composite terms"; using dictionaries and textbooks for this seemed to him a way to economize in classification schedule size, but it was no economy in the classifier's time. He finds "Appendix L[P] 27219" and from that can work in the schedules through to L27219:415 for "Vermiform appendix inflammation or Appendicitis" and to L27219:415:77 for "Appendectomy." If he has found in a dictionary that nephritis is inflammation of the kidneys, in the index he then finds "Kidney G [P], K [P2], L [P], 51"; the last is obviously in Medicine; G is Biology; and K, Zoology. In the schedules he can work from L51 for Kidney and with the opening formula L [P]: E [2P] get out L51:415 for Inflammation; and if the item to be classified is on hydrotherapy as a form of treatment, the number would be L51:415:65.

CC has 14 small-page columns for its medical facets and their foci; DDC (17th ed.) has 75 large-page single columns giving full numbers. The DDC index refers from Appendicitis to Vermiform appendix diseases and on page 2625 gives "Vermiform appendix, anatomy human, 611.345; other aspects, see Nutritive organs; diseases, surgery, 617.5545; anesthesiology, 617.975545." The 1957 edition of CC in one volume costs 36 shillings outside India. DDC, of course, costs very much more, for more than one reason, and in not many countries can many libraries afford to buy an edition even now and then, and certainly not every five years. But labor costs in America are high, time is indeed money, and class numbers are expected even more directly. Both LC and DC numbers are given in bibliographical announcements and there is even what began as Cataloging-in-Source and is now Library of Congress Cataloging in Publication Data.

The indexing just considered is that of classification tables, to provide numbers more or less ready-made, or means of making them. But there is also the indexing of classified catalogs, which of course are not alphabetically self-indexing. Crestadoro's indexing of unclassified books in closed access has been considered, and the development which came out of the British Battle of the Catalogs in public libraries and the battle for open access; as this was won there had to be classified arrangements. These became mainly DDC, but the accepted indexing was a crude form of title word indexing with reference to the numbers of the class including the titles. There is evidence that classification makers have not paid much attention to the ways in which catalogs in which their classifications have been used have been provided with necessary alphabetical indexing. One thing that may be credited to Ranganathan is that in one sense he was thorough; he did attempt a complete reconstruction of library science in all its branches, and for cataloging with his classification scheme he developed a method of indexing he called "chain indexing," which could be used with any hierarchical classification and certainly with DDC. It is apparent that his CC was not likely to be used in Britain, and it was even less likely in America. But the use of his chain indexing with DDC classification in the newly established British National Bibliography (BNB) could be regarded as his major triumph and advertisement. How it came and went is told in the next section.

6.7 Ranganathan's Influence in Britain

Ranganathan's influence in Britain came not through his CC but the generalized theory which in his new terminology became facet analysis and his facet categories, and through what he called "symbiosis of the classified and the alphabetical catalog"[160] and the expression of this which he called "chain procedure," applicable to the indexing of any hierarchical classification with an hierarchical notation. Coates, writing on terminology with general application to subject catalogs, said: "CHAIN--also to be credited to Dr. Ranganathan--is a hierarchy of terms in a classification scheme, each term containing or including all those which follow it. CHAIN PROCEDURE is a method, first propounded by Dr. Ranganathan, of constructing subject index entries, without permutation of components, by citing terms contained in particular chains." While it is not permutation in a mathematically formal way, and is selective as most IR use of permutation is, it nevertheless seems to be essentially permutation of hierarchical classification notation with verbal representation which can be arranged alphabetically as indexing. How did Ranganathan's influence take effect?

In 1948 he said he spent a whole Sunday in Chaucer House, headquarters of the Library Association (LA) in London, with D. J. Foskett, Bernard Palmer and A. J. Wells in what he called "experiencing the subject of faceted classifiction." Of these three, Palmer had sat at Ranganathan's feet while on war service in India in 1940, and again after the war; by 1951 he was Education Officer of the LA. Wells was Editor of the British National Bibliography. Both were thus in influential positions. In 1951 they published their Fundamentals of Library Classification; in its dedication to Sayers and Ranganathan this was off with the old love and on with the new. In its Preface tribute was paid to Bliss, "whose unparalleled work on ... helpful order we largely accept." They thought Bliss, however, would oppose some of their conclusions, that fundamentally there is a "pattern of thought activity which coincides with the basic concepts of physical science--matter, energy, space and time ... such a pattern enables a classifier to construct a formula which is valid for the analysis of any subject into its fundamental constituent elements. From these elements the complex derived composites that form the subject of books, etc., can then be built up. So far as our experience goes, and that of Dr. Ranganathan on whose researches this work is largely founded, this hypothesis is valid." This shows that Ranganathan was thought by some to be finding his categories in nature, not imposing them. However, the Palmer-Wells book became very much required reading for the LA examinations in the theory of classification and became for many unquestioned gospel.

Ranganathan said the Chaucer House meeting eventually led to the formation of the Classification Research Group (CRG). It could have been an influence but there was a chain of events beginning with a resolution of the Royal Society's Information Conference in 1948 for the constitution "through existing organizations or otherwise, of a standing committee on subject classification in science," with a suggestion that alphabetical arrangements should come within the terms of reference; Ranganathan separately referred to this conference.[161] According to A. C. Foskett, a Royal Society committee in 1951 invited Vickery to form a group to take over its work; the LA refers to "interested librarians"[162] and, while it published their first "memorandum" in 1955 as received by the LA Library Research Committee, does not suggest that CRG was an LA creation. The Group apparently began in 1952, and the LAR listed 15 members in 1955; these included Palmer as Chairman, Vickery as Secretary, Wells and Coates of BNB as members, and D. J. Foskett. The influential memorandum of CRG published in 1955 was headed with its conclusion: "The need for a faceted classification as the basis of all methods of information retrieval." Its argument leads in the text to the merely verbal variant, "that an essential tool in constructing any [their emphasis] retrieval system is a classification of knowledge." Preference for a facet classification is not pursued here, except that the memorandum seems to advocate single entry of a compound subject item "under the compound class number which uniquely represents it," with indexing--preferably Ranganathan's chain procedure indexing--as a substitute for added entry in the classified catalog. This was used with DDC in BNB for about 20 years.

6.8 BNB, Its Classification, Notation and Indexing

BNB, organized by a council of librarians, booksellers and publishers, was to be self-supporting as a national bibliography. It began as a weekly list in January 1950, but without an index, use of DDC's own index being assumed.[163] This was not satisfactory and Ranganathan's chain indexing was adopted, and for the coextensive heading--for entry only once, "under the compound class number which uniquely represents it," as the CRG Memorandum said--there was verbal extension as required after a uniform token numeral [1]. Perhaps Wells had hopes of something better coming from Ranganathan himself, who must have been persuasive. In an article in the Indian Librarian for June 1958, Wells went so far as to say:

> ... if specific indexing is to be undertaken some way must be found of making the Decimal Classification numbers coextensive. It is a serious dilemma which will ultimately destroy the effectiveness of the classified catalogue. In this respect, of course, the Colon Classification offers a better basis than the Decimal Classification but if the Decimal Classification is to be used, then the dilemma must be solved. As you are no doubt aware, we have resolved it temporarily ... by adding ... 1 to a deficient class number and developed the class by naming the further subdivision in words.[164]

Ranganathan seems to have assumed hierarchical notation and the coextensive single entry heading or number as all the terms in a compound which could be arranged in one hierarchy. Suppose a book on virus diseases of apples, then the classificatory hierarchy for BNB would be "634.1 - Pome fruits, 634.11 - Apples," this verbal translation of the numbers being called "featuring." But as 634.11 was the limit of the DDC number it had verbal extensions of further specification of the book as in "634.11[1] Diseases, Viruses." This was sufficiently representative of the book, which Coates in 1960 called "summarization of its unified content."165 An actual book, however, was on virus diseases of apples and pears, which are coordinate as pome fruits, so that in Coates' sense there is no unity of content; the book was multitopical and could require more than one entry; in this case, two, the second being an entry or reference under "634.13[1] Diseases, Viruses." Now, using the apples heading to exemplify indexing, this would be "Virus: Diseases: Apples: 634.11[1] ... Diseases: Apples: 634.11[1] ... Apples: Fruitgrowing 634.11." Coates, who was BNB's head cataloger, admitted a defect in this, in that with specific approach in an alphabetical or classified arrangement, an inquirer would expect "Apples - Diseases - Viruses," apples being the specific object and the rest aspects; and even if he looked under Viruses first, he would have to know the system and have to work through to find out if anything was entered for "Apples - Diseases - Viruses," and could draw a blank. This, however, Coates argued, was the price to be paid for the saving of permutation, but he did not identify the number reversals of the method with permutation, assuming that permutation means all or none. Coates himself, however, showed knowledge of IR permutations which, like most in IR use, are selective, providing primarily for getting each term first, which for example only requires the simple form--sometimes called cyclic-- of ABC, BCA, CAB, without the other possibilities with three terms of ACB, BAC, and CBA. The trouble with Ranganathan's chain procedure is that the original chain is reversed, which is a permutation, with progressive dropping off of links, so that the inquirer finds "Apples, Fruitgrowing 634.11" and "Apples, Cookery 641.6411," but not "Apples - Diseases - Viruses" in that usual specific order.

For direct alphabetical indexing purposes in the British Technology Index (BTI) in 1962, Coates produced a purely verbal version of chain procedure, his own example being "Hydrogen peroxide - Bleaching - Cotton, see Cotton - Bleaching - Hydrogen peroxide; Bleaching - Cotton see Cotton Bleaching." Without being subordinate, as in indexing of classified cataloging, this is much simpler, but essentially the same in its defects. BNB in the sixties developed a new form of permutation selection and display which has been called "Precis," an acronym for "preserved context index system." Both the BNB and BTI systems need further consideration; the point here is that Precis, which superseded the chain indexing used in BNB for about its first twenty years, is not in any symbiotic way tied to the classification; it is a systematic selection of permutations independent of the class numbers to which reference is made.[166] In 1964 Ranganathan published a paper, "Subject Heading and Facet Analysis," in which he said it had been a mistake to think that "facet analysis is either by itself classification or ... a technique designed exclusively for classification"; he used an example from Coates' BTI but adapted it in his own inimitable way to his own ideas and definitions,[167] meanwhile repeating his criticisms of Cutter's original rules, without regard for later modifications in dictionary catalog practice. He did this also in his 1949 paper called "Self-perpetuating Scheme of Classification."[168] Both papers appeared in the Journal of Documentation and are probably the shortest and best available expositions of Ranganathan by Ranganathan.

Of the general classifications considered, beginning with Dewey's and including Ranganathan's Colon, the latter had less adoption for use, American or British, than the others, but had most acclaim in its general theory, and "Facet" became better known than any other word in his teeming, bewildering terminology. But how has this fared? In Britain the self-constituted Classification Research Group did much to establish the idea of the need for a faceted classification as the basis of all methods of information retrieval, an idea which could hardly have been more sweeping. This was in 1955, but even by 1950 there were other innovations emerging, and beginning to compete with facet classification where it was most successful--in special libraries in competition with UDC.

One innovation was more of a gradual development, overcoming Cutter's name problem in his dictionary cataloging and serving what Coates called an alternative concept of specific entry, related to specific information on objects rather than the objects alone, and serving what Coates thought might have been distinguished as what he said Ranganathan called "coextensive subject cataloging."[169] In Britain this was called "pre-coordination" when "coordination" became established in America as the name of the other more radical innovation which was then distinguished in Britain as "post-coordination." Bernier said in 1956 that they differ "from alphabetical subject indexes in enabling simultaneous correlation of two or more terms not necessarily in alphabetical order. They differ from classified indexes in that subjects represented by single or correlated terms are not arranged in hierarchies."[170] This was certainly something new, breaking as it did into the dichotomy of the classified and alphabetical index or catalog. The next chapter is on pre-coordinate indexing systems and the one following it on post-coordinate systems.

Chapter 7

PRE-COORDINATE INDEXING
WITH PERMUTATIONS AND COMBINATIONS

7.1 Definitions

Pre-coordinate indexing here means systematic subject heading--not influenced by Cutter's principles of public usage and names according to natural, narrative language in sentences with their grammar and syntax--or concordance title word transposition methods producing a combined subject and title "entry word" and, as possible, the economy of "title-a-line" entries. It implies multiple terms which are words or phrases. When the later indexing (considered in the next chapter) was first called correlative and then coordinate, there was confusion because while the indexing considered in this chapter is essentially association of terms, that in the next chapter is dissociation up to the point of actual retrieval. Pre-coordinate and post-coordinate then came into some British use to avoid ambiguity, but in American usage coordinate alone has usually meant the latter (i.e., post-coordinate).

Subject terms must of course be words, such as Crops as a noun in the plural, and Crop rotation as an adjectival phrase, with the prepositional phrase, Rotation of crops, and its inversion, Crops, Rotation of, as alternatives. Haykin in 1951 preferred prepositional phrase inversion to formal subdivision such as Crops - Rotation, as preserving "the integrity of the commonly used phrase," but there is also Crop rotation as an adjectival phrase.[171] LoC has Rotation of Crops with a see reference from Crop rotation and Crops, Rotation of, but going back to Cutter's Movement of fluids in plants as description, which was not a name, LoC used Plants, Motion of fluids in, along with Plants, Protection of; by contrast, it used Aeroplanes - Motors - Ignition and Aeroplanes - Turbojet engines - Ignition. These examples demonstrate the inconsistencies which have developed and persisted in dictionary cataloging over the course of a century.

Pre-Coordinate Indexing 175

With UDC numbers, pre-coordinate has been used with what have been called reversals, meaning permutations; the 1957 example from the Science Museum, London--575.17:591.3:599- has already been used with permutations for multiple entry of an item called <u>Genes in Mammalian Development</u>, the colon compound representing Genes (in relation to) Embryology (in relation to) Mammals, these verbal terms also being permutable. With three terms in any form six permutations are possible; only three are needed for each term as the first word, and the crude or simple method called "cyclic" or "rotating" has been used, which may be left to right (clockwise) or right to left (anti-clockwise) with reference to the first order, thus producing ABC, BCA, CAB, or ACB, CBA, BAC, these being only two out of the possible six. The development of systematic, consistent pre-coordination with permutation for multiple entry is shown in the following systems, beginning with Kaiser's, which had some special library use in Britain into the 1920s, and ending with Austin's PRECIS, which superseded Ranganathan's chain indexing in <u>BNB</u> about 1970. Something more is attempted in all of these systems besides mere multiple entry under the coordinated terms, and one--Sharp's SLIC--is mathematically a system of combinations, as distinguished from permutations.

Permutations are combinations, with arrangement as an added consideration. Combinations are simply combinations, without consideration for the arrangement of the combined terms. The use of selected permutations in IR might have been called "Selected Listing in Permutations," or SLIP; it wasn't, but in 1965 John R. Sharp introduced "Selected Listing in Combinations," or SLIC, and it may be true, as he said, that what are mathematically combinations are an alternative to permutations. However, he seems to be the only authority who has developed a combination system, and consideration of combinations as an alternative to permutations will be left until later in the chapter. Kaiser's, Farradane's, Coates', Sharp's and Austin's systems are considered in their chronological order.

7.2 <u>Kaiser's Systematic Indexing</u>

Kaiser's systematic indexing is so named after his book, <u>Systematic Indexing</u>, published in 1911 in London by Isaac Pitman & Sons Ltd., as the second and last volume in "The Card System Series." The first volume of this series, called <u>The Card System in the Office,</u> had been published in

London in 1908 by Kaiser himself. His starting and his finishing point was data processing and control in business by elaborate card indexing, which even as late as 1911 had some of the novelty that electronic data processing had fifty years later. The second volume was on commodities or goods and the use of the card system in their buying and selling; he hardly touched on services as commodities, and in his book was not greatly concerned with manufacture and thus with science and technology, although Kaiser himself, and others, did use his system for indexing in the fields of applied science and technology. On the title-page of Systematic Indexing he is described as Librarian of the Tariff Commission, but the only references to the Commission in his index are to an example of alphabetical arrangement and to two pictures of filing cabinets and card cabinets, with one or two men and three women at work. He does not seem to have thought of himself as a librarian, and certainly examined the bibliographically-based methods of librarianship and rejected what he conceived them to be. Had the terms been current he would have distinguished himself as a documentalist, or even more to his liking, as an information retrievalist. He said in his 1911 book that,

> this scheme of indexing was worked out in Philadelphia in 1896-1907, and after some years of constant application involving an index of some 50,000 cards it was rewritten in the light of experience gained.

References are many to his 1911 book and to its paragraph numbers; he did not give page numbers. His only further explanation was in an ASLIB Conference paper in 1926, also called "Systematic Indexing," reprinted in R. K. Olding's Readings in Library Cataloguing (Melbourne, 1966).

Julius Otto Kaiser (1868-1927) was born in Stuttgart, Germany, March 10, 1868; with his parents he went to Australia, and particularly to Brisbane, when he was nineteen, in 1887. His education was continued, and then he was a school teacher of languages and music until 1892, when he went to South America, and taught, until in 1895 he went to Philadelphia and was employed in the Philadelphia Commercial Museum. In 1899 he went to London and was employed on indexing by the Westinghouse Company, the Tariff Commission, Vickers Ltd., and Nobel's Explosive Company. In 1914, after war with Germany had begun in August, both his name and a somewhat Germanic or Prussian appearance, according to the popular image, made him unpopular, and his employ-

Pre-Coordinate Indexing 177

ment record may have made him officially suspect. He returned to America and was engaged on miscellaneous indexing work until he went into the employment of the Hercules Powder Company on January 10, 1927--"for the purpose of organizing the library and correspondence, and developing a central index of technical information"--only to be knocked down by an automobile on February 2 and to die of his injuries on February 4, 1927, just short of being 59. This biographical data is from an obituary notice in the house magazine of the Hercules Powder Company, the Hercules Mixer, March 1927 (p. 5).

In a paper he wrote for the ASLIB conference in 1926, he said he "was working the Dewey system at a Philadelphia library"--that of the Philadelphia Commercial Museum--"just thirty years ago," which would be 1895. Either he had had commercial experience in South America which gave him an informed commercial viewpoint, or he very quickly absorbed and rationalized a commercial viewpoint in the museum. He certainly doesn't read like the usual teacher turned librarian, common in librarianship then and later. He certainly had unusual powers of independent and analytical thought, along with some fixed and prejudiced ideas. For example, he seems to have been mathematically adept, yet remained to his death unable to reconcile himself with the ordinal or indicative use of zero in DDC's notation; to him zero was quantitative; it was nothing, and nothing couldn't or shouldn't be something. But his thinking about IR was thinking about what is now called IR, without entanglement in a bibliographical or librarianship tradition.

There seems to be no trace of what he did in the Philadelphia Museum. My inquiries at the Museum in 1964, and my later correspondence with the Museum revealed, if anything, less than the average knowledge of him and his thinking in America, which has been low. This has meant lack of evidence and knowledge about the development of his thinking, and his terminology, from about 1895-6 when, he said later, he first worked out his scheme, until 1911 when he published his Systematic Indexing, the principal source of information about it. In this there is a comparative study of classifications as a means of information indexing--which is still worth reading--and a much more superficial view of alphabetical cataloging; he shows knowledge of Cutter's classification but none of his Rules for a Dictionary Catalog.

This was not peculiar to Kaiser; what is peculiar is

his use of the term "concrete." Cutter had used this, and in 1895 was said to prefer the principle of concrete cataloging, in a sense very close to Kaiser's. This preference of Cutter's was cited in the preface to the ALA subject headings list of 1895, and it is quite likely that this was acquired and was discussed in the Philadelphia Commercial Museum at the time Kaiser was a new man on its staff. On the other hand, there appears to be nothing to disprove mere coincidence. Kaiser rejected hierarchical classification as a means of information indexing, and certainly had no thought that it should be a basis of all methods of information retrieval. He rejected cataloging, which he called "catchword," and opposed cataloging and indexing in a way which was common and has continued. But then, even of indexes (meaning alphabetical indexes) he said, "of available indexes in print,"

> they give entries under titles, authors and catchwords of books and ... of articles ... Even an article in a newspaper ... may treat on a subject or subjects ... entirely foreign to the indication at its head ... Subsidiary subjects are almost invariably drawn into an argument, and these in themselves may be the subject of our inquiry, but they are nowhere accounted for; printed indexes leave the contents almost entirely untouched.

Continuing his Introduction on this line, Kaiser said that information could not be limited to that in published literature; for the purposes of a business it must include correspondence and any other useful material: "We require an index to the information contained in our materials ... not a catalogue of publications," and "our" index must be so constituted that "we can exercise systematic control over the information.... You cannot buy a ready-made intelligence department on which to run your business."

> We shall take literature to pieces and rearrange the pieces systematically ... we must try to dissociate INFORMATION from literature; we do not want books, we want information, and although this information is contained in books, it should be looked upon as quite a different material and must be treated quite differently from books.

In a guessing competition, one might well place this statement at about 1953, with other writing about a new kind of literature needing a new method of indexing, in Mortimer

Pre-Coordinate Indexing 179

Taube and Associates' Studies in Coordinate Indexing, and in American Documentation. In fact, Kaiser's comments were contemporary with Hulme's finally stating his literary warrant theory in articles in the Library Association Record, 1911-12, and in the same city of London. Hulme was rejecting the "snippet" literature, which was Kaiser's meat and drink, so that Olding has argued that Hulme's literary warrant must be supplemented by an information warrant, and Olding's thinking is informed by a knowledge of Kaiser as well as of Hulme.

Kaiser could hardly not have known of the Patent Office Library off Chancery Lane, and may have met Hulme, but there is no evidence that they knew each other's work, and none that Kaiser took any interest in the Library Association. For convenience he was called a librarian, but as noted above, the Hercules Powder Company engaged him in 1927 "for the purposes of organizing the library and correspondence, and developing a central index of technical information." As in some later developments with coordinate indexing, the maintenance of a library and of an information index could be associated, even coordinated, but hardly integrated. In his 1911 book, Kaiser talked about the Intelligence Department of a business which his indexing was to serve. Then, in his chapter III on Literature, he said first that "Literature is a descriptive record ... the manner of recording is that of description by means of letters, hence literature." There is no nonsense here about identifying literature with imaginative or creative literature and treating informative literature as only something the cat dragged in. "What we record is what we OBSERVE, what we REASON OUT. The subjects of our observing and reasoning are THINGS in general, real or imaginary, and the conditions attaching to them. We shall call them CONCRETES AND PROCESSES respectively...." In more general terms these are "objects" and "aspects," which had already been distinguished by Cutter, though not to the same effect. Kaiser then identified these with names or terms, these being the forms or representations of things in literature and in indexing, and went on to distinguish a third category:

> we shall divide our stock of names or terms into those of CONCRETES, PROCESSES, and COUNTRIES, concretes being the commodities with which we are concerned, processes indicating their actions, and countries indicating the localities with which the concretes are connected.

In his Introduction Kaiser referred students to textbooks of logic, but without citing any particular one. He could have had in mind Mill's System of Logic, which was Hulme's authority; the logic of Kaiser's distinction of concrete and process is that of "Substance" and "Attribute," and logically he was never quite comfortable about country, because it seems really to be a sub-category of Substance or Concrete.

After his chapter III Kaiser examined classification and classification schemes, and indulged in one of his rare uses of sarcasm when he said about a UDC number at the point of 100,000 subdivisions that it had "only just emerged far enough from the fog to mistake an Icebreaker for a Ferryboat." He preferred what was basically Cutter's specific entry, but systematized exactly where Cutter had failed to systematize it, in subdivision of object by aspect. Kaiser's chapter IV on Classification may be dismissed, because for his purpose he dismissed classification, in the sense of the classifications of Dewey, Cutter, Brown, and Otlet's UDC. His chapter V is called Systematic Indexing, and is on the construction of entries, but it has to be read with chapter VI on Application to the Card Index. Three points of fundamental importance are his three categories of terms--Concrete, Country and Process--his citation order, and selected permutation.

There is always a minimum of two terms, Concrete and Process, and a maximum of three: Concrete, Country, Process. In an example he stated all the possible permutations of "Nitrate ... Chile ... Trade," which are six, as follows,

Nitrate...Chile...Trade	Chile...Nitrate...Trade
Nitrate...Trade...Chile	Trade...Nitrate...Chile
Chile...Trade...Nitrate	Trade...Chile...Nitrate

He had already argued that the process relationship to the concrete is an "of" relation, meaning a prepositional relationship requiring that there must be first the concrete; in pursuance of this, with reference to the phrases "Trade in nitrate" and "Trade of Chile," he said,

> it follows that concretes and countries are indispensable, while processes are not, for information on a process must include either a concrete or a country.

Pre-Coordinate Indexing

He admitted the possibility of exceptions to this only with great reluctance; a business might be only in one commodity, so only process would be relevant; or it could be restricted to only one country. The most important exception--of the business interested only in a process--he didn't seem to have realized, but then, given this assumption, it would only be interested in applications. However, Kaiser arrived at one practical rule: write as many cards for each statement as it contains concretes or countries. This implies multiple entry apart from permutation.

For the same item there were to be two entries, one under concrete and one under country, though not one under process. The selection of permutations was not based on any mathematical formula of cyclic permutation, or any theory of what Ranganathan and the Indo-British School called chain procedure, or any theory of single entry supported by cross reference. But there was also to be multiple entry if there were two concretes in the same item. Kaiser's example was the use of water power to generate electricity, in which waterpower and electricity are both concretes, and he arrived at two statements, or headings for entry, each with its process, <u>Waterpower - Application,</u> and <u>Electricity - Generating.</u> There was fudging on this, however, as there was also in a consistent, systematic distinction of concrete and process in that order. On the one hand Kaiser was insistent on no departure from names--though here he was in the eternal dilemma of his logical distinction--and the basic principle of known names in known order. But then, because rules without exceptions was a cherished principle of Kaiser's, he separated Agriculture into <u>Land - Cultivation,</u> and Bibliography into <u>Books - Description,</u> and even Education into <u>Children - Instruction.</u> Yet he had said,

> Our index contains information under NATURAL INDIGO, ARTIFICIAL INDIGO, SYNTHETIC INDIGO, and INDIGO. These terms have been drawn from various sources and for obvious reasons the indexer is not at liberty to change names.

Nevertheless, anticipating Ranganathan's distinction of "Fundamental Constituent Terms" and "Derived Composite Terms," he did change the names, in some cases, though not in all. Having said that use of waterpower for the generation of electricity meant two "statements" and so two entries, he admitted multiple-word concrete terms, including <u>Hydro electric power plant;</u> and although the order of "Sewing machine" is process-concrete, he concluded lamely that "sewing machine is one term although two words; for our purpose sewing is inseparable from machine."

Kaiser was in the same difficulty as Taube with his uniterms--that terms of logical consistency cannot be identified with single words; Taube had to accept what he called "bound" terms, what others called concepts. So, inconsistently, Kaiser both breached and accepted the principle of known names in known order. But most importantly he embraced multiple entry for the literary or bibliographical unit, because his unit of entry was neither literary nor bibliographical; it was subject itself, which he called concrete. He gave an example of an article, only a page of his book in length, which was itself a snippet from another periodical; the article was titled "How paper affects metal." As a whole Kaiser thought Wrapping paper - Chemical action would be sufficient for it, but then went on to list the concretes in it, with differing processes, which could be analytically indexed, such as Wrapping Paper - Composition, Silver ware - Corrosion, "etc. etc.," according to different standpoints or interests. And he not only indexed; in his own words, he "reconstituted the information." His statement or heading, for him, was information; for example, Sheep - Australia - Shearing would in itself be information that sheep were being shorn in Australia, which might therefore be a market for shears. There was then on his card an "amplification," which could be the whole information, or an abstract which he called a "condense," and the reference. He also had his own formal method of upward and downward references on guide cards, which need not be considered here, but is worth study.

What was right and/or wrong with Kaiser's Systematic Indexing? It was not a general system of information indexing; but then, he didn't say that it was, and he certainly didn't label himself as a librarian. What was wrong with it as a general system was his absolute distinction of concrete and process; that is, not only as a distinction of relationship but as a fundamental distinction of terms. His processes were not processes merely because of their "of" relation to his concretes; they were in an "of" relation because they were processes. But Ranganathan, a boy of three when Kaiser went to Philadelphia, later fell into the same error with his fundamental category of Personality, and only scrambled out of it with his later second rounds of Personality in his Energy category, and then with the generalized "isolate" idea of fundamental terms, taken, at least in name, from Farradane, who mentions Kaiser in his ancestry.

The Indo-British School made much of Kaiser in post-Cutter development because, according to Coates, he was one of three who made attempts to get "to closer grips with the problem of the relative significance of the various components of a compound subject";[174] the other two, according to Coates, were Ranganathan and Farradane. He said "the basis of Kaiser's scheme and that devised from Ranganathan's 'facets' is the classification of isolated terms into categories." The isolated terms are then what Farradane called "isolates." There is something in this, as long as Kaiser is not cast in the role of stumbling forerunner, along with Cutter and Dewey.

There were other elements which were quite alien; Kaiser's system, above all, was not a single entry system, which is an important practical difference, and there is no reason to suppose that he would not have rejected Ranganathan's Colon Classification as he did earlier ones, including UDC with its colon punctuation relations. Moreover, Kaiser was not concerned with a compound subject of a literary unit or document; he was concerned with a simple object, his concrete. He qualified this with the process he felt it must have, but only with one term, and the same was true with his country limitation. He said nothing of specification of a document's subject, every jot and tittle and so on, and found his limitations not in the document but in user interest.

Had he not died as the result of injuries in an early automobile accident, he could have lived, as Hulme did, into the coordinate indexing period, about 1950, and it is far more likely that he would have thought himself a forerunner of co-ordinate indexing than of facet classification. But in his time he was the contradiction both of UDC and of Hulme's literary warrant. He did not maintain consistency in the distinction of his concretes and processes and of subject names, as he intended, and his concrete-country-process formula was too rigid, perhaps even for his limited field; but he did distinguish subject names, in his statements or headings, from the summaries of information he called amplifications, and he did not confuse them in the coextensive heading. He did not establish a school because, although he wrote a book, he was not a propagandist, and although he had to deal with bibliography and librarianship, he remained a business systems man or analyst. He did not begin with a bibliographical bias; he never had one.

7.3 Farradane's Isolates and Their Relations[175]

Farradane's theory is one of what he called "isolates" in information or knowledge, and of relations between them, which he distinguished as "operators." He related this theory to both classification and indexing and its practical applications in a 1950 paper and in a 1952 supplement. In the latter he increased his relations or operators from four to nine, with elaboration of his ideas of developmental psychology rather than logic as their basis. Neither in these papers nor others does he seem to have arrived at any practical applications of his general theory to classification in the usual sense of hierarchical classification; he did offer a method of alphabetical indexing. Broadly, he seems to have thought of distinction of isolates as an inductive way of arriving at the material to be classified, as opposed to the divisive method traditionally applied to the whole body of preconceived tree of knowledge; however, classification is not in question here.

He seems to have been the first user of the term "isolate" in IR, and even its coiner for any use other than as a verb. Ranganathan preceded him as a writer, and was an influence on his thinking in some respects. Farradane was a signatory to the British Classification Research Group's 1955 "Memorandum on the Need for a Faceted Classification" as the basis of all methods of information retrieval, which, after generally adopting facet analysis as a means of arriving at subject categories, devoted a paragraph to "another technique of analysis, developed by Farradane." With his own system, Farradane was always an odd man out in the Indo-British School. In his alphabetical indexing he did not derive his indexing terms from a classification. And Ranganathan's use of the term isolate has its own twist and seems later than Farradane's. Farradane said of Ranganathan's Colon Classification that,

> in providing a system of conjunction of related subjects ... [it] still remains partly dependent upon an initial group of arbitrarily selected headings, and the relations are not accurately characterizable.

Of Kaiser's systematic indexing his criticism (along with some praise) was that it led "to oversimplification of relations; and consequently unwieldy types of concepts." It may be worth noticing that Kaiser used the words isolated and relationship when he said,

Pre-Coordinate Indexing

isolated terms must be connected, brought into relationship, so that we shall be able to report fully on any subject required.

But this is not dealing with relation of subject terms.

Farradane went on to what he called "items of knowledge," but this may be ambiguous; speaking of classification and concepts he said,

> an item of knowledge will thus be an object or class of objects, a process or class of processes, or an abstract term or class of such terms, which is clearly, and, at its own level of complexity, uniquely definable, as far as may be possible. Any other item would in reality be composed of two or more concepts, leading to logical confusions. Let us call these items, as defined, isolates.

So his items of knowledge are his isolates, and he was particularly interested in "all possible relations between them, including interactions of any kind." But his isolates have to be individually definable; they have to be words or names, or terms. Objects and processes may interact, for example sheep and their shearing, but to what extent and in what way do terms interact? They have relations of a grammatical, of a logical, kind and of an IR kind, one modifying another, but do they have the interactions which some physical counterparts may have? Farradane's isolates are what are usually meant by terms, which are the subjects of items of information, singly or in some combinations. And his examples indicate that his items of information were the usual literary or bibliographical items, mainly articles in periodicals.

This is important in distinguishing Farradane from Kaiser; his isolates may be identified with Kaiser's concretes and processes as distinctions of elements of subjects, but they do not for him distinguish items of information. He went on to speak of his system of being of the greatest value, "in preparing an index of scientific literature, in particular ... because scientific papers mostly concern one subject at a time." He meant subjects which could be compounds of terms or isolates, in what he called "analets." A statement in syntactical form, such as that "cats eat mice," could be turned into one that "mice are food for (or of) cats," and this into one that "cats' food equals mice." This then can be written for IR purposes as Cats - Food - Mice, or Cats -

Feeding - Mice, with any variation of punctuation such as the colon. The relation of the terms or isolates can be understood, although as far as possible only the noun as a grammatical form, or the adjectival phrase, is used; verbs are eliminated, but there may be prepositions and these are in fact disguised in his signs of operation or relation. By means of this "analysis of statements," Farradane produced an "analet," which represents the statement of an item of information. This again is not Kaiser's taking literature to pieces and dissociating information from it; Kaiser did not relate three terms except when there was geographical limitation, as in his Nitrates - Chile - Trade relation; otherwise he related only two. Perhaps, as Farradane said, Kaiser oversimplified relations, but in such a subject as "mice as food for cats," however expressed, Kaiser would have recognized two concretes, cats and mice, and two processes to make two of his statements or subject headings, Cats - Feeding, and perhaps Mice - Uses, for two entries for the same item of information. The final result may, however, be much the same, because Farradane was not a single entry man; he allowed permutations of his analets, and so could allow at least three entries for Cats - Food - Mice. His major interest was relations distinctions--in the example cited, between cats and food, and between food and mice.

Farradane began with four distinctions of relation between two isolates; these he called operators, with typewritten distinguishing signs as follows: $\neq$ for the equivalence operator; /[for the "appertaining to" or appurtenance operator; /- for the reaction operator; and /: for the casual operator. The diagonal or slash sign is common and equivalent to a dash or colon; the bracket indicates direction of appurtenance. For example, in Cats/[Food/Mice, the bracket shows that the food appertains to the cat; this applies also to the other signs, with the exception of the equals sign which is in a neutral position. Another of his examples is Structure]/Dextran:/Sucrose-/Leuconostoc, the analet of "Structure of the dextran synthesized from sucrose by Leuconostoc"; in this the structure appertains to the dextran, presumably caused or synthesized from sucrose, by its reaction with Leuconostoc. Farradane was Scientific Information Officer in a sugar company's laboratories, and it becomes apparent that if these distinctions of relations or reactions between things are important for IR, then technical knowledge in specialized fields may be necessary. Another example was Morphine/-Respiratory centre]/Rabbit, for the "Action of morphine on the respiratory centre of rabbits." The morphine reacts on

Pre-Coordinate Indexing

or affects the respiratory centre of the rabbit. These examples show that relation is independent of order. The food is the food of cats, though the order is Cats/[Food; the structure is the structure of dextran, and in Structure]/Dextran the sign is reversed; if in a permutation the order were Dextran /[Structure, then, as shown, the sign is reversed.

The system isn't easy, though perfection might come with practice, and might, as Farradane said, be left at least in part to clerks, and then perhaps to machines. In particular, permutation isn't easy, especially with analets in which there are square-bracketed interpolations. Finally, as it seems in reading, he said,

> ... alphabetical arrangement of the analets, and their permutations, according to their first isolates, provides a complete and entirely logical subject index of the available material.

But then it appears, almost by the way, that the operator notation is not for use in a published index,

> The material can easily be analysed in card index form in the first place. The conversion into a printed index as, for example, for an abstracts journal, is a simple matter, the choice of the short connecting words between the isolates, where necessary, being as a rule obvious; for example: 'Bauxite/[Aluminium-/Production/[Electrolytic Process' is 'Bauxite, Aluminium by electrolytic process form'.... It will be seen that these versions form normal index entries.... The logical discipline provided by the construction of analets renders correct indexing a simple process, with certainty of logical order and completeness of cross referencing, as far as may be desired.

This is a rather cursory and questionable assertion about normal and correct indexing, and certainly about "logical order and completeness of cross-referencing, as far as may be desired." One interesting contrast is that between his repeated assertions of a logical product and his assertions that the foundations of his relations are not drawn from logic.

Besides square bracketing there is round bracketing; for example, "Technical editing" becomes Editing, (technical) ≠ Career]/Chemists, because technical is not considered an essential indexing word or not one that should come first; in purely verbal expression, it should come last, with this result: "Editing, Career for chemists of, technical," which reads like title concordance indexing and title-a-line economy in their heyday. Why not "Chemists - Careers - Editing, Technical," with more punctuation but no prepositions? However, on the logic of the system generally and beginning with the Cats/Food ≠ Mice example, mice are not the only food of cats, and Farradane himself said the equivalence may be only partial, when there is no conflict; but mice are a species of the food of cats--why not then, with much talk of logic, a genus-species relation in the system? Even with his operators extended from four to nine, there does not seem to be provision for this relation, and no discussion of it, even though it has been the most used relation in IR.

In his 1952 supplementary paper Farradane showed awareness of symbolic logic, offering his "logical" rules as "the basis of a new type of experimentally based symbolic logic expressing scientific method." Whatever it might be (and it could be symbolic), it was hardly logic--i.e., the science of reasoning--in the scientific or any other method. A majority of Farradane's analets seem to result in a hierarchical, or dependence, or specificity order of terms, as in cats, food, mice. When they don't, a question may be raised; for example, why Morphine, Respiratory centre, Rabbits; why not Respiration, Drug effects, Morphine, Rabbits? The statement, "The action of morphine on the respiratory centre of rabbits," seems to be a title, and some of Farradane's conversions seem to be no better than title entry in title term order. The original statement of the Dextran example reads "Structure of the dextran synthesized from sucrose by Leuconostoc"; the conversion begins Structure]/Dextran. But what if the original statement had read "Dextran structure with synthesis from sucrose by Leuconostoc?" In 1960 Coates concluded,

> The system ... offers no rule for component order in a neutral subject catalogue. It does, however, once the desired component has been chosen as entry word, prescribe logical limits on the way in which the remaining terms may be arranged. [176]

There is, however, danger of ambiguity in Farradane's insisting on something being logical while also insisting that its foundations are not those of logic. In 1962 Coates was still interested in what may be called "guidelines" for what he

Pre-Coordinate Indexing 189

called "concrete-abstract order of terms," but he had concluded that the omission of actual relational terms was of little importance for IR purposes. And in 1965, J. R. Sharp, while crediting Farradane with a contribution to semantic research, himself adopted alphabetical as a standard arrangement of combined terms.[177] First and last, classes and subclasses of literature are being indexed according to the subject characteristic; it may be desirable to index in an increasing order of specification or specificity of the literature, but do Farradane's operational relations of actual things give much help in this? Isn't there a basic confusion? He does not seem to have published any development of his scheme since 1952.

7.4 Coates' Chain Procedure Cross Reference

Coates' chain procedure cross reference in alphabetico-specific indexing was exemplified in the British Technology Index (1962)[178] of which he became the Editor, and which he presumably devised. He had previously been Chief Subject Cataloguer of the British National Bibliography, and had made himself an authority on its chain procedure classifying and indexing, and on the possibilities of the derivation or adaptation from it of some form of direct alphabetical cataloging or indexing. He wrote on these topics particularly in an article in 1957 on "The Use of B. N. B. in Dictionary Cataloguing," and in his 1960 book, Subject Catalogues: Headings and Structure.[179]

Here is an example from BTI, 1962, of single entry under a coextensive heading,

> POTATOES, Fungicides, Triphenyltin acetate, residues
>
> Triphenyltin acetate residues on potato leaves in blight spraying trails. G. A. Lloyd, C. Otaci & F. T. Last. J. of Science of Food & Agriculture, 13 (Jul 62) p. 355-8. refs.

Here are see references to the heading, and so to the entry,

> RESIDUES, Triphenyltin acetate, Fungicides, Potatoes. See POTATOES, Fungicides, Triphenyltin acetate, Residues

TRIPHENYLTIN ACETATE, Fungicides, Potatoes.
See POTATOES, Fungicides, Triphenyltin acetate

FUNGICIDES, Potatoes. See POTATOES, Fungicides.

With these headings in alphabetical order, no reference, of course, is needed from POTATOES to POTATOES. This item does not appear in BNB, which is not an index of periodical articles as BTI is, but if it were in BNB its entry in the classified section would be like this:

633.491[1] - Fungicides. Triphenyltin acetate. Residues

[entry]

BNB's subject indexing for this item, in its alphabetical author, title and subject section, would have been like this before its chain indexing was dropped for PRECIS (considered below):

Residues: Triphenyltin acetate:	
Fungicides: Potatoes	633.491[1]
Triphenyltin acetate: Fungicides:	
Potatoes	633.491[1]
Fungicides: Potatoes	633.491[1]
Potatoes: Agriculture	633.491[1]

There has to be indexing of Potatoes, in the aspect class, Agriculture, which includes Potatoes, and the class number for Potatoes in Agriculture. The figure one in square brackets was the standard sign in BNB for verbal extensions, when the class number from DDC was not sufficiently extended; these verbal extensions are necessary to make the coextensive heading or number, for what is more often than not the only item requiring such specification.

As pointed out just above, a cross reference from Potatoes is not necessary in BTI because this is the specific entry heading. This is common to both Cutter and Coates, although in Cutter's sense Coates is not always as specific as Cutter in his entry word. The essence of chain procedure, however, in both BNB's classified single entry indexing and in BTI's alphabetical single entry cross referencing, seems the same. There is what Ranganathan has called a "Forward rendering of the terms of a compound subject," as heading

Pre-Coordinate Indexing

for an item entry; then there is the reverse rendering of this, reduced term by term or "link by link" in the "chain" so that each term in the reverse order, from most specific to most general, is the entry word for item indexing or cross reference, this indexing or cross reference being intended to take the place of what otherwise would have to be multiple or added entries. Coates' own example in the 1962 volume was:

COTTON, BLEACHING, HYDROGEN PEROXIDE

HYDROGEN PEROXIDE, Bleaching, Cotton
    See COTTON, Bleaching, Hydrogen peroxide

BLEACHING, Cotton, See COTTON, Bleaching.

The method he compared this with was entry under each term separately. But certainly more commonly used about that time would be the method employed in the Wilson Applied Science and Technology Index. Using Bleaching, cotton, with a see reference from Cotton bleaching, it also refers from Bleaching materials to particular materials, and enters items on "Bleaching Cotton with Hydrogen peroxide" under Bleaching, Cotton and under Hydrogen peroxide. Whatever BTI's advantages, the inquirer looking under Bleaching doesn't find a reference there to "Bleaching materials including Hydrogen peroxide." The see reference system is analogous to chain procedure for particular entry headings, in this case Cotton, Bleaching, Hydrogen peroxide. Ranganathan's claims for it as his facet analysis applied to subject heading have been examined in chapter 6.[180] The PRECIS permutation system has satisfactorily superseded Ranganathan's chain procedure in BNB and has been considered as suitable for direct alphabetical indexing, but the chain procedure might be considered as suitable for periodical indexing, despite the many special claims made for BTI which are hardly relevant to what seem to be the essence and defects of the chain procedure method.

7.5 Sharp's Selective Listing in Combination[181]

In his book, Some Fundamentals of Information Retrieval (1965), J. R. Sharp found himself involved in coordinate indexing, and so with symbolic logic or Boolean algebra, or the calculus of classes. He explained the "logical sum, difference and product" of symbolic logic, using Venn diagrams, and then went on to say,

> if we ignore the problems of provision for search-
> ing for logical sums and logical differences and can
> solve the problem of providing for retrieval by the
> logical product of any number of the elements of a
> subject designation which are used in indexing, then
> we have solved the major problem.

This became a premise of his SLIC, as explained in his book and more simply and briefly in a short article in American Documentation. His combinations, it should be made clear, are mathematically different from permutations. In his book he argued and stated his combination principle in mathematical terms, and took as a suitable subject--"to demonstrate the working of this principle"--"the lift produced by blown flaps during take-off." There may be one or more items on this particular subject to be entered under or indexed by combinations of its terms. "Descent produced by blown flaps during landing" would be another subject with one or more related items using different terms. A limited universe of discourse seems taken for granted, but there may be assumed to be a cross reference from Aeroplanes or some intermediate term to Take-off, and perhaps others. Sharp was demonstrating term combination at a point of specificity. He continued:

> the elements in the compound heading can be con-
> sidered to be LIFT, BLOWING, FLAPS, TAKE-
> OFF. As we have to cite each combination in a
> standard order, alphabetical is the obvious one to
> use and we may as well cite them in this order be-
> fore we begin to make selections: BLOWING:
> FLAPS: LIFT: TAKE-OFF.

This alphabetical horizontal order for the terms of compound headings may be considered standard for the SLIC system, but is not a standard or starting order for combinations or permutations in other systems, in which the order has been one of relation and increasing specificity of the subject. Sharp's formula gave a maximum of 15 combinations, consisting of four single terms, six dual, four triple and one quadruple term, as follows:

Blowing	Blowing: Flaps	Blowing: Flaps: Lift
Flaps	Blowing: Lift	Blowing: Flaps: Take-off
Lift	Blowing: Take-off	Blowing: Lift: Take-off
Take-off	Flaps: Lift	Flaps: Lift: Take-off
	Flaps: Take-off	

Pre-Coordinate Indexing

      Lift: Take-off

      Blowing: Flaps: Lift: Take-off

As many of these as are finally used are arranged in alphabetical order--which may be called vertical--and are, of course, inserted into a general alphabetical arrangement, which in a specialized aeronautical index might range from Aerobatics to Zeppelins.

With 15 possible combinations the problem, as in other systems, was reduction, or economy. Sharp said:

> Bearing in mind that our purpose is to provide for certain retrieval by reference to a single place in the file regardless of whether we search for any one, two, three, or all four of the terms ... suppose we seek information on 'lift produced by flaps.' The relevant search terms are obviously 'lift' and 'flaps,' and if we arrange these in alphabetical order, FLAPS: LIFT, and consult the file at this point, we find that there are two relevant entries, one comprising the two terms plus the term 'take-off.' The philosophy of these principles has been based on the premise that we will accept any entry provided it includes the search terms, regardless of whether any additional terms appear with them.

He had rejected, at least as a minor need, retrieval of logical sums and logical differences, by which he meant A + B not related, and A and B perhaps related, such as Blowing and Flaps, but not take-off. He went even further when he declared, in effect, that finding stated search terms regardless of whether any additional terms appear with them is desirable;

> Indeed, our purpose is to make this specific provision and it is this which conventional systems do not normally give, and which is the very raison d'être of non-conventional systems.

His system distinction here may not be quite clear. He seemed to treat BTI as a conventional system, yet in it such a cross reference as "Bleaching, Cotton see Cotton, Bleaching" leads to all extensions of the latter. Similarly, if one looks up "Gas" in LC cataloging, Gas, Natural is found with it, Gas, Natural - Pipelines with this, and Gas, Natural -

Pipelines - Taxation with this; also Aeroplanes leads to Aeroplanes - Jet propulsion, with here the further subheading, - Air intake.

Let us arrange Sharp's maximum combinations alphabetically and number them like this:

1 Blowing
2 Blowing: Flaps
3 Blowing: Flaps: Lift
4 Blowing: Flaps: Lift: Take-off
5 Blowing: Flaps: Take-off
6 Blowing: Lift
7 Blowing: Lift: Take-off
8 Blowing: Take-off
9 Flaps
10 Flaps: Lift
11 Flaps: Lift: Take-off
12 Flaps: Take-off
13 Lift
14 Lift: Take-off
15 Take-off

If we proceed to eliminate, using "10 Flaps: Lift" and "11 Flaps: Lift: Take-off" to illustrate--if 11 is used to index both items on Flaps and Lift and items on Flaps and Lift and Take-off, it does not matter if the latter are found in a search for the former (it may in fact be found interesting by the inquirer), so "10 Flaps: Lift" is not necessary. Proceeding this way, in order from 1 to 15, the first three are not necessary, because all of them are in 4 in the same order, with only the addition of Take-off; in this way, 1, 2, 3, 6, 9, 10, and 13 can be eliminated, leaving only the following:

4 Blowing: Flaps: Lift: Take-off
5 Blowing: Flaps: Take-off
7 Blowing: Lift: Take-off
8 Blowing: Take-off
11 Flaps: Lift: Take-off
12 Flaps: Take-off
14 Lift: Take-off
15 Take-off

On the distinction of "conventional" and "non-conventional" as applicable to his own system he also said,

> though this is a matter of combinations, and such indexing might perhaps be better called 'combination indexing,' the principle of 'logical products' of the selected terms is a legitimate way of regarding the method, and as logical sums and logical differences can also be provided, the expression 'co-ordinate indexing' is now generally used for systems which make such provision.

But the necessary implication of symbolic logic in this coordinate indexing, meaning post-coordinate here, has been questioned. Basically SLIC seems to be a pre-coordinate system which cannot be grouped with post-coordinate systems.

Attempting to make it clear--perhaps not without error--may have made Sharp's system seem difficult, even impractical, but all systems tend to seem like this until they are studied and practiced. Sharp gave a fairly simple description and rules in his American Documentation account, even for those for whom permutations and combinations seem like higher, if not highest, mathematics; and it certainly seems simpler than a coordinate system heavily laden with roles and links such as the E. J. C.-Battelle system, or an unconventional, "conventional" alphabetical system such as BTI's. Sharp seems to have shown that his system can be mechanized and computerized to the point of print-out of a page-form index, and it is a weakness that post-coordinate indexing cannot be done in page form, and that page-form adaptations of conventional alphabetical indexing from it do not have the associations of terms which are the advantage of page-form pre-coordinate indexes.

Sharp's SLIC, Selected Listing in Combination, has a close rival in what might be called SLIP, for Selected Listing in Permutations, which is already known in several more or less loose forms, mathematically speaking. Sharp has made a contribution in his study of combinations and permutations, and of course in his development of a mathematically sound combination system, but his is a selective system, and does not seem as easily workable as the SLIP system.

7.6 Austin's PRECIS[182]

PRECIS is an acronym for Preserved Context Index System. It results in systematic permutation exemplified by ABCD, BACD, CBAD, DCBA. This, however, is set out in two lines, an upper and a lower beginning as A, BCD. Austin and Butcher, in a BNB publication in 1969, used the subtitle, "a rotated subject index system," but rotated had been used in different senses, and the PRECIS method has since been called "shunting." Permutation selection could, of course, be haphazard, the only requirement being that any one of the permutations beginning with each term should be used. One purpose is simply to insure that each term is used as an entry term and this can be made systematic by the cyclic method; but there can be other factors determining selection, and preserving context became one, involving linguistic and semantic considerations, and in purpose the development was more complicated than this.

PRECIS seems to have arisen out of the unsuitability of BNB's chain procedure indexing for conversion to a MARC system, i.e., one producing machine-readable copy, to be produced by computer, and read or printed or projected by computer. Austin, who seems to be regarded as its principal author, had worked with classification interests of the kind set out in the CRG Memorandum of 1955, in favor of faceted classification systems based on a classified schedule. But if a subject index for BNB could not be based on Ranganathan's chain procedure and had to be a systematic alphabetical subject index of terms giving only class numbers and location reference, with computer requirements of logic and consistency, thinking had to be turned to linguistics and semantics. This thinking can be studied in papers and a book by Austin. One emerging need with even simpler requirements was the reduction of each item's subject to terms, and the already established coextensive subject cataloging idea of specific entry as established by Ranganathan and Coates had to be considered. The coextensive subject expression could not be derived from an hierarchical classification, however, to provide a systematic and consistent method of permutation.

The ABCD generalization may, then, be misleading; at least it is not given as a starting point. A term order for each subject has to be determined on principles calculated to express context, to allow its preservation in permutation, and to facilitate computerization. One example is:

United States. Library school. Teachers. Recruitment.

The computer is programmed to begin by recording these in positions called "Lead," "Qualifier," and "Display," and what is called the string becomes, for another entry:

United States
Library schools, Teachers Recruitment

Next Library Schools becomes the lead, with United States the qualifier on the top line:

Library schools. United States.
Teachers Recruitment

Pre-Coordinate Indexing 197

This continues until there is only one line consisting of lead and qualification and display:

Recruitment. Teachers. Library Schools. United States.

There are then four permutations, out of a possible total of $4 \times 3 \times 2 = 24$, but each begins with a different term, and is still in context, left or right, with the order of the original string. On various grounds, including differing experience, it is possible to be critical of the order of the original string, but what is to be remembered is that context is maintained, and every one of the four terms is a lead to the indexing, and every entry will have the same location number, possibly 020.71173, independent of the indexing.

The system has had gratifying adoptions and has attracted international attention, although there has been some questioning, for example of its suitability for indefinitely cumulating dictionary catalogs, without some selection. Of course, some items will only require one term, and some only two, and so on; but there may still be some desirable application of Cutter's principle of dividing or subheading entries under headings only when the entries are numerous. There are verbal problems with PRECIS, too, some of which have been considered and solutions offered. Clearly, neither the use and acceptance of PRECIS, nor the doubts about it for some situations will be settled by 1976.

Chapter 8

POST-COORDINATE INDEXING AND MECHANIZATION

8.1 Definitions and Limitations

The terms "post- and pre-coordinate" avoid possible ambiguity. Pre-coordinate indexing has already been considered and seems to fall clearly within the ambit of contrast to what have been called conventional. Pre-coordinate systems might, however, themselves be called established systems compared with the post-coordinate systems which began about 1960-61, and they are still in wider use. Pre-coordinate systems, still developing as shown by Austin's PRECIS system of permutation, are in the established class if one uses the positive definition that they are systems with already complete, though not necessarily unique entries, in predetermined orders distinguished as alphabetical and classified. These seemed to divide the IR world into two parts, a true dichotomy, nothing else being conceived until the development of post-coordinate created a trichotomy, a Gaul in three parts.

Bernier distinguished what he and others were still calling correlative indexes from alphabetical indexes, saying that they enabled "simultaneous correlation of two or more terms not necessarily in alphabetical order." He went on to say that they differed from classified indexes in that subjects represented by single or correlated terms are usually not arranged in hierarchies; this, however, may need some qualification. Once terms with entries under them in some form have been correlated to produce term coordination, what may be done with the product by way of further indexing does not seem to affect the basic question of their term arrangement for coordinated recovery; and while terms in isolation may have to have some arrangement and/or indexing so as to be found for coordination, the form of this does not matter and in some examples has been according to the schedules of a conventional classification.

Post-Coordinate Indexing

Maltby, in an added chapter for his 4th edition (1967) of Sayers' Manual, said that "unlike classification, co-ordinate indexing techniques do not attempt to map out knowledge in a systematic pattern." Six pages later, in the same chapter, however, he adds that "co-ordinate indexing systems make more use of classification and classificatory principles than some of their supporters might wish to confess," although he goes on to show that he does not mean the established and accepted library sense of classification.[183] Needham, in his Organizing of Knowledge (1964), in a short end chapter on "other retrieval devices," having already described the best and only commonly known post-coordinate system at that time--a "term entry" or "item on term system"--said that "it is important to note that term entry devices do not obviate the need for classification--whatever claims to that effect may have been made at one time ... in fact, some classification and standardization of terminology is needed." Needham does seem to have classification in the established library sense in mind as the necessary source. But, of course, it was not easy for those who saw the CRG faceted classification as the established basis for all IR methods to drop it without some salvaging.[184]

However, considering differences, it may not be apparent that when an inquirer correlates or coordinates two or more terms--as in some relation which for him has subject interest, and on which he wants to retrieve information--whatever the method by which he might retrieve or have items of information finally retrieved for him, there has to be anticipatory cataloging or indexing. An information item may be term-indexed in some way as one on "Scurvy or Scorbutus," "Limejuice," "Vitamin C," and "Acne" and "Zinc oxide"; but there is not what has been considered in the previous chapter as pre-coordination of either the first three or the second two for established alphabetical cataloging. Nevertheless, it is cataloging or indexing as a human mental procedure, expressed in the devices used for post-coordination. With A, B, C as terms which he knows are or may be related, an inquirer can go to any established type of catalog looking for these terms as headings of the pre-coordinated kind, and direct alphabetical arrangement or an alphabetically indexed classified arrangement will reveal fairly shortly what there is in the collection in which he might hope to find something. He does not have to go through some matching or sorting process, with the possibility, as it were, of nothing out of the slot, or what have been called "false drops." It is, therefore, desirable to have a list of terms in the particular system available for prior consultation; this has become known as a "thesaurus" and will later be considered separately.

While indexing for post-coordination and post-coordination itself are functionally related, they should not be confused; attempted simplification in either can produce difficulty and inefficiency in the other. Bernier first came across a form of correlative index in the thirties; a man named C. W. Foulk "prepared an index in which serial numbers assigned to a private file of reprints were recorded in numerical order on cards bearing single terms related to the subject matter of the reprints. Selection of the reprints (shelved in numerical order) was effected by comparing serial numbers on two cards bearing terms related to the subject(s) of the reprints sought. Identical numbers found on both cards were the serial numbers of reprints related to subjects associated simultaneously with both terms. This is one type of manipulative correlative index. 'Manipulative' in this case refers to the selection of cards bearing terms pertinent to the search and the process of comparing their serial numbers ... the term 'manipulative' is taken to exclude manipulations which are usual in searching alphabetical indexes and classifications."[185] Manipulation in its literal sense, and in derivation, means "handling," in the literal sense of that term, but there have been complications with what may be called appliances, and then with machines--first with punched card sorting machines and then with computers. Foulk handled his cards with term headings and item numbers on them, and this exemplified what sellers of systems hoped would be a major field. Gerald Jahoda in 1960 presented a useful DLS thesis at Columbia University on "Correlative Indexing Systems for the Control of Research Records," and in 1970 his Information Storage and Retrieval Systems for Individual Researchers, on both conventional indexes and (post) coordinate indexes, was published by Wiley. In 1967 A. C. Foskett published A Guide to Personal Indexes Using Edge-notched and Peek-a-boo Cards (Melbourne: Cheshire). Both books dealt with indexing systems involving appliances used with specially prepared cards. However, though books on systems for personal use are published, it is not apparent that many of those who take up a system for purely personal use persist with their indexing and manipulation.

Manipulation does not make post-coordinate systems suitable for miscellaneous reader use, and substitutes for the established alphabetical or classified catalog have not been found adaptable to page- and card-form catalogs, indexes

Post-Coordinate Indexing

and bibliographies. The scope, or field of practical and economic use, of post-coordinate systems is limited, but they have had their uses, though perhaps with not always intended limitations. These uses have been mainly in special indexing on a comparatively small scale, and for auxiliary purposes in an ordinary library; possibilities and needs for auxiliary indexing of special materials increased in the period of development of post-coordinate systems during and after the 1939-45 war. Two early and different systems were Batten's Optical Coincidence System in Britain, which also became known as Peek-a-boo, especially in America, and the American system which its developer or inventor, Mooers, called Zatocoding.

Development from earlier and different uses is not always obvious or certain. In the classification chapter of his Principles of Science, however, Jevons in 1874 did distinguish what he called diagnostic systems of classification, with particular reference to George Bentham's "Analytical key to the natural orders and anomalous genera of British flora," in his Handbook of British Flora (1866), and Jevons said that Linnaeus appeared familiar with the idea under the name "Synopsis."[186] The characteristics by which plants became scientifically classified are not obvious, but more superficial characteristics would be used to enable amateurs to understand the scientific classification. They may then be diagnosis from characteristics which are not superficially obvious, employing the method of syllogistic argument in logic, as in: "all conductors of electricity are metals or metallic; this is metallic, therefore a conductor; but on this infallible test it does not conduct, therefore it cannot be a metallic substance." An appliance for identifying birds from their appearance was the use of a printed transparent overlay over a printed card, so that obvious characteristics such as a curved beak and white feathers with sulphur crest would identify the bird known as a sulphur crested cockatoo; comparable devices seem to have come into some use for mineral prospecting, and a patent was taken out in America by Taylor in 1915 for a selective device for bird identification.

Post-coordinate indexing devices may be generalized as diagnostic classification devices, it being understood that this is not the systematic relation and association of subjects which librarians commonly call classification. In the more numerous of these IR devices, items which have been recorded as on terms, and as on the same terms, have to be diagnosed--these are what have been distinguished as "item on term" devices; the less numerous but perhaps more useful devices, which can diagnose whether an item is on certain terms, have been called "term on item" devices. Devices emerged in the forties without it being immediately apparent that they were of a kind or a sub-kind. That they developed from such devices as Taylor's in 1915 is surmise, but if--as seems more likely--there was independent development, this does not preclude essential likeness, even going back to Jevons' diagnostic classification of 1874, although this does not seem to have been suggested. Although Jevons went on to distinguish alphabetical arrangements of names as index classification useful in librarianship and bibliography, he did not anticipate IR methods which might be essentially what he called diagnostic classification.

Well known "item on term" systems have been those called optical coincidence or peek-a-boo, in which optical coincidence is an indirect method of item number coincidence and direct number coincidence systems; "term on term" systems have been edge-notched card systems with needle sorting or vibrator sorting, and punched card systems. Computerized systems seem to be in a class by themselves, but in principle they are nearest to "item on term" because there is a linking of terms with items--that is, identifying descriptions of actual items, for which the name data base may be used--although data retrieval has been distinguished from bibliographical item retrieval. A computer may have what, in effect, is an index of, say, "debtors" linked to the store of data about them--their creditors and so on. This use of a data store to which reference may be made for more than one fact or set of facts is part of computer economy; for example, if a bibliographical item base gives authors' names, titles, and subjects, as the usual catalog card does, then it may be consulted within the computer for author as well as subject information. Computer techniques, however, are not considered in detail here.

The "item on term" and "term on item" methods to be considered have been most economically used with material which could be found by numbers in files and which did not warrant traditional full cataloging: reprints, off-prints, and what has been called report literature, which increased greatly in America with government-sponsored and financed research which required that there be wide distribution of reports on research. On the other hand there was limitation of the manipulative methods required, and of quantity. Batten, in England, had to think of dealing with plastic patents for his company when, as a wartime measure, publication of indexed

Post-Coordinate Indexing 203

abridgements ceased and the full patents required laborious examination and analysis. But the number of patents in his field at that time was not overwhelming. In America, Mooers, with his Zatocoding "term on item" system, in a 1954 case history of installation, spoke of "bulging files" holding about 3,000 files with more coming in every day, after four years' operation of his system with about 8,500 documents. These are obviously not figures comparable with those of wide-ranging bibliographies and literature indexes or volume collections in general libraries which today with increasing rapidity build up to a modest 100,000 or even a million. However, the post-coordinate systems have had their own situations and economies, and there they have worked.[187]

8.2 Batten's Optical Coincidence and Taube's Uniterm Number Coincidence

Batten, looking for a solution, arrived at one which may have been somewhat anticipated, even suggested, in France. In general, in Batten's system cards for terms have numbers carefully distributed over them by reference to coordinates of the map reference type, and numbers may not be individually printed. Thus, supposing three terms in an item of plastic literature--A, B, C--with A at a number around 800, more or less, representing the item; B might then be on the term card for B with the same number for the same item, and similarly with C. Perforations will have been made through each card at the corresponding numerical points. Knowing a correlation for which an information search is being made, the term cards may be taken out of a pack; they can then be held up or over a source of light, and if the light shines through at the coinciding number points, it can be assumed that the item so numbered has information on all three terms, almost certainly in some correlation.

The filing arrangement of the cards was according to a special classification, apparently not facet; this had led to the Batten system being called "classified" (Holmstrom included it in what he called "A Classification of Classifications," though this had a wide range, including alphabetical orders).[188] In an informative article on optical coincidence origins Wildhack and Stern in America described something like an alphabetico-classed arrangement, speaking of categories with alphabetical subarrangement.[189] But the arrangement of term cards for extraction could be--and apparently has been in several systems in America--entirely alphabetico-

specific. Holmstrom showed that he used "classification"
very broadly, to include phonetic or alphabetical arrangement,
but he distinguished punched card systems from both "classified" and "alphabetical." It was alphabetical indexing which
Jevons had earlier distinguished as index classification.

Taube seems to have been aware of Batten's system
and the Royal Society's Scientific Information Conference, 1948,
in which it was considered. He had had experience in LoC,
especially in its Technical Information Division where LoC was
getting out of its depth. About 1950 Taube left LoC and established a company, Taube and Associates, which he also
called Documentation, Inc. He also lectured on documentation in the Columbia University Library School, maintaining
an attitude of academic impartiality while becoming a paid
consultant and casting around for a simple system of his own
which would deal with "a new literature of scientific and technical literature" alien to "the established patterns of ...
publication and dissemination."[190] What he produced was a
simplified version of the Batten optical coincidence system
which might be called a direct number coincidence system.
Morris, in 1954, quoted Mooers' critical remarks about the
time taken for retrieval using Taube's simplified system, and
Taube's somewhat hasty retort describing Mooer's Zatocoding
as a "patented nostrum." Mooer's system, in fact, was only
partly patented, and what Taube called his Uniterm system,
though not patented, might be more aptly described as a
nostrum.[191]

It was in its operation an "item on term" system,
using numbers to identify items, and simple manipulation to
take out supposedly related term cards and match or compare
them for number coincidence; this was aided by putting numbers in columns according to their unit digits from 0 to 9.
It worked in this respect, but Taube called it Uniterm because
he began with an idea of using single words; so, for example,
there would be term cards for clay and pipes, iron and pipes,
steam and pipes; this meant more of what was called "post-
ing" (meaning entering). For example, there would be six
postings for three items on steam pipes, and then coordination of the adjectival and noun terms. The indexing was usually limited to a subject area which was not likely to include
three such similarly named objects. Taube soon gave way on
this, calling the adjectival phrases "bound terms" while still
retaining the attractive name Uniterm. Criticism introduced
the name concept for names without regard for their conception, and this became established, along with his name "co-

ordinate indexing," which gradually ousted "correlative." But Taube also chose to identify coordinate indexing with Boolean logic; this became prestigious and was even accepted by some authorities who should at least have recognized that logical methods and processes are reasoning processes, not IR processes, even though some analogies may be drawn between the two. Logical authorities began to question the Boolean logic claim and when Documentation Inc. prepared a report, by Jaster, Murray and Taube on the State of the Art of Coordinate Indexing (1962) for the Office of Science Information Service, National Science Foundation,[192] Documentation Inc.'s conclusions were: "a plague on all our houses, including ours." The report implied acceptance of criticisms by logicians such as Bar-Hillel, and suggested that "the I.R. problem be viewed in part as a problem of the optimum design of an engineering system and not solely as a problem of basic research into linguistics and meaning. Such systems work would tend to bridge the gap between linguistic research and actual operation of systems." This could be applied to some of the byways or cul-de-sacs into which the Classification Research Group in Britain has gone in search of something that might prove better or more scientific than the facet classification with which it began.

Taube's Uniterm system is generally considered to have done most to advertise coordinate indexing, and it and Batten's optical coincidence have been the two best-known examples of "entry on term" indexing. Batten was not in business but Taube was, and seems to have made money for himself and his corporation by selling library service, especially to NASA, the National Aerospace Agency. What he provided in staff and services cost a lot, but it was still but a drop in NASA's bucket at the time, and might otherwise have shown up in increases in public servants if NASA had organized its own indexing. Contract cataloging was not new in America or England, even in the time of Poole and Crestadoro, but consultant services and service provision by consultants had begun to increase. Taube, unfortunately, did not live much longer to enjoy his fame or his fortune.

8.3 Edge-punched Cards, Notching, Needle-sorting and Mooers' Zatocoding[193]

Early "term on item" systems were those known as edge-punched card and needle-sort, and these seem to have been the source of Mooers' Zatocoding vibrator system. Edge-punched cards came with a variety of names from the sellers of the cards--McBee, Keysort and E-Z Sort in America, and Copeland-Chatterson or Paramount in Britain, the latter apparently identical with Keysort in America. The material indexed was likely to be the same as the reports, reprints, and so on, for which the "item on term" systems were used, but the face of the card could carry a bibliographical description and a reference or location number. Because of the method of sorting for IR, the cards can be in any order, and if the method is reserved for subjects or subject terms the cards may be author-alphabetical, though this will involve refiling since cards would have to be taken out in packs for the sorting operation. It seems to have been common to keep the cards in a changing order or lack of order following any particular sorting operation.

The body of the card is intended for item description, and location holes are punched on the edges. Each hole is numbered for reference to its term and representation, and a maximum number of holes might be 100, allowing a hundred terms. Only one of these or two or three might be used for one item, but different ones for another, and so on. Let us suppose common personal use by someone working with the literature of apples: he might use three holes--for "barrels," "cases," and "cartons"--but if he thinks he may not have enough holes, may resort to generic terms suggested perhaps in the alphabetical listing of terms and codings which may be honored by the name thesaurus, in which there can be collateral references. This is a general problem of post-coordinate systems because of coding limitations and/or desirable economy of operation. He might then use "containers" or "packaging" as one generic term, and have little trouble in hand sorting what came out.

When a hole is used it is snipped out into an open notch, and this is where the needling came in. In a pack of cards, in a line from front to back or the reverse, there will be holes and notches covering each other, but a needle or bodkin or icepick may be pushed through what is either still a hole or an open notch. Then, when the cards hang on the needle and are loosened and shaken, those which still have unbroken holes will hang on, but those with opened holes or notches will fall off or can be shaken or pulled off. If the enthusiast has used three terms--"barrels," "boxes," "cartons"--and he wants entries on all three, he might use one needle three times or three needles at once.

Post-Coordinate Indexing 207

There have been complications with edged-punched cards and needle sorting for "term on item" coordination, and special equipment and other attempts have been made to overcome its limitations. These cannot be pursued in detail but the source references will provide descriptions and illustrations. Mooers' development, however, broke new ground with mechanization and with coding.

On the physical operation side, Mooers invented what may be called a "vibrator." This was a box in which a pack of cards was supported on rods which were movable so as to be in line with edge-punchings from front to back or the reverse; an electric motor then vibrated the pack so that on the rods as placed, the notched cards dropped about a quarter of an inch, while those with holes in the same line or lines were held up. The latter could then be lifted out, and those left behind would be the wanted cards. Mooers said that cards could be sorted at the rate of 800 a minute.

He called his terms "descriptors," and even if he had not unfortunately added that a "subject headings list" would call to mind a rough approximation of what he meant, "descriptor," like "keyword," would still have become a misleading and ambiguous term. A better comparison is with Basic English with a vocabulary limited to about 800 words; these do not include, for example, "thermometer," but this can be got round with "heat measuring instrument." Mooers' descriptors, carefully worked out for a given subject field and a particular customer, are like Basic English; six may be used where one special word or phrase would do, but his descriptors were a major part of his solution to the coding problem with the limitations of edge-punched cards, and he considered between 250 and 300 quite enough in any subject field.

He used four "Zatocodes" for each descriptor on a card: for example, 3 11 15 39 ... 1 11 34 40. It may be noticed that 11 is in both groups here, but this was part of his superimposed and random coding; the groups of four numbers are combinations even though a number is common to both. These combinations were selected at random, and while he admitted that there could be some false drops, statistically the possibility would be low and he considered his method the most economical in use of available holes. Twenty-six things taken four at a time produce 14,950 combinations and so provide distinctions with little possibility of confusion. The principle seems to be that of the combination lock.

Mooers has the first reference in this study as the well identified inventor of the term "information retrieval," which he said was first used at the Royal Aircraft Establishment in England, in reports which helped to establish it in America about 1954. This British use, almost unknown in England, arose out of the interest of Fairthorne, Senior Principal Scientific Officer in the Mathematics Department at the Royal Aircraft Establishment, who had become interested in indexing and corresponded with Mooers, before actually meeting him in 1950 on his first visit to America, when they were able to discuss common mathematical interests. Mooers first made public use of the term in a paper read to the Association for Computing Machinery, March 29, 1950, and then published it as Zator Technical Bulletin 48, which almost certainly was taken back by Fairthorne. The latter's Towards Information Retrieval, 194 a collection of papers, was first published in 1961 with introductory comments, "From a point of view of Mathematical etc. Techniques" by Mooers, with reference to Fairthorne in it. The story is a minor one of the meetings of men and minds affecting development.

8.4 Photography, Shingling, and Roles and Links

With hindsight the situation in 1876 seems pretty clear-cut: the choice was between Cutter's alphabetico-specific entry and the Amherst or Dewey classification. Getting back to 1876, however, reveals the conflict of Poole and Cutter producing the latter's specific entry, and some doubts about DDC not certainly emerging as a system until 1885, Cutter having been deflected from producing by then what could have been strong alphabetical notation competition. Then in the 1890s there was the battle of the catalogs in LoC which might have had a different result and produced different effects on American indexing generally. In the 1940s and 1950s postcoordinate indexing may have been a development from what Jevons in 1874 called diagnostic classification, with the aid of a gadget appearing at least as early as 1915, Taylor's patented Selective Device. In the third quarter of the 20th century conflicts and supersessions seem mainly to have arisen from the speed-up of technological developments generally, which of course helped to produce information explosions and development of techniques in IR.

The influence of photography has been neglected, possibly because like printing and, later, television, it has been identified with amusement and recreation. Especially with the introduction of film instead of glass plate photography and micro-photography with enlargement, however, enormous possibilities were opened up, and some of them were realized. One product was Shaw's Rapid Selector, which could be classed as "term on item." Entries with abstracts could be put on microfilm with "frames" which could be searched sequentially and at speed; this was called "stroboscopic" indexing. Each frame for an entry included coding spots for subject terms, with perhaps a mixture of pre- and post-coordinate indexing; with photographic recognition of a coding pattern there was momentary arrest of the film's passage and the entry and its abstract were photographically reproduced. Though it had some use, Ralph Shaw's Rapid Selector did not realize all his hopes for it.

Contemporary with the Rapid Selector there was the manual method of cumulation called shingling. In reminiscences E. A. Savage, City Librarian of Glasgow, recalled a practice from the days when books were much more stably in print, of ordering for a new library all the books in the printed catalog of an established library, then cutting up entries from this catalog and pasting them up, perhaps with a few additions, as copy for the printing of a catalog for the new library. Shingling was somewhat different: legitimate entries in a bibliography or index, in perhaps weekly or monthly parts, were cut up for cumulation and printing after pasting on sheets. Methods using photography did away with shingling.

From 1957 to 1961 the National Library of Medicine in Washington developed mechanization of its Index Medicus production; mechanization of punched cards for input and output and interfiling before printing was highly developed but there was no mention of a computer alternative at that time. [195] This became part of the MEDLARS (Medical Literature Analysis and Retrieval) system which had international use, and at least from 1967, in Maltby's 4th edition of Sayers' Manual, was described as computerized; Artandi said it became operational in January 1964. [196]

Mooers showed himself aware of computers as communication instruments in 1951, and of course of Hollerith body-punched cards. These had been developed for sorting out various classes of data on census returns, and would have become a fairly obvious device for IR. Mooers distinguished "invariant" and "alternative position" scanning, the latter being pushed by a Frenchman, Samain.[197] Holmstrom listed Samain in his "Classification of Classifications" as an improvement on Hollerith. Mooers, with reference to Samain, said: "alternative position scanning is a very powerful technique. However, it requires an elaborate and expensive technique because of the need to search many alternative locations in the field." Samain went over to film with patterns of transparent and opaque spots, under the trade name Filmorex. Punched cards of the invariant or pre-determined position type had some use and seemed suited to UDC (or UDC to it), though there wasn't agreement on this. This system might have been developed and displaced Mooers' Zatocoding, but on the evidence computer potential and developments seem to have displaced cards as in the National Library of Medicine's mechanization, although it may have found it could use its cards, at least in the beginning, for input into a computer.

A particular difficulty with post-coordinate indexing must be considered here. In pre-coordinate headings, term relations are fairly apparent, especially with reference to catalog entries under them. In post-coordinate indexing, terms are dissociated, and may have different relations in different parts of the same item, and their indexing is analytical without particular references being given. This means that there may have to be literature searching within an item after post-coordinate indexing has drawn attention to it. An item may deal with Coating of and Coating with Concrete, in relation to Iron pipes, magnesium and spinel. Iron pipes are internally coated with concrete, concrete may be coated with magnesium, and magnesium with spinel. Two of what have been called "roles" are <u>coating of</u>, and <u>coating with</u> concrete; in their context pre-coordinated terms may need no more than an occasional parenthetical preposition. For post-coordinate indexing some opinion developed that varying roles of objects needed distinction, and what were called "links" in a post-coordinated set might need to be shown by adding letters to numbers. This linking is of terms in an item, not of items themselves, but term roles can hold for several items. Roles and links were especially emphasized in a system prepared mainly by Costello of the Battelle Memorial Institute for or in conjunction with the Engineers Joint Council, with teaching material. The course was sold in America, Australia and Great Britain, only to participating fee-paying students, and was probably most influential in Britain in suggesting an alternative to facet classification, which still held sway in the sixties. The Zinc and Lead Development Associa-

Post-Coordinate Indexing 211

tion in England got a research grant requiring it to have an IR system in operation by January 1962; because of this it switched from its intended facet classification to coordinate indexing, but it seems not to have distinguished the Battelle Costello system from Taube's Uniterm system, although Taube never had any enthusiasm for roles and links.

Blagden,[198] who had been librarian of the Zinc and Lead Development Association before becoming librarian of the British Institute of Management, wrote an article for JoD in 1966 which he called "How Much Noise in a Role-free and Link-free Coordinate Indexing System?" "Noise" is American IR jargon for "False drops," which is also jargon. Blagden decided against roles and links as not being worth the saving in false drops. Costello's EJC-BMI system distinguished 14 roles, which have some relation to the question of relations of terms and their dissociation in post-coordinate indexing. Mooers, however, said his descriptors were each true "in some way of the information content of the unit of information." They might have "formed some interacting combination in the original document, or it could just as well mean that they related to independent ideas scattered through the document." But this seems to imply the question of the multi-topical item needing to be treated as if it were two or more items, or a need for some indication of related and unrelated descriptors. Mooers said that using descriptors "drops all relationships between the ideas represented by them"--that is, omits all consideration of relationships, which Mooers said were "subtle things depending upon the point of view in most information situations." He seems to have realized that there was some confusion in this, and in a later ASLIB paper in 1955 did not touch on it either way. Taube answered the same relations question facetiously by saying that in fact the man does not bite the dog, and Venetian blinds and Blind Venetians are not likely to be in the same field, but he too seemed to see later that there could be ambiguity in what he called the direction of terms. Mooers wrote of an index of descriptors, usually an alphabetical listing of single descriptors and their simpler combinations; although not developed sufficiently, this appeared to imply the thesaurus idea.

8.5 The New Thesauri

The new thesauri are the subject heading or term lists used mainly with, and adapted to, coordinate indexing. They may have more in common with the subject heading lists proposed about 1876 than is apparent. A useful account by Vickery in 1960 is titled "Thesaurus--A New Word in Documentation";199 clearly the word was not a new one in documentation or IR, but no evidence has been uncovered that those who brought it into use again were aware of its earlier use, and I have found only one contemporary mention of its early use. Vickery heard Brownson use it in 1957, referring to mechanized text searching and indexing with "the application of a mechanized thesaurus based on networks of related meanings." Brownson may have been referring to the word's use by Luhn, also in 1957, to which Vickery also refers. Vickery also mentions that Bernier used the name "technical thesaurus" for an index of complicated relations of terms he called "semantemes."

The name thesaurus has not been uniformly applied, and one list conservatively called a list of headings may be comparable to another called a thesaurus; for example, there is Medical Subject Headings (MeSH) of the U.S. National Library of Medicine and the NASA Thesaurus of the U.S. National Aeronautics and Space Administration. MeSH has more of what might be regarded as definitive characteristics of thesauri than, for example, the Engineers Joint Council Thesaurus of Engineering Terms, which is subtitled "A list of engineering terms and their relationships for use in vocabulary control in indexing and retrieving engineering information"; this is not essentially different from a subject headings list. These and other lists and thesauri are specialized, and thus categorization or class listing can be achieved which is not possible in a large general list. The earlier proposals for a universal thesaurus with both classification and alphabetical indexing of terms along the lines of Roget's Thesaurus seem to have proved impossible of useful achievement, and the end result was only the indexing part, with "refer to's" and "refer from's." Roget gave his classified section what could loosely be called synonyms and antonyms for "concepts," and the word thesaurus, especially in American usage, seems to have come to mean any dictionary of synonyms, however organized. What was wanted with coordinate indexing was indexing of synonyms, with reference to the preferred term, especially in technical vocabularies which sometimes have a degree of synonymity above the general average. Also, for its own technical reasons a general rule of specific entry ceased to apply in coordinate indexing; upward cross reference from specific to generic terms became necessary.

Post-Coordinate Indexing

A user of coordinate indexing might be expected to sit down with a thesaurus for a pleasant half hour or so, in which he works in and out, up and down, until he has a list of terms used in the system which he thinks might be coordinated in some information item. A manual or mechanical search is then made for items in which the terms or "concepts" named are used, presumably in some coordination. The coordination of coordinate indexing is, of course, in the act of retrieval or consultation, not in compilation. A manual thesaurus is used in this way even in consultation of on-line computerized indexing. Because thesauri, so-called, are specialized, it is scarcely worthwhile examining any in detail, especially as their use remains fluid. The possible use of one, however, may be briefly stated. The U.S. Bureau of Reclamation's Thesaurus of Descriptors (Oct. 1963) is a list of keywords and cross references for indexing and retrieving the literature of water resources development. The thesaurus has a list of "Descriptor fields" for reclamation engineering; one of six fields is Civil Engineering, and for this particular field there is reference to Descriptor Groups with numbers from GP 01 to GP 47. A Descriptor field reference under Civil Engineering is GP 08 Construction; in GP 08 there is Bulldozers, and in the main alphabetical index appears Bulldozers GP 08. The user therefore has access through the six "fields" as listed, through the 47 "groups" as listed, and through the alphabetical, more or less specific, term list. MeSH (Medical Subject Headings), not called a thesaurus, is on these same lines.

8.6 Computers and IR

Computer use for IR and for service to libraries may eventually prove to have been in about mid-career in 1976. Body-punched cards of the kind introduced by Hollerith for statistical analysis of census returns came into some use and were obviously a threat to edge-punched cards and Mooers' development, but the computer from about 1940 was initially developing strictly as a calculating machine of the kind known as the electronic digital computer--as distinguished from the analog computer which is related to slide rule-type calculation rather than calculation using numerals or digits. Being digital in operation, computers are in the line of development from the ancient abacus. One of their great advantages is the high speed of electronic operation and their capacity to hold data in memory units or stores, including their own instruction or programming. In relation to the photographic film method of Shaw's Rapid Selector and punched hole systems, computers use arrangements of magnetized spots. Like Shaw's Rapid Selector they can produce data copy by "print-out," but they can also use television-type projection, for one form of what is called "on-line" consultation. In contrast to "on-line" is "batch" processing, which can result in delays, as is also the case with shared computer time. Libraries hope that eventually lower costs or better budgets will result in their acquiring their own computers which can have wider uses in a library than indexing or cataloging. Like many uses of photography, computerization requires its own technicians, including computer engineers and programmers, but there is a growing body of librarian specialists known as systems librarians. Computer technology and operation for IR and what has been somewhat magniloquently called "Information Science"--with its rather unscientific jargon such as "noise," "false drops" and "slop," "hardware" for the machines and "soft-ware" for their stationery--can be initially studied in such a book as Artandi's Introduction to Computers in Information Science (2d ed., 1972). A British introduction of wide range is Meetham's Information Retrieval (1969).

The application of computers to IR became possible once it was proved that they could handle logical operations, especially those of Boolean or symbolic or mathematical logic, as well as purely arithmetical tasks. Shannon in 1938 published a paper called a "Symbolic Analysis of Relay and Switching Circuits," and in 1948 a book called Cybernetics was published by Norbert Wiener--cybernetics being defined as "the study of control and communication in the animal and the machine." These publications and a futuristic essay by Vannevar Bush in 1945 on the possibilities of mechanization, entitled "Memex," gave rise to the idea of computers as "mechanical brains" and journalists began to call the simplest communication devices, even of the bell push-type, computers and/or mechanical brains. But it has not been found possible to program the machine with the semantic capacity of the human mind or brain; even if illogical, the latter can still identify subjects and terms in language implying meaning. It can state the meaning of an item for pre-coordinate permutations such as "Houses - Heat loss - Insulation - Thermoplastics," and only then can the computer be used, very valuably, for the "shunting" permutation of PRECIS (itself in its purpose and method entirely a human mind product). But the computer does not in any way recognize more than the coding of the terms in it. Coates had introduced computer permutation in the production of his BTI, his purpose being efficiency and economy in getting out issues on time without human error, which can (and does) result in faulty programming. In an account of his BTI computerization he stressed that, like BNB indexing by the PRECIS method a little later, his BTI indexing was human-based.201

Within limits, however, a means was found of producing computer indexing, and thus were born the two acronyms, KWIC and KWOC. An introduction to Chemical Titles in 1959 (Feb. 24) described it as "A concordance to chemical research papers. The use of electric computers has made it possible to provide a 'current awareness' service in the form of an index. The particular form of this concordance is that of the keyword-in-context-type." This type of index does not seem to have any manual predecessor. In Watt's Bibliotheca Britannica in 1824 there was what became known later as KWOC or Keyword-out-of-context, title words being used as headings with abbreviated repetition in the titles. In the indexing developed by Poole in America and then by Crestadoro and/or his employer Low in England for the economy of "title-a-line," there was title word transposition in that a keyword or indexing word became the first in the line, the entry word, and out of its context.

In his KWIC Luhn used two devices; one was "wrap-around-titles"--the title in its item order, if necessary with some cut-off at either end so that indexing title words come approximately in the middle of a column page; these are truly in title context. The other device of Luhn's, more relevant to computer use, was the "stop list." The titles of articles in chemistry have been fairly literal and authors and editors have been encouraged to make them more so. The computer could be programmed to shift titles round so as to bring every word into the central position, with the repeated titles, of course, finally being printed out in alphabetical order for published reproduction. The computer could also have respect for what was called a "stop list" of words of little subject significance; prepositions and conjunctions, for example, could remain in the titles but not be brought into the indexing position. The computer, having been programmed, could do this, and it was no mean achievement; but it hasn't a clue to the linguistic or semantic significance of what it is doing, whereas the monks in their original Bible concordance indexing, and Watt, Poole and Crestadoro in their adaptations, knew what they were doing and why.

Verse and title concordance methods and limitations of

indexing should not be confused with source limitations of term selection for coordinate indexing, pre- or post-. Cutter said "enter books under the word which best expresses their subject, whether it occurs in the title or not." Without limiting indexing to some title corcordance method, term selections can be limited to titles, abstracts, chapter headings, likely looking headings in book indexes, and so on. There were hopes of what was called automatic indexing based on texts and word relations and clusters in texts. This was related to automatic translation from one language to another, but while there are theoretical possibilities, the complexities and costs seem insuperable. After a "state of the art" report in 1965 not much seems to have been forthcoming.[202] A distinction emerged between assigned and derived terms (i.e., derived from titles), with echoes of Crestadoro's 19th century arguments that authors should be regarded as authorities on their titles. One statement was that "source indexing can originate only with the generator of information, not with the reviewer or librarian. Within the creative manipulations required to originate and finally to communicate, lie the elements of a very powerful indexing system."[203] But one may doubt or suspect whether this suits a system. Automatic indexing, apart from questions of method, would need computer record of texts such as magnetic tapes; the computer would certainly not read the natural language text. Tapes, because of cost, have been scarce even for experimental purposes, and it may be ironical that producing concordances of authors' writings, usually in poetic fields, seems to have been one of the few justifications for reducing complete texts to machine-readable copy. Another one, an IR one, has been the reproducing of centrally produced and copied cataloging such as that of LoC and BNB.

The now inevitable acronym appeared in America-- MARC, for Machine-Readable Cataloging; there followed a British MARC and there is, for example, an Australian one, and an Australian agency through which extracts can be acquired from the others for particular books. The MARC records, of course, have to be computer read or translated, and there have to be format adjustments for the MARC records, but in Australian experience MARC resulted in libraries getting LoC cataloging much quicker than ever before. "MARC based cataloging was introduced into the University of New South Wales in March 1974; in the same year it provided 20% of current cataloging, and should eventually provide 80%."[204] This could be typical of Australia; the University of New South Wales, tending to be angelic in its tread, has certainly not rushed in, though among about sixteen Australian universities it is fairly progressive.

Another perhaps delayed and tentative development was one of geographical regional centers of service linked by general communication services. The British Library was one of these and there had been proposals, not realized, for regional centers through the United States; the federal capital was obviously one in Australia.

In IR itself, speed of access was constantly improved. The original tapes had to be searched sequentially, but a distinction must be made between sequential arrangement and sequential searching. Alphabetical and numerical arrangements are sequential, but with knowledge of alphabetical and numerical order what was rather confusingly called "random access" is possible. Knowing the place of MN as in the middle of the alphabet, one can go to it fairly directly, and so with other letters or numbers. Needle-sorting and Mooers' vibration box provided what could be called simultaneous access; within a computer there can be fractional scanning, either side of a central point. With discs and multiple searching heads and other devices there can be approximation to direct access which has been rather confusingly called random, on the "near enough" principle. Vickery quoted Bucholz on these difficulties: "we may vary the approach ... but sort we must."[205] Sequential sorting through tape, like sequential sorting through punched cards, proved comparatively too slow, and discs comparable to gramophone records were a substitute because they allow multiple simultaneous searching in different circles. But tapes may be short or long, and sequential searching of the long tape took too long; the long tape has therefore been superseded in later generations of computers by magnetic "cores," magnetic drums and discs. A further important breakthrough was the availability of choices of different type-styles in computer print-out copy for reproduction.

ABBREVIATIONS AND ACRONYMS

(Note: these abbreviations are used in both the text and the references)

ALA	American Library Association
AM DOC	American Documentation
Aslib	Association of Special Libraries and Information Bureaux
BC	Bibliographic Classification (Bliss)
BML	British Museum Library
BNB	British National Bibliography
BSI	British Standards Institution
BTI	British Technology Index
CC	Colon Classification (Ranganathan)
CRG	Classification Research Group (British)
DAB	Dictionary of American Biography
DDC	Dewey Decimal Classification
DNB	Dictionary of National Biography (British)
EC	Expansive Classification (Cutter)
FID	Fédération International de Documentation
ICSL	International Catalogue of Scientific Literature
IIB	Institut International de Bibliographie (afterwards FID)
IR	Information Retrieval
JoD	Journal of Documentation
KWIC	Keyword-in-Context
KWOC	Keyword-out-of-Context

Abbreviations and Acronyms

LA	Library Association (British)
LAR	<u>Library Association Record</u> (British)
LC	<u>Library of Congress Classification</u>
LJ	<u>Library Journal</u> (American)
LoC	Library of Congress
LQ	<u>Library Quarterly</u>
MARC	Machine-Readable Cataloging
PLUSA	<u>Public Libraries of the United States ... Special Report ... 1876</u>
RBU	<u>Répertoire Bibliographique Universal</u>
SC	<u>Subject Classification</u> (Brown)
SHF	Subject Headings File
SHL	Subject Headings List
UDC	Universal Decimal Classification

REFERENCES AND NOTES

Note: These references and notes have interlinear numbers in the text in one sequence and are in these forms,

3   Edwards, E. <u>Memoirs of Libraries</u>, 2 vols. 1859; 1:8, 12-13.

22 Edwards (3): 266-268.
    The bracketed figure is that of the first and fuller reference to Edwards' <u>Memoirs</u>.

29 Sayers, W. C. B. "Some Canons of Classification," <u>LAR</u> 9:425-42, 468-475, Aug. 1907.

44 Sayers (29).
    <u>LAR</u> for <u>Library Association Record</u> is in the preceding list of Abbreviations and Acronyms. There is more than one reference at some numbers, mainly as bibliography for information not pursued in the text. The notes are occasional and mainly bibliographical or critical.

Chapter 1 (references 1-19)

1   Mooers, C. N. "Comments on the Paper by Bar-Hillel," <u>Am Doc</u> 8:116, Apr. 1957. A note by Mooers on his introduction of the term information retrieval in 1949-50.
    Fairthorne (194) 536.

2   <u>Australian Library Journal</u>, Editorial, 23:89, Apr. 1974.

3   Edwards, E. <u>Memoirs of Libraries</u>, 2 vols. 1859; 1:8, 12-13.

4   Richardson, E. C. <u>Classification Theoretical and Practical</u> 1930:59. (Shoe String Press Reprint)

References and Notes   221

5   Hessel, A. History of Libraries. Scarecrow Press
    1955:2.

6   Hessel (5) 129.

7   Edwards (3) 1:22.

8   Richardson (4) 89.

9   Turner, E. G. Greek Papyri: an Introduction. Oxford,
    Clarendon Press, 102.

10 Richardson (4) 90.

11 Sayers, W. C. Berwick. Manual of Classification, 3rd.
    ed. rev. 1959:96. A 4th ed., 1967, after Sayers'
    death, was edited by Maltby; it largely follows the 3rd
    but here the 3rd ed. is generally cited. In both edi-
    tions index references are to paragraph numbers, but
    here page numbers are given, in keeping with gener-
    al practice, except for Kaiser's Systematic Indexing,
    1911, which has only paragraph numbering (see note
    172).

12 Turner (9) 101, 140.

13 Reichmann, F. "The Book Trade at the Time of the
    Roman Empire," LQ 8:40-76, Jan. 38.

14 Irwin, R. The Heritage of the English Library, 1964:
    87, 110.

15 Irwin (14) 110, 129.

16 Savage, E. A. "Cooperative Bibliography in the Thir-
    teenth and Fifteenth Centuries," in his Special Li-
    brarianship in General Libraries, and Other Papers,
    1939:207, 292-3, 301.

17 Daly, L. W. "Contributions to a History of Alphabetiza-
    tion in Antiquity and the Middle Ages," Revue d'E-
    tudes Latines, Brussels, 1967:76-77, 79.

18 Wormald and Wright. The English Library before 1700,
    1958:23, 26.

19 Encyclopaedia Britannica, 11th ed., 1910: Concordances;
    Langton, Stephen.

Chapter 2 (references 20-65)

20 Besterman, T. Beginnings of Systematic Bibliography, 1936.

21 Besterman, T. (20).

22 Edwards (3) 1:226-268.

23 Richardson (4) 57.

24 Bliss, H. E. Organization of Knowledge and the System of the Sciences, 1929:328-9.

25 Bliss, H. E. Organization of Knowledge in Libraries, 1933:194.

26 Edwards (3) 2:783.

27 Sayers (11) 90, Division 2.

28 Richardson (4) 53.

29 Sayers, W. C. B. "Some Canons of Classification," LAR 9:425-42, 468-75, Aug. 1907. This was the first publication of his Canons, criticized in discussion at their delivery; afterwards, in various editions of his Manual and other works, they were amplified and altered out of recognition.

30 Sayers, W. C. B. Manual of Classification, 1st ed., 1924.

31 Sayers (11) 104.

32 Newman, L. M. Leibnitz (1646-1716) and the German Library Scene, 1966:28, 30. (L.A. Pamphlet 28)

33 Edwards (3) 2:764-5.

34 LaMontagne, Leo E. American Library Classification with Special Reference to the Library of Congress. Hamden, Connecticut: Shoe String Press, 1961.

35 Sayers (11) 112, 141. Maltby, in the 4th ed., seems to have followed first Sayers and then LaMontagne.

References and Notes

36 LaMontagne (34) 175.

37 Wheatley, H. B. How to Make an Index, 1902. ch. 1.

38 Jevons, W. Stanley. Principles of Science: a Treatise on Logic and Scientific Method. 2d ed., 1877:714-16. Reprinted, New York: Dover Publications, 1958.

39 Bar-Hillel, Y. "A Logician's Reactions to Recent Theorizing on Information Search Systems," Am Doc 8: 103-112, Apr. 1957. For comments on what Mooers thought of Bar-Hillel's confusion of item retrieval and item searching see note 1.

40 Edwards (3) 2:95.
    Wheatley (37) 15.

41 Edwards (3) 2:80.

42 Richardson (4) 41-42, 107-8.

43 Richardson (4) 41-2.

44 Sayers (29).

45 Esdaile, A. The British Museum Library, 1948:94, 340-42.
    Garnett, D. R. "On the System of Classifying Books on the Shelves of the British Museum," Essays in Librarianship, 220-224.
    Edwards (3) 2:776, 796.
    Hill, F. J. "Shelving and Classification of Printed Books in the British Museum," from a thesis in the L.A., 1933.
    Brunet, J-C. Manuel... 1860-65: 1, Introduction, v-vi.
    Panizzi, Sir A., quoted on classifying, cataloging and Watts Bibliotheca, in Wheatley (37) 191-3.
    Wheatley's How to Catalogue a Library, 1889, is a useful source of extracts from the Enquiry which may not otherwise be available.

46 Harris, G. W. "The British Museum System of Press Numbering," LJ 12:331-334, 1887.
    Reichmann, F. "Cornell's Reclassification Program," Coll. and Res. Libraries, Sept. 1962:369-374, 440, 450-55. What had become known as Harris's classification was a version of the BM system he admired

in 1887.

G. W. Harris is not to be confused with T. M. Harris [LaMontagne (34) 104] or W. T. Harris [LaMontagne (34) ch. 10].

47   Mason, T. "A Bibliographical Martyr," The Library 1, 1889, 56-63, reprinted in Selected Readings on the History of Librarianship, 2d ed., LA, 1966:233-250.

48   LaMontagne (34) 1988:200, on John Edmands.

49   Williamson, W. L. William Frederick Poole and the Modern Library Movement, N.Y., 1963. As a librarian's life and times this is well above the average in length, impartiality and scholarship, compared for example with Dawe on Dewey (66) and Rider on Dewey (78), although the latter is certainly superior to Dawe.

50   Jewett, C. C. "A Plan for Stereotyping Catalogues by Separate Titles; and for Forming a General Stereotyped Catalogue of Public Libraries in the United States," Am. Soc. Adv. of Sci. Procs 1850:165-76.
Williamson (49) 18, 34-35.
Cole, J. Y. Ainsworth Spofford and the National Library, 1971, 13-25. A good account of Jewett's National Library efforts with the Smithsonian Institution.

51   Cutter on Jewett's Boston Public Library Headings, PLUSA, 539.

52   Poole's IR Use of the Word Thesaurus, LJ, 53:110, 1878.
"The Plan of Poole's Index," LJ 3:109-10, 131-151, 326-9.
"Library Symposium: the Plan of Poole's New Index," LJ 3:141-151, 1878.

53   Low's British catalogue--Cutter on his concordance of titles purpose, PLUSA, 535.

54   Axon, W. E. A. On Crestadoro, in Handbook of the Public Libraries of Manchester, also reprinted in Library World 24:87-101, July 1921-2.

55   Cutter on Crestadoro, PLUSA, 535.

56   Axon on Crestadoro in DNB.

References and Notes

57 Crestadoro, A. Art of Making Catalogues. 1856.

58 Cutter, C. A. "New Catalogue of Harvard College Library," North American Review, Jan. 1869.

59 Coates, E. J. Subject Catalogues: Headings and Structure, London: L. A., 1960:36.

60 Cutter on comparison of alphabetico-classed at Harvard and alphabetico-specific, PLUSA, 540.

61 Esdaile, A. (45) 136.
    Jenner, H. "G. K. Fortescue, a Memory," The Library, 3rd ser. 4:1-45 Jan. 1913.
    Pollard on Fortescue in DNB.

62 LaMontagne (34) 181-2.
    Shurtleff, N. B. A Decimal System for the Arrangement and Administration of Libraries, Boston, privately printed, 1856.
    Edwards (3) 2:928-9.
    Poole. "Shelf Marks," in his chapter 25 on the "Organization and Management of Public Libraries," PLUSA, 106.
    Dewey in his DDC Introduction, "Notation."

63 Sayers (11) 111-12. Discussing decimal systems before Dewey he made no reference to Poole's chapter, and decided that Shurtleff's notation had no relation to that of Dewey because it wasn't used relatively, but that is not the essential question.

64 Edwards (3) 2:928-9.

65 Daly (17) 96.

Chapter 3 (references 66-101)

66 Dawe, Grosvenor. Melvil Dewey, Seer, Inspirer, Doer, 1831-1931. Essex Co., N.Y.: Lake Placid Club, 1932. 43, 10, 25-27, 31-65, 46-47. This compilation of about 400 pages was commissioned by the Club and was written and published in about six months after Dewey's death in December 1931. Dawe had some, but apparently not completely unreserved, access to club papers by and about Dewey. The

writer was not a librarian, and has to be read critically and between the lines, because neither Dawe nor the Committee overseeing him, including Dewey's second wife and his son, seemed to understand the implications of what he quoted and wrote as eulogy. This reference is only one of many made to it, and it is further considered where it comes into the story.

67 Dawe (66) 13, 49, 52.

68 Dawe (66) 52, 53, 157.

69 DDC, 18th ed., vol. 1:2.

70 Dawe (66) 49-50, 167.

71 Rider, Fremont. Melvil Dewey, Chicago: ALA, 1944 (American Library Pioneers VI).

72 Comaromi, J. P. (1937-). A History of the Dewey Decimal Classification, Editions One through Fifteen, Univ. Michigan, 1969, Ph.D. Library Science. Ann Arbor, Michigan: University Microfilms, Inc. Comaromi's interest was mainly in the classification used and developed in the Amherst College Library by Dewey and others, and later by him and his editors. Comaromi did, however, write on how it "got into the world," meaning out of Amherst, and about the bibliography of the so-called 1st ed., and he had access to Dewey papers in the University of Columbia library. Dawe, Rider and Comaromi can be said to be complementary as primary sources, Rider having known Dewey well, been related to him by marriage, and even lived in his home.

73 Dawe (66) 49-50.

74 Dewey, Melvil. "A Decimal Classification and Subject Index," PLUSA, ch. 28. This is the first of four new classifications described in this chapter, and either the Preface he prepared for what he reckoned as the 1st ed. of DDC was used in this account or the reverse.

75 Comaromi (72) 4, 79.

76 Dawe (66) 155.

References and Notes

77 Foster, W. E. "Five Men of 76," ALA Bull. 26:312-323, 1926.

78 Rider (71) 28.
   Dawe (66) 278-87.

79 Rider (71) 104-5.
   Dawe (66) 324-6.

80 Rider (71) 104-5.
   Dawe (66) 22.

81 Rider (71) ch. 11.

82 Dawe (66) 13, 224, 229-50.

83 Dawe (66) Frontispieces.

84 Dewey, 1873 Amherst submissions. In Dawe (66), 176, 319-322; in Rider (71) in part, 29-30. Dawe and his committee were fortunately impressed by what Dawe called "Three Genetic Papers" and printed them as documents of historic value, with a facsimile of a page of one called "Library Classification System." This, as does not seem to have been generally realized, explains difficulties in the printed version. Dawe and Rider clearly did not understand the technical significance of these papers--that they outlined notation but not what became the 1876 notation. Dewey did not even seem to have realized in 1873 that the arabic numbering system on which he was supposed to be an expert has only nine, not ten, digits in the strict sense, because the abacus place values for ten and multiples of ten were adapted in the written system. Dewey himself, while he claimed invention in 1873, did not in 1876 mention his submissions of 1873, nor his use of William Torrey Harris in the one on classification, nor that they did not include an alphabetical index.

85 Maass, John. "Who Invented Dewey's Classification?" Wilson Library Bulletin, Dec. 1972, with letters in Feb. and Apr. 1973.

86 Leidecker, K. F. "Debt of Melvil Dewey to William Torrey Harris," LQ 15:139-42, Apr. 1945. Graziano, E. E. "Hegel's Philosophy as Basis for the Dewey

Classification Schedule," Libri 9:45-52, 1959. Comaromi (72) on Graziano, 13-62.

87 Dewey references to Battezzati, LJ 1:120, Nov. 3rd; 2: 33, Sep. These were in discussion of the possibility of catalog card supply through publishers, without any reference to classification. Dewey was certainly interested in card supply but not with any disclosed relation to his classification, though he may have thought of cards with his classification, not Brunet's, as some of Battezzati's cards for booksellers had on them.
Bottasso, E. "Le origine delle classificazione decimale," 182 Annali della Scuola Speciale per Archivisti e Bibliotecari dell'Universita de Roma, Anno V, N. 2, July-Dec. 1965.

88 Hulme, E. Wyndham. "Principles of Book Classification," LAR 13-14, 1911-12. Reprinted by the Association of Assistant Librarians and in Olding, R. K., Readings in Library Cataloguing, Melbourne, 1966.

89 Dawe (66) 63. Dewey at this stage wanted to get his classification into Wellesley, but didn't for some years.

90 Dawe (66) 160, 167. Cutter was advising Miss Godfrey, Wellesley's librarian, and had apparently not then changed his own mind about DDC.

91 Cutter, C. A. "Classification for the Shelves with Some Account of the New Scheme for the Boston Athenaeum," LJ 4:236, 1879.

92 Cutter, C. A. "Classification on the Shelves," LJ 6:64-69, 1881.

93 Cutter, William Parker. Charles Ammi Cutter. Chicago: ALA, 1930 (American Library Pioneers) 41. William Parker Cutter was a librarian and C. A. Cutter's nephew; he assisted him with his EC in every respect before and after C. A.'s death.

94 Dewey, M. "Principles Underlying Numbering Systems," LJ 4:7-10, 75-78.

95 Cutter, C. A. "Thirty-five versus Ten," LJ 7:62, April 1882.

References and Notes 229

96 Larned, J. N. "A Nomenclature for Classification," LJ 9:62, Apr. 1884.

97 Cutter, C. A. "A Notation for Small Libraries," LJ 12:324-326, 1887.

98 Larned, Josephus Nelson (1836-1913), DAB 11.

99 "Dewey's 35-Character Notation with a Book Classification by C. A. Cutter and an Enlarged Edition of Dewey's Index." Dawe (66) 101. Apparently this was never issued, but at the time Dewey seems to have been interested in possibilities of commercializing his relative index.

100 Dawe (66) 178. Rider (71) 35. Apparently in reply to inquiries from Dawe in 1932, W. P. Cutter said he had not seen a published copy of the Cutter-Dewey 35-base pamphlet and did not think it had ever been published. In 1944 Rider was satisfied to say that it was never published.

101 Lamb, E. "The Expansive Classification in Use," LQ 4:265-269, Apr. 1934.
Doyle, J. M. "Library of Congress for the Academic Library," Univ. Illinois Graduate School of Library Science, Role of Classification... 1959:76-92.

Chapter 4 (references 102-121)

102 Coates, E. J. (59) 69.

103 Cutter, C. A. "The Editor to the Proprietors." This is Cutter's final report in and on his Boston Athenaeum Catalog to the full subscribing, owning members, called Proprietors. The first column is highly critical of what was the new catalog as he took it over from Poole, becoming its editor, and in effect chief cataloger as well as librarian in 1870. It is pp. 3399-3402 in the last volume.

104 Jevons (38) 702.

105 Haykin, D. J. Library of Congress Subject Headings: a Practical Guide, 1951.

106 Public Libraries in the United States (PLUSA), ch. 27, "Library Catalogues" by C. A. Cutter, with Part II as the 1st ed. of Cutter's Rules for a Dictionary Catalog.

107 Hulme, E. Wyndham. "Principles of Dictionary Subject Cataloguing in Scientific and Technical Libraries," LAR 2, pt. 2, 571-576, Nov. 1900.

108 Hulme, E. W. "On a Cooperative Basis for the Classification of Literature in the Subject Catalogue," LAR 4, Pt. 2, 317-326, 1902.

109 Olding, R. K. Wyndham Hulme's Literature Warrant and Information Indication. Univ. California School of Library Service, 1968. "Inaugurating a lecture series on cataloging and classification in honor of Professor Emeritus Seymour Lubetzky"--Foreword.

110 Coates, E. J. "Alphabetical Subject Catalogues," JoD 9:58-63, Mar. 1953. A review of Haykin (104) including comment on specific entry definition with reference to Ranganathan, p. 62.

111 Lilley, O. L. "How Specific is Specific?" Journal of Cataloging and Classification, 11:3-8, Jan. 1955.

112 Mills, J. (review of) Davison, K. Classification Practice in Britain, JoD 23:85-88, Mar. 1967. Incidental opinion on American subject cataloguing, 87.

113 Angell, R. S. "Library of Congress Subject Headings--Review and Forecast," in Subject Retrieval in the Seventies, Univ. of Maryland, School of Library and Information Services, 1972, and also separately.

114 Coates (59) 15, 31-38.

115 Cole, J. Y. Ainsworth Spofford and the "National Library," 1971.

116 Mearns, D. C. "The Story up to Now," in the Annual Report of the Librarian of Congress, 1946.

117 Butler, Pierce. "J. C. M.," LQ 4:127-130, Apr. 1934.

118 LaMontagne (34) 51, 60, 221-2.

References and Notes 231

119 Hanson, J. C. M. "Subject Catalogues of the Library of Congress," ALA 31st Conference, Bretton Woods, Catalog Section, 1909.

120 LaMontagne (34) 315-16.

121 Dunkin, Paul. Cataloging USA, 1969, ch. 5.

Chapter 5 (references 122-142)

122 Sayers (11) 216-220. The following are references which have been used and are essential, but particular points have not been dealt with in the text:
Jast, L. Stanley. "Classification in Public Libraries with Special Reference to the Dewey Decimal System," The Library 7:169-178, 1895.
———. "The Dewey Classification in the Reference Library and an Open Access Lending Library," The Library 8:835-53, 1896.
——— and J. D. Brown, "The Class List," The Library 9:41-44, 1897.
———. ———. "The Compilation of Class Lists," The Library 9:45-69, 1897.
Dent, R. K. "The New Cataloguer and Some of His Ways," The Library 9:173-178, 1897.
Doubleday, W. E. "Class Lists or Dictionary Catalogues," The Library 9:179-189, 1897.
Barrett, F. T. "Alphabetical and Classified Forms of Catalogue Compared," 2nd International Library Conference, London, 1897, 66-71.
Jast, L. S. "Classification in British Libraries," LAR 5:173-182, 1903.

123 Munford, W. A. James Duff Brown, London: L.A. 1968.

124 Munford, W. A. Penny Rate, London: L.A. 1951, 103-105.

125 Jevons (38) 715.

126 Munford (123) 16, 33, 69.

127 Munford (123) 86, 91-95.

128 Sayers (11) 175.

129 Brown, J. D. Library Classification and Cataloguing, 1912, and 1916, 147-8. This was a revision of his Manual of Library Classification, 1898, and Sayers suggests its updating in H. A. Sharp's book (130).

130 Sharp, H. A. Cataloguing... 4th ed. London, 1948, 23, 25-6, 157, 331.

131 Cranshaw, J. "The Public and the Catalogue: Dictionary or Classified?" Library Assistant, 30:72-77, 1937.

132 Bradford, S. C. Documentation, 1948, reprint 1953: 140.

133 "International Catalogue of Scientific Literature," Report of the Committee of the Royal Society of London, 1898, 31; Second International Conference... 1898.

134 Murra, K. O. History of Some Attempts to Organize Bibliography Internationally, 1950, 40.

135 These references are not specific but give the background of the development which produced Aslib in Great Britain and special library services in industry. A good general study with excellent references is A. W. Johns, Special Libraries, Development of the Concept, Their Organization and Their Services, Metuchen, N.J.: Scarecrow, 1968. It is a comparative study of developments in Great Britain, America and Australia, first written for a master of librarianship degree in the University of New South Wales, School of Librarianship. These references show development in Great Britain and something of the battle in detail:
"Technical Libraries, Bureau of Industrial Information," LAR 20:176-82, Mar. 1918.
Pearce, J. G. "The Future of Documentation," LAR 20:162-6, 1918.
"The Technical Library," LAR 22:122-157, May 1920. This includes: Simnett, W. R., "Technical Libraries and Intelligence," and Matthews, R. B., "The Technical Library."
Savage, E. A. "Technical and Commercial Libraries," LAR 20:159-166, Aug. 1920.
Ridley, A. F. "Special Libraries and Information Bureaux in Great Britain," LAR 27:242-255, Dec. 1955.

Hutton, R. S. "The Origin and History of Aslib," JoD 1:6-20, June 1945.

136 On the philosophy of Otlet and La Fontaine in their organization of Répertoire Bibliographique Universel and its classification, I have been indebted to conversations with Mr. Boyd Rayward, and use of parts of his Chicago Ph. D. thesis while it was in progress.

137 Otlet, P. "Sur la structure des nombres classificateurs," Institut International de Bibliographie Bulletin 1:230-42, 1895.

138 Dewey, Melvil. "Suitability of the Decimal Classification." ALA Atlantic City Conference, 1899, College and Reference Section, Discussion on Classification for college libraries by Olive. Cutter spoke on his E. C. LJ 24:41-49, 154-157.

139 Sayers, W. C. B. "The Institut International de Bibliographie: Its Work and Possibilities of Cooperation," LAR 23:345-351, Nov. 1921.

140 Hopwood, H. V. "Dewey Expanded," LAR 9:307-322, 1907.

141 Ditmars, E. M. R. "Coordination of Information, a Survey of Schemes Put Forward in the Last Fifty Years," JoD 3:209-22, Mar. 1948.
_____. "A Chapter Closes: Bradford, Pollard and Lancaster," College and Research Libraries, 10: 322-337, Oct. 1949.
_____. "Dr. S. C. Bradford," JoD 4:369-374, Dec. 1948.

142 Lloyd, G. A. "UDC as an International Switching Language," Subject Retrieval in the Seventies. Univ. of Maryland, School of Library and Information Service, 1972, 116-126.

Chapter 6 (references 143-170)

143 Irwin, R. Librarianship: Essays... London, 1949.

144 Classification Research Group. "The Need for a Faceted

Classification as the Basis of All Methods of Information Retrieval," LAR 57:262-268, July 1955.

145 Ranganathan, S. R. Prolegomena to Library Classification. 3rd ed. Asia Publishing House. 23.

146 Ranganathan (145) 95-101.

147 Bliss, H. E. Bibliographic Classification... 1953. 4 vols. in 3. v. 1 first published, 1940. 1:20-21.

148 Bliss, H. E. "A Modern Classification for Libraries with Simple Notation, Mnemonics and Alternatives," LJ August 1910:351-354.

149 Bliss, H. E. (25) 318.

150 Bliss, H. E. (25) 283.

151 Irwin (140) 645-6.

152 Bliss (147) 1953, v. 3:45.

153 Bliss (143) 106.

154 Sayers (11) 106.

155 (112) 86.

156 "Ranganathan, Library Classification on the March," Essays in Memory of ..., Sayers, 1961:80.

157 Ranganathan (145) 23.

158 Ranganathan "Self-perpetuating Scheme of Classification," JoD 4:225, Mar. 1949.

159 Ranganathan (145) 399.

160 Ranganathan (156).

161 Ranganathan (145) 297.

162 Foskett, A. C. Subject Approach to Information, 2d ed. 1971:363.

163 Foskett (162) 233.

References and Notes

164 Wells, A. J. "Some Comments on the Indian National Bibliography," Indian Librarian, June 1958:13.

165 Coates (59) 16.

166 Austin, D. "The Development of PRECIS," JoD 30:47-102, Mar. 1974.

167 Ranganathan. "Subject Heading and Facet Analysis," JoD 20:109-119, Sep. 1964.

168 Ranganathan (158).

169 Coates (110) 62.

170 Bernier, C. L. "Correlative Indexes, I: Alphabetical ...," Amer. Doc. 7:283, Oct. 1956.

Chapter 7 (references 171-182)

171 Haykin (105) 24.

172 Kaiser, J. Systematic Indexing, London: Pitman, 1911. Kaiser, J. "Systematic Indexing," Aslib Report of Procs., 3rd conf., 1926:20-55. Also in Readings in Library Cataloguing, ed. R. K. Olding, Melbourne, 1966, 141-162. The 1911 book is paragraphed, not paginated; references to the paragraphs are given by number in the text.

173 Olding, R. K. (109).

174 Coates (59) 39.

175 Farradane, J. E. L. "A Scientific Theory of Classification and Indexing and Its Practical Applications," JoD 6:83-72 June 1950.
"Further considerations," JoD 8:73-92, June 1952. References to Farradane's papers in the text are by page numbers and volume numbers.

176 Coates (59) 48.

177 Sharp, J. R. (181) 198.

178 Coates, E. J. "The Use of BNB in Dictionary Catalog-

uing," LAR 59:197-202, June 1957.

179 British Technology Index, 1962, ed. by E. J. Coates.

180 Ranganathan, S. R. (167). In this Ranganathan put his own mark on Coates' BTI method, using an example from it and explaining it in terms which were not Coates', whom he did not mention; Coates had not mentioned him either.

181 Sharp, J. R. Some Fundamentals of Information Retrieval, 1965. References are given to page numbers for his Selective Listing in Combination (SLIC).
Sharp, J. R. "The SLIC Index," American Documentation 17:41-44, Jan. 1966.

182 Austin, Derek, and Peter Butcher. PRECIS: a Rotated Subject Index System. London: Council of the British National Bibliography, Ltd, 1969.
Austin, D. "The Development of PRECIS: a Theoretical and Technical History," JoD 30:47-102, March 1972.

Chapter 8 (references 183-205)

183 Maltby, A., ed. Sayers' Manual of Classification (11) 4th ed., 1967. This is posthumous, largely Sayers' 3rd ed. with additions by Maltby.

184 Needham, C. B. Organizing Knowledge in Libraries: an Introduction to Classification and Cataloguing, 1964, ch. 21:219 230. Apart from this last short chapter the book follows the facet principles of CRG and Coates.

185 Bernier (170) 283.

186 Jevons (38 710-13.

187 Casey, R. S. and others, eds. Punched Cards: Their Applications to Science and Industry, 2d ed., 1958. In effect this is a good account of post-coordinate systems before computers. For example, Wildhack and Stern on Peek-a-boo is a very good account with historical development and careful references to authorities.

References and Notes

188 Holmstrom, J. E. "A Classification of Classifications," Royal Society Scientific Information Conference 1948:501-516.

189 Wildhack, W. A. and Stern, Joshua. "The Peek-a-boo System--Optical Coincidence Cards in Information Searching," in Casey and others, eds., Punched Cards, 2d ed., 1958:125-151. (see note 187)

190 Taube and Associates. Studies in Coordinate Indexing, 1953.

191 Morris, J. C. "Evolution or involution? Notes Critical of the Uniterm System (with) A Reply ... by M. Taube," Journal of Cataloging and Classification 10:111-21, Jul. 1954.

192 Jaster, Murray and Taube. The State of the Art of Coordinate Indexing, 1962:204-7.

193 Mooers, C. N. "Zatocoding Applied to Mechanical Organization of Knowledge," Am. Doc. 2:20-32, Jan. 1951.
"Zatocoding and Developments in Information Retrieval," Aslib Procs. 8:3-22, Feb. 1956.
Brenner and Mooers. "A Case History of a Zatocoding Information Retrieval System," in Casey and others, eds., Punched Cards, 2d ed., 1958:340-356.

194 Fairthorne, R. A. Towards Information Retrieval, 1961. This is a collection of papers but includes "comments" by Mooers, xvii-xxiii, with an account of his personal relations with Fairthorne, especially about 1950 when he was introducing the term "information retrieval."

195 National Library of Medicine Index Mechanization Project, July 1, 1958-June 30, 1960.

196 Artandi, S. An Introduction to Computers and Information Science, 2d ed. Metuchen, N.J.: Scarecrow, 1972:135-145.

197 Mooers (193) 30, with reference to Samain.

198 Blagden, J. F. "How Much Noise in a Role-free and Link-free Coordinate Indexing System?" JoD 22:203-209, Sept. 1966.

199 Vickery, B. C. "Thesaurus--a New Word in Documentation," JoD 16:181-189, Dec. 1960.

200 Bush, Vannevar. "Memex," Atlantic Monthly, 1945.
Taube, M. and Associates. "Storage and Retrieval Ideas by Means of Association of Ideas," Am. Doc. 6:1-17, Jan. 1955.

201 Coates, E. J. "The Computerization of the British Technology Index," in Houghton, B., ed., Computer-Based Information Retrieval Systems, 1968:45-63.

202 Stevens, M. E. Automatic Indexing: a State of the Art Report. U.S. National Bureau of Standards Monograph 91, 1965.

203 Cheydleur, B. F. Colloquium on Technical Preconditions for Retrieval Center Operations, Washington, 1965: 119.

204 O'Mara, Robin. "Use of MARC in the University of New South Wales," Lasie 5:3-17.

205 Vickery, B. C. On Retrieval System Theory, 2d ed., 1965:106-107.

INDEX

Abacus 40, 45, 213
Abbot, Ezra 37-38, 43
Abbreviations (notation) 6, 9
Akers, Susan 102
Alembert, Jean de la Rond d' 18
Alexandrian libraries 5-6
Alphabet and letterpress printing 12-13
Alphabetical subject heading arrangements 103-107
Alphabetico-classed catalogs 36-39, 87, 106
American Library Association 51 and Library of Congress 95-96, 99, 101
Amherst plan 46-47, 49-50
Angell, Richard 87, 107
Antony and Cleopatra 5, 7
Arabic numerals 40, 56
Artandi, Susan 214
Aslib 134, 138, 143
Assyria 5
Augustus Octavius, Emperor of Rome 7
Austin, Derek 195-197
Axon, W. E. A. 35

Bacon, Francis 17-19
Banks, Sir Joseph 22-24
Barnard, Professor 52-53
Barrett, Franklin 27
Batten, W. E. 203
Battezzati, Natalie 62
Bernier, C. L. 198-200
Bible concordance indexing 10, 20
Bibliographies and catalogs 9-10
Bibliography, definitions 15
Bibliography, medieval 9-10
Billings, J. S. B. 29, 36, 130-131

Biscoe, W. S. 48
Blagden, J. F. 211
Blake, W. P. 57, 59
Bliss, H. E. 153-161, 163
Book trade, Alexandria and Rome 7
Boolean logic 143
Boston Athenaeum Library 74
Boston Mercantile Library 80
Bottasso, Enzo 62
Bowker, R. R. 51
Bradford, S. C. 128, 138-139, 142-150
British Museum Library Classification 27-28
British National Bibliography 94, 170-173, 196
British Society for International Bibliography 138
British Standards Association 141, 146
British Technology Index 189-191
Brown, James Duff 121-124, 126
Brunet, Jacques Charles 24-25
Burgess, Prof. 46, 53
Bush, Vannevar 214

Callimachus 5-7, 15
Campbell (1896) 114
Card catalogs and Dewey 48
Card cumulation and filing 99
Cassiodorus 8-9, 15-16
Chambers's Encyclopaedia 19
Charron, Pierre 18
Class lists 119
Classification, diagnostic 201
Classification, notation and numbers 8-9
Classification and logic 20

Classification "Canons" (Sayers) 16, 27-28
Classification Research Group 169-170, 184, 205
Classified and alphabetical arrangement 4, 16
Classified catalogs and classification indexing 124-127
Clay tablets and cuneiform writing 5
Cleopatra 5, 7
Closed access in public libraries 119-121
Coates, E. J. 37, 85-88, 189-191
Codex and codices 2, 8-9
Comaromi, J. P. 48, 49, 50, 62, 67
Computers 202, 213-217
Comte, Auguste 134
Concordance, Bible and literature indexing 10, 31
Concretes, processes and countries (Kaiser) 180
Coordinate indexing 174-197, 198-217
Cornell University Library 29
Correlative indexing 198, 200
Costello, J. C. 210
Cranshaw, James 125-126
Crestadoro, Andrea 33-36
Cross references 38, 80-82, 102-103
Custer, Benjamin 68
Cutter, Charles Ammi 43-44, 68-89
Cutter, William Parker 45, 69, 72
Cybernetics 214

Davidson, H. E. 52
Decimal numbers 40, 56, 58-59
Descriptors 207
Dewey, Melvil 44-68, 130-131, 136
Diagnostic classification 210
Diodorus Siculus 4
Ditmars, E. M. R. 138
Document specification (UDC) 143
Donker Duyvis, Frits 134
Dryander, Jonas 22-23

Edge-punched cards 205
Edwards, E. 22, 45
Efficiency and Dewey 52, 55-56
EJC-BMI system 210
Elastic system (British Museum Library) 28
Eratosthenes 9

Fairthorne, R. A. 208
Farradane, J. E. L. 184-189
Fellows, Dorcas 55
FID (Federation Internationale de Documentation) 128
Filing letters, ancient 6
Finding lists 21, 23-24
Fortescue, G. K. 38
Foxe's Book of Martyrs 19

Gesner, Conrad von 15-17
Ginn and Heath 49, 50-51
Glanvil, Joseph 19
Glasgow Public Library, classified catalogs 125-127

Hanson, J. C. M. 94, 96-97, 98, 101, 108, 109, 115-116
Harris, George W. 29
Harris, William Torrey
   on Bacon 18-19
   used by Dewey 60-61
Haykin, D. J. 80, 96, 98, 99, 106-107
Henry, Joseph 31, 90
Hierarchy and expressiveness in notations 42
Holmstrom, J. C. 203-204
Hospitality in notations 42
Hulme, E. Wyndham 7, 27, 67, 85, 113-114, 137

IIB (Institut International de Bibliographie) 128
Index, definition and derivation 9
"Index learning" 19
Indexed catalogs and index-catalogs (Crestadoro) 34-35
Indexes, book--page and paragraph 15-16, 19-22, 176
Indexing, title-word
   Alphabetico-classed catalogs 36-39

Index 241

Classified catalogs 127
  Dryander's 22-24
  KWIC and KWOC 215
  Low and Crestadoro 33-36
  Poole's 33-34
  Watt's 29-30
Indicators and closed access 120-121
Information explosions 3, 13
Information retrieval 2, 208
International Conference on Bibliography (Brussels, 1894) 129-130
International Catalogue of Scientific Literature 128, 131-133
Irwin, R. 8-9
Isolates 184
Item-on-term 202
Items, definition 2

Jahoda, Gerald 200
Jast, L. Stanley 7, 16, 27, 119, 136-137
Jevons, W. Stanley 20, 34, 84, 210
Jewett, Charles Coffin 31-32
Johnston, E. W. 18

Kaiser's systematic indexing 175-183
KWIC and KWOC 30, 215

La Croix du Maine 39
La Fontaine, Henri 128
LaMontagne, Leo 18-19
Lancaster-Jones, E. 138
Lane, W. C. 95
Larned, Josephus Nelson 70-71
Leibnitz, Gottfried Wilhelm 17
Leidecker, K. F. 61
Leypoldt, Frederick 51
Libraries, medieval 10
Library convention (New York) 26, 31
Library indicators 36
Library of Congress 90-111, 115-116
Library of Congress cards 115-118
Library of Congress Classification 108-114
Lilley, O. J. 86-87
Lindsley's takigraphy 45-46

Location reference 21, 24
Logic and classification 20
London Institution classified catalog 24
Low, Sampson 33
Lubetzky, Seymour 100, 105
Luhn, H. 215

Maas, John 57
McNair, M. W. 102-103
MARC 216-217
Martel, Charles 94-98, 108-109, 111
Medieval bibliography and cataloging 9-10
Medieval libraries 9-10
MEDLARS 209
Meetham, Roger 214
Merlin, R. 26
Metric Bureau, Dewey's 51
Mill, John Stuart 114
Mills, J. 87
Mond, Ludwig 129, 131
Montague, Professor 45, 48-49
Mooers, Calvin N. 207-208, 267
Murra, Kathrine O. 128-129, 132
Museum in Alexandria 3

National Library of Medicine (USA) 209
Needle-sort cards 208
Newberry Library 109
Nineveh 5
Notational hospitality 42
Numbers, notation and classification 8-9

Omar (581-641) 7
Open access public libraries, classified 119
Optical coincidence indexing 202-203
Otlet, Paul 128, 130, 133
Ozymandias 3

Panizzi, Sir Antony 128
Peek-a-boo (optical coincidence indexing) 202-203
Poole, William Frederick 31-33, 41, 53, 77, 83, 114-115

Pope, Alexander, on "index learning" 19
Post-coordinate indexing 198-217
PRECIS (Preserved Context Index System) 195-197
Pre-coordinate indexing 174-197
Press marks 21
Prevost, M. L. 85, 205
Printing
    Chinese and European 12
    Letterpress 11
Procrustean bed 66
Prynne, William 19
Ptolemys of Egypt 5
Public library technical departments (Britain) 136-137
Publishers' classified lists 16
Punched cards
    Body-punched 209-210
    Edge-punched 205-206
Putnam, Herbert 91

Ramesseum 3
Random codes and random access 207, 217
RBU 129-130, 132, 137
Ranganathan, S. R. 167, 169-170, 171-172
Rapid Selector, Shaw's 209
Readers' and Writers' Economy Co. 51-52
Report literature 202
Richardson, E. C. 4, 6, 9, 16, 26-27
Rider, Fremont 47, 67
Roles and links 210-211
Roman libraries 7-8
Royal Society of London 128-132
Rudolph, A. J. 93

St. Louis Mercantile Library 18
Samain, J. 210
Savage, E. A. 9-10, 133-134
Savigny, Christophe 17
Sayers, W. C. Berwick 16, 22, 27, 137
Schwartz, Jacob 10, 66, 85, 105
Science Museum, London 138
Sears' List of Subject Headings 87, 102
Sequential searching 227
Seymour, May 55, 66

Shannon, Claude 214
Sharp, J. R. (SLIC) 191-195
Shaw, Ralph R. 209
Shingling 208
Shurtleff, N. B. 39
Simplified Spelling Association, Dewey's 51
Single entry and title-word indexing 126-127
Single entry of items 124, 126
Single-place subject classification, Brown's 124
SLIC (Selective Listing in Combinations) 191-195
Smithsonian Institution 31, 90, 93-94
Special libraries in Britain 134, 136-137
Specific entry and specificity 85-88
Spofford, Ainsworth 90-92, 108, 110
Stereotypes, for catalog printing 31-32, 90
Stewart, J. D. 122
Stop lists 215
Swift, Jonathan 19
Synoptical table 81

Tapes, computer 217
Taube, Mortimer 204-205
Term-on-item 202
Thesauri 32, 211-213
Thirty-five base notation 70
Title-page development 14-15
Tritheim, Johann 15
Typewriting 12

Ulpian Library, Rome 8
Unit card 18
United States Surgeon-General's Library 36
Universal Decimal Classification (UDC) 134-136, 137, 138, 141, 146

Vellum 2, 7, 11
Vocalized notations 41
Volumen 2, 8
Volumes, medieval 10
Volumes as rolls and codices 2, 5

Washington, George 1
Watt, Robert 29-30
Watts, T. 28
Wellesley College 53, 68
Wheatley, H. B. 19, 24
Wiener, Norbert 214
Wilson, H. W. 32, 160
Writing 3-5
Writing materials 2, 5, 11

Young, John Russell 90-92, 94

Zero in decimal systems 40, 65

Z
693
A2
M47

SEP 8 1976